Don't Rhyme For The
Sake Of Riddlin'

Don't Rhyme For The Sake Of Riddlin'

The Authorized Story of Public Enemy

Russell Myrie

CANONGATE

Edinburgh · London · New York · Melbourne

First published in Great Britain in 2008 by
Canongate Books Ltd., Edinburgh

Printed in the United States of America

FIRST AMERICAN EDITION

ISBN-13: 978-1-84767-182-0

Canongate
841 Broadway
New York, NY 10003
Distributed by Publishers Group West
www.groveatlantic.com

09 10 11 12   10 9 8 7 6 5 4 3 2 1

Contents

Introduction

Public Enemy is without doubt one of the greatest hip-hop groups of all time. And according to many music connoisseurs, be they pundits or punters, Public Enemy is the foremost hip-hop group of all time bar none.

If the eighties were about hip-hop introducing itself and the nineties about the culture establishing itself as a force to be reckoned with, then the new millennium is about it enjoying its success while continuing to evolve. Public Enemy were crucial to hip-hop's development. They were responsible for making hip-hop lyrics more progressive and politically aware. No other act within hip-hop music has ever dealt with politics as forcefully as Public Enemy. The production of The Bomb Squad elevated the music to new sonic heights.

As Adam Yauch – better known as MCA from The Beastie Boys – puts it in the sleeve notes to 2005's *Power to the People and the Beats: Public Enemy's Greatest Hits*, 'No one has been able to approach the political power that Public Enemy brought to hip-hop. I put them on a level with Bob Marley and a handful of other artists – the rare artist who can make great music and also deliver a political and social message. But where Marley's music sweetly lures you in, then sneaks in the message, Chuck D grabs you by the collar and makes you listen.' They present undiluted black anger so articulately and stylishly that even those beyond their core audience can't help but take notice and be affected. Public Enemy have been responsible for creating and maintaining a powerful sense of black pride for an entire generation; but a quick glance at any crowd at a Public Enemy concert will reveal fans of all backgrounds.

Public Enemy were one of the first hip-hop groups to have a dedicated following among rock fans – this is the legacy of their tours and collaborations with groups like Anthrax, The Sisters of Mercy and U2. They are one of the most powerful examples of popular music being able to effect social change. 'The reason we made albums is to say something, to push the envelope of music, and our challenge is to see if we can perform them or not,' is how Chuck D sums it up. 'If we can't perform them then we've lost our challenge.'

Public Enemy are one of those classic bands whose music is continually discovered by new generations. Their second album, 1988's *It Takes a Nation of Millions to Hold Us Back*, is hip-hop's *Sgt. Pepper's Lonely Hearts Club*, its *Kind of Blue*. In short, the leading example of brilliance in its field. Their stage show is one of the best in the hip-hop business. Over the years it has evolved to include live musicians the baNNed, who add a new element to Public Enemy's noise.

Public Enemy are alive in the spirit of newer-school rappers like Dead Prez, Mos Def and Talib Kweli, Immortal Technique and Kanye West. It is no exaggeration to surmise that they are the closest thing the current generation has had to a Malcolm X or a Marcus Garvey. Similarly to the two freedom fighters, they made a lot of people question that which they had previously accepted with no complaints or qualms.

When it comes to politics and protest songs Public Enemy are the most respected hip-hop group and Chuck D its most respected intellectual. Those who tire of the more hedonistic, materialistic stance, which much of the more commercially successful hip-hop has taken, constantly look to Chuck and Public Enemy as the ideal of what rap music can do for the black community and race relations in general. Public Enemy are among the first hip-hop groups who have enjoyed long and fruitful careers. They are a band who cannot be ignored.

1

Origins of Public Enemy

Unless you were tuned in at the time, it's difficult to appreciate the extent to which Public Enemy shook up the world, inspiring love and hate in equal measures. Today, when no taboo has been left unbroken, it's almost impossible to shock the masses any more. But when PE exploded on to the hip-hop scene they were an extremely frightening prospect. They made the powers that be nervous in ways that even the likes of NWA and Tupac could never have imagined. PE were largely responsible for creating the conditions that led to hip-hop being feared by the establishment in the first place. But they might not have been such a tight unit if it hadn't been for the hundred square miles that form Long Island.

Like any section of the eternally influential New York City, Long Island has produced its fair share of famous sons and daughters. Among them are the Murphy brothers, Eddie and Charlie; the basketball player Dr J and Mariah Carey. Long Island's other musical offspring include classic hip-hop pioneers like De La Soul and Rakim. Newer artists include Chrisette Michelle and Nyckz. But would it be too outlandish to claim that PE are the sixth borough's most important band?

Long Island certainly owes a debt to hip-hop's version of the Black Panther Party for Self-Defense, if only for the simple fact that, were it not for them, it would never have become known as 'Strong Island' (soon after PE made their presence felt, 'Strong Island' by JVC Force hit big on its way to becoming a hip-hop classic) and, as a result, wouldn't have been able to attain the local pride that previously only existed elsewhere across the rotten apple. New York, like any other city, has its own localised regional rivalries. Such a

nickname – similar to Brooklyn's Crooklyn, Money Earnin'
Mount Vernon or, perhaps most famously, the Boogie Down
Bronx – was needed because Long Island was, and (to a
degree) still is, perceived as 'soft and country' by other New
Yorkers. It has a reputation as a quiet suburban place. It's
the place you go to escape the everyday grind and grit
of the city. Long Island's reputation as a 'nice place' meant
that those parents who had high hopes for their children
flocked there. Such a move has always held particular appeal
for ambitious young black couples who wanted to escape
the trials and tribulations in places like Brooklyn and Queens.
Years before Carlton Ridenhour became Chuck D, the
incendiary lead rapper of PE, his parents were one such
couple.

Long before they considered making Long Island home
Mr and Mrs Ridenhour resided in the black cultural and
business mecca of Harlem. 'They lived on 151st, they're
both from the same block and their birthdays are a day
apart,' Chuck says. The harsh realities of supporting a family
meant that they had to leave uptown and up sticks to Queens
where Mrs Ridenhour's parents lived. The support from the
extended family helped seal the deal. Consequently, Carlton
Ridenhour was born in Flushing, Queens, on August 1, 1960.
The future sports fan was born right next to Shea Stadium.
Coincidentally, Richard Griffin, aka Professor Griff, who
would grow to become PE's Minister of Information as well
as one of their most controversial figures and best producers,
was born on exactly the same day. But unlike Chuck, his
family already lived in Long Island.

'Queens was affordable for a young black couple. I mean, my
parents were young so they moved around . . . in affordable
housing,' Chuck hastens to add. 'We moved to about eight or
nine places in Queens before we settled in one spot.' Chuck's
grandparents' house and the infamous Queensbridge Projects,
the biggest housing projects in the entire United States, were just
two of these eight or nine spots. But Chuck's family eventually

left Queens altogether. It's tempting to wonder for a split second what kind of hip-hop Chuck might have made had he grown up in Queensbridge. But he was just nine when his family moved out to Long Island. It was a move that wasn't popular with the young Chuck. Leaving Queens for the country was a stark and refreshing contrast, even though it was only a short drive across an imaginary line.

'I remember clearly thinking, "Ohh, we about to move to the country," and then all of a sudden after a fifteen-minute drive we were in Roosevelt. The only major difference is a border.' The short journey wasn't the only thing that surprised nine-year-old Chuck. 'I was in fourth or fifth grade, so I just thought it was incredible that we were coming to a town with a house that we could call our own. It was an influx of white folks moving out and black folks moving in.' During the second half of the twentieth century, America watched many formerly predominantly white towns and cities slowly become black. 'All of the black folks came from all of the other parts of New York City. That migration just happened '68, '69, '70, '71, '72. My people moved out '69.'

In the years immediately following Martin Luther King's assassination in April 1968 Roosevelt changed from being a mixed town into a virtually all-black town. 'It was a little tense,' Keith Shocklee, an integral member of the legendary Bomb Squad production team, remembers. His family had also moved to Long Island after residing in Harlem. 'It was a small town on the brink of just wildness. I had a lot of white friends growing up. And all of 'em moved out.'

Whether or not this 'white flight' affected Hofstra University's Afro-American studies programme (some refer to it as the Afro-American experience) in any way is debatable. The Afro-American studies programme gave young black kids from all over Long Island (participants were aged roughly between nine and eleven) a chance to learn about black history and knowledge of self. The stuff they would never be taught at school. Their teachers were former Black Panthers, members of the Nation of Islam and, as Chuck puts it, 'highly conscious community folk'. Those summer programmes meant Long Island would prove to be a great place to develop the consciousness of the children who would grow up to become PE. It also gave them a chance to become familiar with each other at a young age, although this wasn't necessary for everyone. Griff's house was situated right behind Hank and Keith Boxley's (they were yet to adopt 'Shocklee'). So they obviously knew each other. Keith also played little league football with William Drayton, aka Flavor Flav, PE's court jester. 'I don't know how he did it,' Keith says laughing. 'His body frame was so small.' The potent combination of his musical and vocal skills mixed with his hectic personal life has made Flav PE's most famous member, particularly in more recent years.

A combination of grants and donations meant the programme had access to buses, lunches and other necessities. 'That was a big thing in the mid seventies,' Keith says.'That opened us up.' As the seventies progressed, the programme moved from Hofstra to nearby Adelphi University. 'That's where I happened to meet Eddie Murphy for the first time,' Chuck recalls. 'This was when he first moved to Long Island.' The Murphy family came from Brooklyn.

Long Island is made up of more than a few small towns, and it's worth noting that many of the main players that would go on to form PE came together in Freeport or Roosevelt. It goes without saying that none of them lived in the Hamptons. Roosevelt and Freeport, according to Freeport's Harry Allen, a journalist, photographer and broadcaster who has been a member of PE's sprawling extended crew since their college days are 'kind of like sister small towns, especially the part that I lived in, the black part, the north part'.

A few members hail from further afield. Johnny Juice comes from The Bronx, the borough that mothered this rap shit, but left the projects to move to a house in Uniondale, Long Island, when he was thirteen. Similarly to Chuck, he was initially sceptical about Strong Isle. 'When you live in The Bronx, you live in the projects and there's a lot of people around,' he says. 'Then you move to the suburbs and nobody's on the street. I was looking around like, "Where's everybody at?"'

James Bomb, an integral member of the S1Ws, was raised in rural Pahokee, Florida, a small town of around 6500 people. As well as being one of the most important reminders that PE are very different to your average rap group, the S1Ws (S1W being short for Security of the First World) form a human rebuttal to the insulting term 'Third World' and are one more element of the legendary PE live show. James Bomb moved to Long Island aged twenty. Tellingly, he had benefitted from the Panthers' lunch and breakfast programmes while growing up in Florida. The impact this had had on his young mind constitutes one more reason why PE would become a lot more than the first rap crew to instill some local pride in their home town. They didn't fashion themselves after the Black Panther Party for Self-Defense for nothing.

2

Spectrum City Come to Life

The mid to late seventies would see New York slowly but surely become hooked by the last great cultural movement of the twentieth century. While it was still very much a ghetto secret for much of the seventies, by the end of the decade hip-hop fever was spreading everywhere. Like rock'n'roll in the late forties or soul music in the early fifties, hip-hop was still very much in its infancy, but the vibe was unmistakeable. Hip-hop probably fascinated its first era of fans more than any subsequent generation. It would never be this fresh and new again. It was into this that the Spectrum City crew came to life.

The first incarnation of Spectrum City consisted of Hank and Keith Shocklee and Richard Griffin. But they took their original name from the childhood partnership Keith and Griff had formed. 'We used to call ourselves the KGs, Keith and Griff.' Keith recalls. 'Eddie Murphy used to come DJ with me too. He used to come to my parties and get on the mic and say his thing in high school.'

The budding mobile DJ crew didn't name themselves 'Spectrum' until 1976 when the trio were in their teens. The 'City' was added for marketing reasons on WBAU radio around 1984. Operations were based at their local youth centre. They managed to convince a lot of the local youths that a radio station was housed inside, although that wasn't strictly accurate. But music was being played in the place, courtesy of some old turntables, a mixer and some speakers. It also meant that their mothers didn't have to worry about them running the streets and falling prey to the many temptations therein.

When Griff left Long Island to join the services, the Shocklee brothers continued doing parties, and watched their local business grow as time progressed. 'Around our way we was just picking up from what the guys were doing up in The Bronx and Brooklyn,' says Keith. 'Brooklyn had a lot of mobile DJs when we was growing up.' Other popular DJs in Long Island included DJ Hig, whose little brother Brian Higgins would eventually become Leaders of the New School's Charlie Brown.

Keith was also making mixtapes and earning a couple of dollars doing beats for local groups as early as 1976. 'A lot of mobile DJs were making mixtapes but I had to make special ones. 'Cos I used to make them for different people, cats would come to me like, "I don't want the same records that you put on his." Or it would be, "I don't want the same records played the same way. I want mine, my own unique mixtape."' Consequently, he would spend literally hours in his basement making sure his stuff was on point.

Mobile DJs became popular because in 1970s New York racism was still very prominent and certain things were understood if not spoken. 'Most of the clubs was white clubs and, you know, they had the white DJs playing there,' Keith says. After a while, a lot of ghetto celebs began to pass through their events. Everybody from Grandmaster Flash to Grandmaster Caz came by. Chuck first saw Grandmaster Flash and Melle Mel aged eighteen at Roosevelt Roller Rink.

He was overwhelmed. 'I had no words, believe me. They came out to Long Island and tore that shit down. I couldn't even believe it, man. It was one of those things where I said, "Shit, I don't know about rapping, 'cos nobody in the world could be better than this." So that kept me away from rapping. Fo' real, I'd just never heard a dude so good. And Flash was a DJ that was just never, never, ever off beat. And these two guys together? There was nothing like that DJ and that emcee, man. They were a million miles ahead of anyone else in my mind.'

Nearly ten years after the Ridenhours moved to Long Island, when he was eighteen, Chuck connected meaningfully with

Hank Shocklee, and their friendship was born. This was the first crucial meeting that would eventually lead to the formation of Public Enemy. But before Chuck linked up with Hank's Spectrum City DJ-for-hire collective as their emcee, he had to pay his dues and watch from afar. Like a large number of Long Island youths, Chuck was already a fan of Hank Shocklee and Spectrum.

Chuck first hooked up with Hank during the early months of 1979. At this time he had returned to Adelphi University, one of the spots that used to host Afro-American studies, to study graphic design. Besides sports, graphic design and the burgeoning hip-hop culture were his main obsessions. Strangely, Chuck has his mother to thank for creating the circumstances. 'Really, my moms hired Spectrum,' he admits with a laugh. Chuck's mother was involved with the Roosevelt Community Theater, and they were looking for people to play music. Hank and Spectrum fitted the bill perfectly.

In late seventies Long Island, if you needed some DJs for a function of whatever kind, you could do a lot worse than the Spectrum crew. Keith emphatically insists, 'From the beginning we were DJs and we knew how to rock a crowd.' Although they wouldn't start playing even a few rap records until the eighties began to loom on the horizon, they did have 'tons of r'n'b records, that had a great vibe and a great funkiness to it'.

So while the likes of Grandmaster Flash and The Furious Five were the first to blow Chuck's mind, Hank and Spectrum were largely responsible for making Chuck decide to form a lasting relationship with this new music. Like many, Chuck was amazed at the way hip-hop DJs used their turntables to extend certain sections of records to make them last longer than their creators had intended. At the time, 'Galaxy' by the LA-based funk and Latin group War was one of his favourite records. One night, while in a basketball gym watching Hank DJ at a local night called Higher Ground, Chuck became more and more stupefied by how long his favourite song was lasting.

Of course Hank was just back-to-backing, or mixing and blending the break section of the record, extending the appropriate section for as long as he saw fit. Not so much of a big deal today. But at the time, that was some shit. 'It was the same record I liked but no words came in. I was bugging out like, "How big is this record?" Ain't no words came in. It just played on and on till the break of dawn,' Chuck says with a 'those were the days' look. 'When I found out that two turntables, two records did this? And it was a mixer in between? That's when I got bitten by the hip-hop bug.'

By this time emcees were just beginning to make their mark and the subsequent rise of their popularity would eventually see them become the main attraction at the DJs' expense. Technology played a part in this too. The echo chambers used by Keith never failed to get the crowd hype. 'That was like, "You're listening to the sound, sound, sound, of the K, K, K, G, G, G". That style was new to people. Words repeating on and on and on and music is changing in the background. That was sorta new.'

'Watching Hank Shocklee and Spectrum was riveting, like seeing a band,' Chuck says. 'But they didn't have an emcee.' This is the gap Chuck would eventually fill. The heads in his neighbourhood were perhaps the first to notice that Chuck was blessed with a voice tailor-made for oratory and performance, and encouraged him to explore these talents further. But another skill would enable him to break the ice with Hank. Chuck was, after all, serious about graphic design. So after one of Spectrum's parties, Chuck decided to approach the local hero he'd been watching from a distance. Even if the thought of becoming Spectrum's emcee existed in the back of his mind, he kept it there, and approached Hank on a design tip. Chuck was specific about the kind of art he wanted to produce. He wasn't about graffiti. Kids did that, and he was already in college. But a combination of graffiti and commercial art was cool.

'I was also into flyers,' he says, 'so after one function, I used to go to all the functions, I approached Hank and also EJ the DJ.' Everett James was Hank's business partner. In years to come he would share PE's headquarters on 510 South Franklin Avenue. But for now, Chuck's main goal was to persuade Hank and EJ that the reason they were sitting outside of a failed gig was because they didn't have a flyer that was good enough to advertise their talents. 'I said, "You guys are too good to not have a flyer nor an artist represent what you guys are doing."' This first attempt didn't really bear much fruit. Chuck recalls, 'They were on some "yeah okay . . . go away" type shit.' Keith concurs: 'My brother Hank was handing out some flyers and Chuck saw one of the flyers and said, "Yo man, your flyers man, they're sorta wack. I can do some better ones." At the time Hank had just met Chuck and he was like, "Man, what are you talking about my flyers is wack? What you mean?"'

Despite this initial rejection, Chuck did do some Spectrum flyers. Meanwhile, his mic skills were developing at a prodigious rate. If only because he could not endure lesser-skilled emcees. He used to get on the microphone every once in a while just to shut other guys up. 'Back then you had a lot of wack-ass cats getting on the mic, and everybody swore they had rhymes for the music.' During the late seventies a song like MFSB's 'Love Is the Message' would prompt a line of hopeful mic controllers to swarm the DJ box. This annoyed the young Chuck. 'Sometimes you'd be trying to get your dance on with a chick and some cat would just get on the mic and disturb the groove, man. I would just joke with my fellas like, "Well I'm gonna get on the mic just to get these motherfuckers off!"'

They say necessity is the mother of all invention and, in order for Chuck to have a good night out, and, perhaps more importantly, some luck with the ladies, he had to invest a little time showcasing his skills. His natural ability would also lead Hank to change his mind about Chuck becoming Spectrum's emcee.

These days any kid with even minimal equipment can knock

out demo-quality songs in a bedroom studio. But nearly thirty years ago, sound equipment, particularly that used for hip-hop functions, just wasn't up to scratch. Therefore, in order to be an effective rapper, for the crowd to actually be able to hear what you were saying, you had to have a voice that could cut through the distortion, feedback and whatever other sonic ailments were present. Carlton Ridenhour just happened to have one of those voices.

As 1979 progressed Chuck decided to sit out a couple of semesters from Adelphi, but he was still regularly attending Spectrum's Thursday Night Throwdowns and getting on the mic. Luckily for many future generations of rap fans, Hank heard him spitting there one night, and was suitably impressed. 'He was surprised to find out that I was the same dude who came to him with the flyers. He was like, "Yo man, I need an emcee. I want an emcee for my group but it's gotta be a special kind of emcee." I was flattered. I was honoured. I was just a fan.' But the fan still managed to play it somewhat cool. 'I said, "Give me the weekend, and I'll think about it."'

'Hank came back screaming like, "Yo, I found this kid, he can do flyers, he can rap, I'm gonna check him out, get him to come to a party",' says Keith. Keith Shocklee was one of the first to benefit from Chuck D's knack for coming up with rap monikers. 'When Chuck came on to the scene I picked up the name KG, Chuck threw in the wizard and so it was like The Wizard K-Jee and from there it just took off. I was DJing at a party right around the corner from his house and not too far from where his friend passed away.'

Sadly, the house party took place on the same day as the funeral of one of Carlton's friends. But he did his best to spit a couple of rhymes. Today's hip-hop kids would struggle to recognise it as rapping. It was most definitely not the type of rhymes you would hear nowadays. What Chuck was doing at the time was more on the MC tip. Instead of spitting sixteen (or more) consecutive bars, he would come up with a series of two- and four-bar phrases. During the next week they hooked up and Chuck did his first gig way out in Riverhead, all the way at the end of Long Island, near the Hamptons. By all accounts it was a great experience, and the first seeds of PE were sown.

While all of this was going down hip-hop was still steadily developing and forging its identity. Chuck describes the summer of '79 as 'just a total hip-hop summer. I never ever recall anything being so hip-hop crazy like the summer of '79.' This was despite the lack of rap records in existence. Everyone just knew that there was something in the air. That something genuinely different was about to take place. Popular DJs at the time included Play Hard Crew, DJ Pleasure, Groovy Loo, Mechanic and Tommy T. Another important milestone occurred when famed DJ Eddie Cheeba premiered 'Good Times' by Chic. A few months later this song would form the bedrock of the first globally popular rap record, 'Rapper's Delight' by The Sugar Hill Gang. This introduced hip-hop to the world, while simultaneously making many of its originators in The Bronx sick to their stomachs.

'Good Times' broke new ground for the band that Nile Rodgers and Bernard Edwards put together. They were mostly known for uptempo records like 'Dance, Dance, Dance (Yowsa, Yowsa, Yowsa)' and 'Le Freak', which at the time was their biggest hit to date. 'Good Times' would surpass both. Chic slowed down the tempo and made it funky. This helped it become an anthem with the emerging hip-hop community, and the hit of the summer. All the while, Spectrum City continued to do their thing, but with the added extra of Chuckie D (as he was originally known) on the mic to hype the crowd.

The lack of a large selection of rap records meant that they were still playing a healthy amount of funk and r'n'b, but hip-hop was changing the way a party got started. 'Rap music was so new you couldn't play it all night long. You know some of these girls like to hear the singing records. They want to hear Midnight Star. They want to hear, "I'm curious about your loving girl"', Keith explains. 'But at the same time they also want to hear the DJ scratch.' Spectrum City also made sure they never played a record twice in one night.

Their party-starting business continued in this vein until 1982 when Chuck met Bill Stephney. This was the other crucial meeting that led to the eventual formation of PE. Stephney was the programme director at Adelphi's college radio station WBAU and he had seen Spectrum doing their thing around Long Island. 'They DJed all the parties where hundreds if not thousands of kids would show up,' he says. 'And they gained a great reputation like, "This is the cool gig to go to".' Chuck D had not only been using his graphic design skills for Spectrum's flyers. 'We were one of the rare DJ groups that all had jackets with logos on them,' he says. 'Bill had seen us running around the neighbourhood as Spectrum. He had noticed this and was like, "Oh, Spectrum, wow". This was marketing before there was such a term.' Bill remembers it well. 'At that point there were 11,000 students enrolled at Adelphi University, and of those 11,000, 10,000 of them were white. So you're gonna notice anybody who's African American anyway. But when I saw this guy walking around the campus with a Spectrum City jacket on. Woah! Yo, who is that? He's down with that crew?' One day Bill happened to go over to this guy and introduce himself. 'It turned out to be this guy named Carlton Ridenhour who was down with Spectrum and was familiar with the radio station and the radio show that I was doing and wanted to bring his crew up there. I said, "That's fantastic, I'm a huge fan of Spectrum."'

The Spectrum parties were still doing very good business, probably better than ever. By this time the guests included nascent versions of now classic groups like the Fat Boys and Kool Moe Dee and the Treacherous Three. 'We'd put 'em on the radio, everybody would hear them on the radio and then we'd go right downstairs to the party and party,' enthuses Keith. 'It was crazy.' Things were good, they were having fun, making a little bit of money and they weren't, as Keith puts it, 'in the streets going nuts like our friends that used to hang out with us used to do'. Significantly, while hip-hop had not yet become the big business it is today, they still had their eyes on the prize. Keith recalls how: 'In the back of our minds we were hoping we could turn it into a big business.'

There were still a couple of legendary members who were yet to join the fold, but some of the key individuals who would eventually be known as PE were forging alliances.

3

The Graduation to WBAU

After meeting Bill Stephney things changed for Chuck, Hank and the rest of Spectrum. If who you know can get you to the next level in life, then making friends with the programme director at the local college radio station was not a bad move for a DJ collective such as Spectrum. Other Adelphi alumni include Hip-Hop Activist and Media Assassin Harry Allen, and Andre Brown, who would become better known as *Yo! MTV Raps* resident DJ Dr Dre.

During the day WBAU reflected its largely white student population with a largely white line-up of presenters who were constantly competing among each other for laughs. During the day you were likely to hear acts like The Police, Cyndi Lauper, The Alan Parsons Project, Howard Jones and Duran Duran. But at ten o'clock on a Monday night the extremely varied playlist of the *Mr Bill Show* allowed the students to hear a cross-section of the best new music around. And for the last hour of the *Mr Bill Show* the Spectrum City crew really let the students know what time it was.

After being impressed by their matching jackets, and more importantly, their skills as a mobile party unit, it was only ever going to be a matter of time before Bill found a slot for Hank and Chuck on the radio. As well as hosting the station's anchor show, Bill was in charge of WBAU's weekend schedule. Importantly for the future development of Public Enemy, this show reflected the eclectic nature of the early eighties New York club scene. Songs like 'Grandmaster Flash on the Wheels of Steel' were a sure bet, but alongside Earth, Wind & Fire and the Ohio Players, you could also hear favourites like 'Buffalo Gals' by Malcolm McLaren and the World Famous Supreme Team, plus groups like The Clash and even Bananarama. 'It was very cutting edge, even though it was college radio,' Bill recalls. 'We were playing rap literally before anyone was playing rap, but we were also playing all this other stuff where no one knows where it's coming from. I think people appreciated the fact that even though we were playing a lot of rap before everybody else, in essence it was a new music show.'

Bill's show had a unique vibe which was rare within black entertainment. 'I wound up finding this twelve-inch called "Cookie Puss" by this group The Beastie Boys and when I put that on people were like, "Where do you get this stuff?" And I'm like, "'Cos I'm in different circles."' Those circles included WLIR, the local rock'n'roll station. The scholarship that had allowed Bill to acquire an all-important college education had also secured him a job at that progressive institution. Bill remembers how, 'They were one of the first commercial stations in the States to play imports and also a lot of new-wave punk stuff.'

WBAU presented many interesting opportunites for Spectrum City. In the pre-WBAU years, Spectrum had continued making mixtapes for their local followers. But while it was costing money to make these tapes, they weren't making much back. Going on WBAU was the perfect way to play music for the people for free while promoting themselves as well as the station. 'We said, "If we can get our mixes on the radio then people can get it for free, we'll build the radio station with our name and we'll get our music out there."' It was around this time that they first began making songs of their own to be played on the radio. Chuck is anxious to clarify that it was 'music on other records'. They were still recording their rhymes over the instrumentals of hit records.

Within a few short months the young upstarts were presenting their own show. On Saturday nights the Spectrum Mixx Show lasted for an hour. But before long that wasn't enough either. Soon they were broadcasting live and direct for a full ninety minutes. It was during this period that Chuck really began to inject pride into the idea of coming from Long

Island, which was still suffering from the lack of self-respect that PE would help to eradicate. When it came to their home town few, if any, puffed up their chest and admitted that that's where they came from. It wasn't unusual for such a person to namecheck another area of New York. But Chuck was determined to change that.

Keith, Chuck and Hank were the phone operators. Chuck began to get the people who phoned in to shout out their friends and interact more with the station. This approach increased the number of callers rapidly. As Chuck describes it, 'We wanted to put it out there like, "Okay, you're in Long Island now. You're in Roosevelt, you're in Hempstead, you're in Freeport, let's do our thing here." Giving towns nicknames really set it off. In the sixties and seventies towns had nicknames but they were unofficial. We would make them official. Those that had shaky nicknames? We'd build it up. We built a scenario out of nothing.' Chuck was well used to the challenges facing Long Island in terms of both local pride and the area's reputation as being soft. He would put his own spin on those that called in and hype them up personally. 'Instead of saying, "Charles Chase sends a dedication to his girl Vanessa today," it'd be like, "C Chase gives a shout out to Nessy Ness out there."' Such nicknames would most likely then stick.

Troublemakers had been a constant at the Spectrum parties that took place at venues like the Korean Ballroom in Hempstead, the ballroom at Hofstra University and the Martin Luther King Jr. Centre in Rockville Centre. Fortunately, a solution was on its way. Due to the long-term friendship between Griff (who had recently returned from the Army), Chuck and Hank, an organisation Griff had started called Unity Force were the perfect choice to do security. Unity Force, like the Black Panther Party for Self-Defense, had sprung to life to combat racist attacks. (They weren't only concerned with militancy. Some members of Unity Force, including Brother Mike, had previously been part of a dance group called Nemesis.) 'It could happen at any time because racism was more overt then,' Griff reflects. 'We patrolled the neighbourhood, that kind of thing.' The fatal shooting of sixty-two-year-old Eleanor Bumpers at the hands of the NYPD was an important turning-point in Unity Force's evolution.

'That was one of the things that triggered Unity Force to come together,' says James Bomb. 'You know: "We got to stop this type of senseless killing. Here's a women who's sixty-two year old!" Even though she had a knife, you don't have to fatally shoot her. You're trained to disarm a lady who has no training at all. Not kill her. It's just senseless, for a man who has training and experience. There's no need to kill a person if you can disarm them. You've got to exhaust all possibilities. That's how Unity Force came about. Our main thing was, we were going to police our community.' Such a unit, with around fifty members, led by an ex-soldier like Griff, could easily adapt to security. 'We basically controlled the parties, and to secure a party was probably harder than dealing with racist attacks because we had to deal with our own people,' Griff reflects. 'People were selling drugs and bringing guns and we had stopped all of that.' Brother Drew, who has been rolling with the PE massive since day one, is far more blunt. 'It was like, "If you wanna come to the party and act out, you can get your ass whupped aiight. You can get kicked out." Cos we wanna make it safe for the kids.'

Griff ran a tight ship and gave his crew matching uniforms. 'Everybody was dressed in a uniform that looked like the S1Ws,' Chuck recalls. 'We knew that people, especially young people, were more likely to conform to order. If you don't set no order, they ain't gonna follow no order.'

The other key acquisition when it came to making sure that no enterprising thugs from, say, Brooklyn or Queens, could come to a Spectrum party on Long Island and wild out without fear of retribution was the 98 Posse. Professor Griff describes them as 'a bunch of cats, man, who just possed up, everybody had the same car. And those cats, man, they were some ruthless cats, bro. They were just brutal with how they went about handling different things.'

'The 98 Posse were basically thugs in the Hempstead area . . . well, they weren't really thugs.' Chuck corrects himself. 'They were like . . . they had their own clique, gang, whatever, don't-fuck-with-them-type guys.'

Initially, the 98 Posse were one of the biggest thorns in Unity Force's side. Long Island wasn't the old Wild West, but before too long something resembling a stand-off occurred between Unity Force and the 98s. One night James Bomb got into some static with one of the posse. 'It was just myself and this guy. We were going at it, and I got the best of him and then the following week we had another party, this time at the Korean Ballroom, and, you know, all of them came down. They were armed down and we ended up being armed down as well.'

Thankfully, the situation could be resolved. Unity Force and their less conscientious counterparts struck a deal. 'As soon as I said, "Squash it", another guy unclipped a sawn-off shotgun that was pointed at me,' James recalls. 'I was like, "Woah", you know what I mean. We could have been finished. That's how the 98 Posse started to roll with us.' As usual, Chuck came up with the name. 'It was a group of guys that all had 98s,' James continues. 'It was almost like a car club or something. The way that we communicated was, "We're all in this together". And if a dude come from Queens, or come from so and so and fuck it up, man, they just fuck up the chance for everybody to do whatever to make their money.'

The 98 Posse were immortalised in PE's 'You're Gonna Get Yours'. Just before the crew shouts the song's title on the chorus Chuck spits, 'Suckers to the side/ I know you hate my 98.' The cover for the twelve-inch single of 'You're Gonna Get Yours' features the 98 Posse in all their glory: matching 98 Oldsmobiles cars, gold chains and confident swaggers. In 'Rebel Without a Pause', Chuck famously spits, 'You see my car keys, you'll never get these/ They belong to the 9, 8 Posse.'

'The 98 Posse became bonded with the security and also with the music,' Chuck comments further. 'We were the music guys, Griff was the security, and the 98 Posse were the thugs and all of us worked together to keep something vibrant and happening so everybody could have a good time.'

The 98s would handle business quietly in darkened areas while helping to make sure there was no trouble and that the female patrons, who the Spectrum crew were especially worried about protecting, were safe. 'When we teamed up with them it was like we had the hood on lock,' Griff reminisces. As a result of the union, any hardrocks that came from New York's tougher areas got a surprise when they started to throw their weight around. 'If there was beef, you just didn't mess with us, cos it was bigger than the seven or eight guys onstage,' James Bomb states.

4

Still on the Come-up

Essentially for the future of Public Enemy, Spectrum City's show on WBAU allowed them a glimpse of how the business side of hip-hop was developing. Their close proximity to Queens also proved to be important when it came to their relationship with Run DMC, a group which achieved so many firsts for hip-hop. The late, and immeasurably great, Jam Master Jay in particular would prove to be crucial in the PE story.

It was Bill Stephney who hooked everyone up. He had a connection with Russell 'Rush' Simmons, who was the group's manager, Run's brother and head of Rush Communications. As well as recalling the nickname Russell had had for a number of years, Rush Communications was a budding conglomerate. Simmons, who had already been involved in the careers of early rap stars such as Kurtis Blow, was well on his way to becoming hip-hop's first mogul.

Bill Stephney had the honour of conducting Run DMC's first ever radio interview, and this gave him an insight into how Russell, Run DMC and Jay were doing what they did. About four weeks after the Spectrum crew received what is rumoured to be the first ever copy of Run DMC's breakthrough hit 'Sucker MCs' a very young Run DMC and Jam Master Jay passed through WBAU on their way to future glory. As they were yet to enjoy even their first hit, the Kings from Queens were nervous. They were uncharacteristically quiet and reserved but nevertheless very happy to be there and happy that they were making their way in the industry.

After another visit or two they relaxed and began to open up. The Spectrum crew were always big fans. When 'Sucker

MCs' was being primed for release, Chuck and Hank were able to get an early copy from Run DMC's record company Profile through the record pool (a loose collection of DJs who received promos from record companies and swapped information about music) they were a part of. These were the days before hip-hop's power became undeniable and when it was widely considered to be a fad that would end in the same way as disco and punk: fallen by the wayside. Disgusted fans of genres ranging from rock to classical music derided hip-hop for many reasons. Rappers didn't play real instruments (failing to recognise both the innovative way hip-hop turned the turntable into an instrument and practices like beatboxing), they didn't see the value of 'talking' on records (they obviously couldn't see that rapping is the ultimate manifestation of the ancient African oral tradition) and where was the melody? To many, hip-hop wasn't 'real music'. It's easy to see who had the last laugh.

'Not everybody wanted to be a hip-hop DJ. It wasn't a prestigious thing in the record pool,' says Chuck. 'If you were a hip-hop DJ they'd be like . . . ' He mimics someone being brushed off by a disinterested third party. As hip-hop DJs, Chuck and Hank were at the bottom of their record pool's list of priorities. A lot of club owners also felt this way, so only a few hip-hop records at most would be played at your average club night.

This didn't matter to Chuck and Hank. They weren't as short-sighted as the other DJs and club owners and were more than happy to take the hip-hop records. As the years passed the amount of hip-hop records with which to form a playlist was increasing considerably. In the early eighties, funk and r'n'b began to take a back seat. But the people who ran the record pool were slow to catch on. As a result, Chuck and Hank's dedication meant they would often actually be buying records to play on their show. The record pool wasn't up to the times.

Run DMC's demeanour was very different to that which

the WBAU family had encountered with the handful of rappers who had been successful during the Sugar Hill era spawned by 'Rapper's Delight'. Run DMC ended that earlier style of rap with their stripped-down beats, street clothes and, most important of all, their harder style of emceeing. Their good attitude only made the WBAU crew all the more keen to promote them. From that point any record that came from the Rush camp would automatically get played.

5

It's the Flavor

In their continuing quest to make a name for Long Island, the Spectrum crew had taken to recording local rappers and playing the tunes on air. The Townhouse Three, a group from Freeport, Long Island, were one of these lucky groups. (In later years, Busta Rhymes, Charlie Brown and Dinco D of Leaders of the New School would be equally fortunate.) While they were careful to keep their own soulful identity, like almost everyone else, they modelled themselves on the Cold Crush Brothers, the innovative collective of pioneers from The Bronx (Cold Crush member Grandmaster Caz had to suffer the indignity of having his rhymes bitten (copied) by Big Bank Hank of The Sugar Hill Gang. If you listen closely to 'Rapper's Delight', Hank even spells out his nickname, 'Casanova Fly'). Later on, the trio struck a chord with hip-hop fans as Son of Bazerk. Chuck remembers their songs being just as good as anything else that was about at the time, if not better.

'People thought they were regular records, better than the records we were playing. 'Cos once you hear it on the radio it wasn't no difference.' In just under a decade, Son of Bazerk would sign to Hank Shocklee and Bill Stephney's SOUL label and enjoy a big hit with 'Change the Style'. The song's video, which features Bazerk dressed up as a reggae singer, a doo-wop crooner and a heavy metal artist, is one of the funniest hip-hop videos ever made and was a favourite on *Yo! MTV Raps*.

The Townhouse Three, aka Son of Bazerk, were another important factor in forming what would become Public Enemy. In 1982 Tony 'TA' Allen, known as TA the DJ, introduced William Drayton, aka Flavor Flav, to the fold. In the early eighties he went by the name of MC DJ Flavor. Bazerk needed someone to play keyboards on a tape he was recording for WBAU. Flavor, who was known as a musician around town – he'd also briefly played drums in a band with future Bomb Squad member Eric Sadler – was his preferred candidate.

This true original made the right impression on the Spectrum crew almost instantaneously. After Flav was introduced to Chuck, Hank and Keith, someone, it's unclear who, made the mistake of starting a game of the dozens while he was present. Flavor Flav remembers this moment well. 'Back in the days the thing was the dozens,' he says of the phenomenon more commonly known as 'yo' mama' jokes. 'We were always snapping on each other's moms, snapping on each other's pops, snapping on each other's cribs, snapping on each other. So, I went up there, and started to snap and everything. Next thing you know I was taking on all three of them. Chuck, Hank and Keith. And I was winning. Matter fact, I wasn't winning, I won.' He turns to Chuck, who was sitting on the other side of the tour bus when I spoke to him, and in an excited, playful voice stakes his claim in the snapping game. 'I showed y'all that fucking night Chuck, you know that shit. That's why y'all kept me around. That's why y'all niggas kept me around 'cos I was murdering y'all. I ain't gonna lie.' Chuck's laughs are enough to satisfy Flav that he's right.

'I had to defend my title that night,' he continues. 'I was killing them that night. Next thing you know I started hanging out at the studio, they let me start staying up there, started letting me get involved. That's how I ended up becoming part of the entity.' The humour and light relief that Flavor would bring to PE had always been there. 'Claustrophobia Attack', one of his pre-PE songs, featured him rhyming over the Ohio Players' 'Fopp' about the perils of getting caught in an elevator with a woman who has bad breath.

Flav was so good he was beating future professionals at the dozens. One night after a gig, the Spectrum crew found themselves chowing down at a White Castle burger restaurant around three in the morning. A local comedian from Roosevelt named Steve White happened to be present, and a snap battle ensued between Steve and Flavor. Steve was no soft touch and would go on to feature in both film and TV. He has appeared in the Spike Lee films *Do the Right Thing*, *Malcolm X* and *Clockers* and Eddie Murphy's *Coming to America*, and has graced TV shows like *Hangin' with Mr Cooper*.

'He was considered the next Eddie Murphy,' is how Bill Stephney sums White up. Despite this, like everyone else, he just couldn't handle Flavor. 'They went back and forth, back and forth and Flavor just killed him and the whole place just started roaring when Flavor came up with this one line. Flavor has always been a star.'

Nevertheless, as Bazerk already knew, Flavor had even more

on offer than his ability to tell 'yo' mama' jokes. He had mastered numerous instruments, and his skills as a musician would become very useful to PE. The first instrument the young Flav learned was the organ. His mother bought his older sister an organ and before long little William had learned to play the theme to *Batman*. Then, in school, he began learning the drums during sixth grade. From there it snowballed. He started to learn how to read music and after he began playing with the school band, MC DJ Flavor picked up every instrument he could lay his hands on and learned them by ear. 'I just started messing with all the other instruments in the band room and everything. Just by myself in school, cutting class and going down to the band room. That's how I learned how to play the flute, the French horn, xylophones, tuba. I can play the oboe, all that.' As someone who had been in bands before he joined PE, he knew what it felt like to perform and was comfortable onstage. In short, he slotted in perfectly. In time, Flavor Flav would become PE's secret weapon.

By his own admission his childhood in Freeport was something of a troubled one. Flav was also well known locally for shenanigans that had nothing to do with his skills as a musician. Like a lot of black ghetto families, or any families living in neglected areas, his family consisted of a few different types. There were extremes of good and bad. 'My family was mixed up,' he says. 'My moms and them went to church, my pops and them were street. You know how regular family life shit go.' Flav describes his young self as 'a real bad kid, real wild, a real handful'. There was the usual petty thuggery: stealing cars, and things of that nature. But this didn't last. Before he joined PE, William went to college and got himself a chef's degree. At one point he was a school bus driver. 'I ended up growing up and being mild mannered,' he points out. Spectrum's good-natured decision to let other young guns knock out some tunes at their beloved headquarters paid off well. By the end of 1982, Flavor had his own show. His Saturday night slot from ten till eleven-thirty led perfectly into the Spectrum show.

6

510 South Franklin Avenue

In the mid seventies Hempstead's Eric Sadler was the first member of Public Enemy to own office space in 510 South Franklin Avenue. He had been in various bands since the early seventies playing either bass, guitar or keyboards. As luck would have it, his dentist Dr Raymond Gant, who lived across the street, was friends with his parents and had talked to his mother about some space that was available in the building where he worked.

Once the rent of $150 per month was agreed Eric moved all of his equipment in and opened a rehearsal studio. This was a few years before he began working with the guys who would become PE. But, as a local youth, he definitely knew who Spectrum City were. 'I'd see the Spectrum guys around town doing gigs,' he recalls. 'A lot of times they'd be doing a gig and my band would be playing so I'd see 'em from time to time. I didn't really know 'em, but I knew of 'em.'

Around eighteen months after Eric moved in, he received a phone call out of the blue from Hank Shocklee, whose long-suffering parents had decided to rid their house of all of his noisy musical equipment. 'I don't even know how Hank got my number,' he says. 'He's like, "You think we can get into the building you're at?" I said, "I don't think it's a problem."' Dr Gant didn't think it was a problem either. So Spectrum took their partnership with EJ the DJ a step further by agreeing to split costs, and moved into the upstairs office.

Chuck's description makes it clear that PE love 510 South Franklin Avenue in the same way that The Beatles loved Abbey Road and DJ Premier loves HeadQcourterz. (The studio was previously well known in hip-hop circles as D and D Studios. This was before the hip-hop legend renamed it after one of his dead homies.) '510 South Franklin was a very key area, it was our headquarters. It was sort of a record studio for DJs and we would make these records, well, we would make tapes to play on the radio station.' It was an exciting time. 'I was just completely taken with the creativity of these people,' says Harry Allen, who after meeting Chuck at Adelphi began rolling with the extended crew. He had already given himself the title of Hip-Hop Activist and Media Assassin. 'A whole conglomeration of individuals were getting together around hip-hop. You'd have people like Run DMC, who were big fans of the *Super Spectrum Show*, come though. You'd have people like Spider D and DJ Divine come through.'

When it came to their radio show, Chuck's rapping (which was still only over the hot instrumentals of the day) was still more of a necessity than anything else – there simply weren't that many rap records – but Spectrum were on their way to becoming a fully-fledged group producing records. Chuck certainly had their listeners thinking this was the case. The promo tapes he would make for the radio, similarly to Son of Bazerk's songs, were perceived as professional records by WBAU's listeners. It wouldn't be long before Spectrum made the jump to actually making records.

Musician and record producer Charles Casseus, who had shared half of Eric's rent at 510 before Spectrum rented space there, was in 1984 chiefly responsible for the first record that would involve future members of PE. As well as Eric and Charles, 'Breakin' In Space' (a record that could only have appeared during the over stylised and slightly pretentious early years of the eighties) by Key-Matic featured some of Charles's friends like Najee, a session musician from Queens and a girl named Sharon. Keith Shocklee, credited as The Wizard K-Jee, was the DJ. 'Breakin' In Space' was a hit in the New York area, and gave those involved a chance to travel a little and do some promotional gigs. One of their gigs, a promo for Kiss FM, featured a young Madonna on the bill. Charles also recorded a single with Butch Cassidy, who used to roll with Spectrum and who Chuck describes as 'my radio partner'. Butch filled the hype-man role Flavor would later occupy. Interestingly, he was using the same studio that PE would later use for *Apocalypse '91: The Enemy Strikes Black.*

The third and most crucial record Spectrum were involved in that year was 'Lies/Check Out the Radio' which dropped on Vanguard Records. This happened through a connection of Hank's who, at the time, was holding down a day job as the manager of a record shop. Tim Olphie, the regional manager for this particular chain of record shops, had links with a dance DJ named Pinky Velasquez and the entrepreneur who funded BT Express's records in the seventies. Tim was their guide to this strange new world of recording rap. Hank brought the rest of Spectrum with him, they booked some studio time in Manhattan and recorded 'Lies', a song made in the Run DMC mode.

It's very important to note that they wanted to promote themselves as radio DJs rather than as a recording group. This is why when they found themselves with some extra studio time they decided to record a cut called 'Check Out the Radio'. Later on, when that song was played on the radio, it became a firm favourite for The Beastie Boys and Run DMC.

Unlike 'Lies', on 'Check Out the Radio' Chuck 'was saying things on there that were kinda fly'. He recalls, 'It was totally the antithesis of "Lies", 'cos "Lies" was a record that we probably knew we wouldn't play ourselves. It wasn't even saying "check out the radio", it was "check us out on the radio". It was all about WBAU.' These songs, and other songs they made around this time like 'It's Working', represented a massive step forwards.

'Check Out the Radio' represented the first time Eric 'Vietnam' Sadler officially recorded with the crew who would become The Bomb Squad. Against the advice of his musician friends who felt that 'rap is garbage, rap is not real music', Eric had accepted Chuck's invitation to 'help 'em out with the music and mess around'. He had a slightly more modern attitude to hip-hop than most musicians: 'I didn't care at all. I was like, "Hey y'all upstairs, I'm downstairs. Y'all don't know how to work this stuff. I'll come up there and do some stuff," because I had been in the studio with my boys for ever.'

PE owe Eddie Murphy, who by now was well known around Long Island, a small debt for Eric's skills. Eric had natural talent and had been a musician for around a decade at that point. But when the comedian asked Eric to look after his equipment, he gave the future Bomb Squad member the chance to familiarise himself with the latest keyboards and relatively new innovations like the DMX drum machine. 'He was like, "Yo man, you guys can help produce my record, I did the *Saturday Night Live* thing, I just made some money and I'm a be moving from one side of town to the other side of town. I was like, "Oh, okay great",' Eric says. 'He didn't have any place to leave his recording equipment so he left it all at our rehearsal studio. I was like, "Damn, I better learn all this stuff while it's there." For twenty-four hours a day, I was learning that stuff backwards and forwards.' Over the years, Eddie had emceed at shows where Eric's band was playing. Occasionally, he was the comedy act before a talent show Eric was involved in.

Unfortunately, Eric and his boys never produced Eddie's record. When Eddie moved from Roosevelt to Baldwin in Long Island his new management felt they had to dish out a dose of reality. 'His managers were like, "You're not understanding what you have here,"' Eric recalls. 'They talked him into getting away from all his neighbourhood friends and moving out to Jersey.'

At the same time a deal was worked out with Prince for the then rising star to produce Eddie's record. So when it was time for Prince to send out the two-inch tapes, he sent them out to 510, where Eddie's equipment was. Eric, a big Prince fan, was suitably impressed. 'When we received the tapes coming from Paisley Park, nothing even said Prince on it, it said Jamie Starr and Alexander Nevermind. It was two songs but I remember one of the songs was called "Chocolate". After a few weeks plans changed again. This time it was decided that King of Funk Rick James was going to shape Eddie's album. So off Eddie went to have many of the adventures that his brother Charlie would eventually relive in the classic 'True Hollywood Stories' segment of Dave Chappelle's all conquering *Chappelle's Show*.

Eric simply shrugged and carried on as normal. 'It was like, "Well at least I got to hold on to the equipment for a while, good luck with what you're doing".'

Although he had spent days and nights learning this new equipment, when he first turned up to the studio to record with Spectrum Eric discovered he was surplus to requirements and was sent home. 'I was like, "Okay, no problem". I went back and started playing cards with my boys. Pinky was going to produce the record so they didn't need me any more.' But on the very next day, Chuck called him back complaining about Pinky's hip-hop studio shortcomings and asking him back to knock out one jam real quick. Eric agreed, he was picked up and driven to the city and they banged out 'Check Out the Radio' in about an hour. 'And that was kind of it,' Eric says. 'After that, I'd still mess around with some junk with them while they were upstairs and I was downstairs.' They weren't about to take over the world just yet.

It was around this time that Eric discovered, quite by chance, that Hank and Keith Shocklee were his cousins. One day after making some beats at 510 South Franklin Eric went to the Shocklee household to hang out. After playing football the three of them went into the kitchen for some drinks. 'My grandmother always sat by the kitchen,' says Keith Shocklee. 'And she looked at Eric and said, "Eh Eric, you look just like Joe Sadler." ' A surprised Eric confirmed that Joe Sadler was his grandfather.

It took Grandma Shocklee about five minutes to piece the whole thing together. She had grown up in a part of St Kitts chiefly populated by Matthews and Sadlers. Of her nine brothers and sisters, some had moved to England and some to America. 'It was crazy,' Keith continues. 'We knew each other for two and a half years, me, him and Hank were all working together, hanging out, going to parties, till my grandmother saw him and that's how we figured it out.'

7

Public Enemy Number One

Even though they were developing artistically, Spectrum City's debut twelve-inch failed to set the rap world alight. In 1984 it was going to be very hard to outdo the likes of LL Cool J, Run DMC and Whodini, all of whom were selling healthy amounts of records.

For a brief moment, it seemed like things were going to fizzle out. Harry Allen was not alone in feeling very nervous that this could end up being the case. 'I always felt like if these guys had a break, if people were to hear their music, it would really be amazing, and so when their first break came with the Vanguard record, I thought that was going to do it and then it didn't. After that, they weren't doing as many mobile gigs and I kinda thought, "Wow, I guess that was it".'

But it transpired that the lull caused by the failure of 'Lies/Check Out the Radio' was only the calm before the storm. Another of the radio promos made was called 'Public Enemy Number One'. It was put together with two tape decks in the studio. This Keith Shocklee production would eventually change everything for the young group. An element of necessity would play its part in the creation of Public Enemy. It was necessary for Chuckie D to defend his lyrical reputation. 'I made "Public Enemy Number One" 'cos there were some elements in the neighbourhood that heard my other promos and one of these cats that was part of a legendary crew called the Play Hard Crew told Flavor he was gonna take me out rhyming.' Sound familiar? This is the cat Flav is talking about at the beginning of the (slightly different) version of 'Public Enemy Number One' that was released on Def Jam just over two years later. He's the dude that complains to Flavor about how 'that brother Chuckie D swears he's nice'.

At first, emcee battles were not top of Chuck's to-do list. He wasn't trying to be 'one of those battle cats'. He was trying to improve things for all of the local emcees by getting them on the radio and building up a local scene. Ironically (and unluckily for the Play Hard Crew), Chuck's mic skills were called into question at the same time that Chuck and Flav began to put together their unmatchable back-and-forth style. Prior to PE, no two rappers had jammed together in the way Chuck and Flav made famous. Run and DMC had traded lyrics and even finished each other's lines, but they did it on a far more equal footing. Chuck was definitely in charge, but Flavor's contribution was priceless, and always funky.

Unbeknown to the Play Hard Crew, they would be the first to be blown away by the combination of Chuck and Flav. Chuck's father had a furniture removal business. Chuck managed to hit his boy Flav off with a job, and by working a job together, they came up with something that would later prove to be one of PE's greatest assets. Their interaction not only made their records memorable. The PE live show would not be the devastating affair it undoubtedly is without their chemistry.

After leaving the offices on 58th street in Times Square Flav would write down ideas if Chuck was driving and vice versa. Once they got back to Hempstead they would work on their ideas in the studio. 'Me and Flavor were driving trucks for my father, for a year and a half, two-year period. Flavor needed a gig, my father was moving furniture in trucks, so we would drive the new furniture and go through new routines while in the truck.'

Their interplay, though unique for hip-hop, was not without precedent. One major influence was the legendary James Brown and Bobby Byrd. The Godfather of Soul didn't only influence hip-hop with the loops that formed the basis of many great rap records. His vocal stylings were equally influential. 'You know the "everybody over there, get on up", that contrast,' says Chuck. All the years spitting on sub-par equipment had taught Chuck a thing or two about voice levels. He realised very early on that he would work well with Flav. Flavor's voice is high pitched and 'trebley' but it has some 'bassy' strength to it. Chuck's voice is of course as bassy as they come, but has the tiniest amount of treble there too.

Their voices, like their personalities, were polar opposites: they were up and down, left and right, north and south. 'Both of us could cut through a recording,' Chuck states. 'Or cut through things that became noise.' The other influence was far more modern. Chuck was paying attention to the Philadelphia rapper Schoolly D, who, alongside DJ Code Money, made his mark with hits like 'PSK'. 'Code Money would open up to say something and set it up for Schoolly like, "Hey Schoolly, why did you do this, duh duh duh", and Schoolly D would come in with "duh duh duh".' Schoolly D's style of making records and his voice style were a big influence on 'Yeah, I'm just going in with the 98,' as Chuck raps in 'You're Gonna Get Yours'. Chuck goes on: 'It's in the same cadence as "PSK what the hell does it mean?"'

Just as hip-hop production developed more rapidly during the mid eighties, so did the vocal styles. At the close of the decade Ice Cube would comment to Chuck on how he was influenced by Chuck when it came to that particular cadence and flow. Chuck responded by saying he got it from Schoolly D and Mr. Magic. When it was brought to Schoolly D's attention he admitted he was influenced by Melle Mel.

But while Spectrum were becoming more and more involved with the recording process they still didn't want to be recording artists. They wanted to work full time in radio. The crew looked up to the likes of the World Famous Supreme Team (who in time would go on to make 'Buffalo Gals' with Malcolm McLaren), who had a show on WHBI, and 'Chief Rocker' Frankie Crocker who played on WWRL. A gig along those lines, and the chance to continue with their DJ gigs, would have suited them just fine.

A big reason for their hesitancy to become recording artists was that during their time at WBAU the Spectrum camp had been observing the harsh realities of the developing rap game. Inflated egos meant that they had to treat the upcoming acts who played at their gigs like kings. But after the shows the Spectrum crew would then drive those acts back to the same impoverished neighbourhoods that they'd always lived in. Driving supposed rap stars back to the projects made an impression. 'None of them were really getting paid off records so I was like, "Damn",' is how Chuck assessed the situation.

8

Johnny Juice in the House

In among everything else that was going on, Spectrum were still actively courting local talent. It was around this time, late '84, early '85, that DJ Johnny Juice joined the crew, after impressing Chuck and Hank at a talent contest they held at Spectrum's headquarters. Juice would also play his part in the future careers of the individuals who would go on to form Leaders of the New School, the Long Island-based group that released hits like 'International Zone Coaster', 'Case of the PTA' and 'What's Next' before their most popular member Busta Rhymes went solo. When the young Juice arrived in Long Island he realised that, unlike in The Bronx, he would have to go looking for hip-hop vibes. 'In The Bronx you just had to look out the window and it was there,' he says.

Juice met a guy named DJ Will who in turn introduced him to Darryl Higgins, aka DJ Hig. Hig had been DJing for a long time around Long Island and this was how he met Spectrum. He was particularly tight with Eric Sadler: 'Hig also had his own little sound system, they were like competing sound systems but they were friends, they knew each other.'

Hig and Will had been teaching Juice, already a natural at breakdancing, how to scratch and mix, with the result that Juice and Hig's brother Charlie Brown, who went to the same school, formed their own little DJ crew. Trevor Smith, aka Busta Rhymes, also attended the same high school as Juice who, because he was a few years older, was helping to tutor the young break-dancer. 'As gifted students if we tutored other kids in certain subjects we'd get extra credit. Busta was a popper and he was nasty. He came looking for me to be a part of my breakdancing group kinda before I even met Brown.'

Before long, Juice would introduce the artists who would

be known as Busta and Charlie Brown to each other. At the time they went by the excellent old-school names of MC Chill O-Ski and KB MC, short for Krush Brown. Rolling with older breakdancers allowed the three youths to shuffle past security and into the Spectrum parties. 'I was with Hig so I was introduced to MC DJ Flavor, Chuckie D, Mellow D and DJ K-Jee.' The B-boy in Juice still makes him speak his mind: 'Honestly, I wasn't too impressed with 'em. But they were still rocking the shit.'

Johnny Juice was back in The Bronx visiting family when Charlie Brown called him up about the talent contest that led to him joining PE. 'I got back and there was a message from Brian like, "There's a contest, they're looking for rappers and DJs". I was like, "Aiight". My moms drove me over. I was only something like sixteen.' Juice and Brown attended the contest with a couple of extra friends: a breakdancing Michael Jackson impersonator called Fame Jackson, and Juice's homie Daqwuan. He was pulled in to replace Busta, who, at the last minute, had decided to spend the weekend with his father in Brooklyn.

When they arrrived at 510 they found a line around the block. Everybody wanted to be a star. Juice and co. were the youngest guys there and Juice the only non-black person. 'I was the only Puerto Rican there,' he reflects, 'but I didn't give a fuck.' 510 South Franklin Ave is a big building. Back in those days, Eric had a demo rehearsal place on the first floor. Directly above him was the dentist's. Spectrum City and EJ the DJ shared the space above Dr Gant's office.

When they finally reached the end of the queue Juice and Brown discovered two things. Firstly, that they would have to audition individually as solo acts. This meant the routine they had practised would have to wait for another day. Even worse, there would be no battling. They would have to showcase their skills in a different way. Juice was especially upset with this. 'Me? I'm the battle dude. I thought I was gonna battle K-Jee and Mellow D. I was like, "I'm dying to fuck these dudes up,

I can't wait!" They were amused by my attitude. I know they weren't worried about it. But I was dead serious.' Instead he had to prove his worth on two SL-1300 turntables. Armed with two copies of 'Funky President' he proceeded to scratch – once he had acquired some milkcrates to stand on.

For their competition, the rappers had to sift through some beats on a drum machine. Once they chose something they liked, each contestant had a minute and a half to show and prove. Brown and Daqwuan grabbed the mic. A week after the talent contest Juice got a job at Burger King. On his second day, a Sunday, Chuck called him with the good news. At 8 o'clock on Monday morning, Juice (and all of the other young guns that were picked) showed up at 510 South Franklin to see if this was something he was really gonna rock with, or if Brown's apprehensions were well founded. Brown hadn't been picked and was perhaps a little green-eyed.

Upon arrival, Juice was shocked to see logos and names for seven groups that didn't yet exist. One of the groups was Leaders of the New School. Another was Terminal Illness Crew, supposedly the first white rap group. There was also the Kings of Pressure, Son of Bazerk, Hellraisers, True Mathematics and The Invisible Empire.

At the time there weren't many hip-hop groups with a lot of members. Stetsasonic were yet to put out any records and the Wu-Tang Clan wouldn't blow up until the start of the next decade. So putting six emcees and two DJs in one group, when four was usually the limit, was unheard of, it was a big deal. But this was the Spectrum master plan: 'Chuck was like, "I've picked you guys for your speed and for your attitude." That's when I realised he liked my whole "fuck you" attitude.' The penny dropped. The names, concepts and logos for these groups had been pre-chosen, and the talent contest had taken place to find members to fit. Juice decided this was something he was gonna mess with and he joined the Kings of Pressure, a name evidently inspired by the nickname of a Philadelphia suburb, 'King of Prussia'.

The Kings of Pressure immediately went to work on some four-track demos that would win them a lightly lucrative deal with Next Plateau Records. Throughout the time Juice was recording with the Kings of Pressure, the future PE personnel heard him scratch and earmarked him for the record that would become *Yo! Bum Rush the Show*. 'They were like, "Yo, we're working on an album for our group Public Enemy, and we want you to come in and do some scratching." I'm like, "Sure, whatever".' In order to familiarise him with the material he would be working on, Chuck began giving Juice rides home in his grey Cougar after recording was finished. Juice's home town of Uniondale was right next to Roosevelt, where Chuck lived, so it wasn't a problem. Along the way he would play the tunes that would become PE's debut album. Juice's 'fairly photographic' memory meant he could memorise each track and then work out which records to bring when he next rolled through the studio. Of course, Keith and Chuck had an extensive (and catalogued) record collection up in 510, but Juice liked to use his own tools. He ended up fitting into the swing of things fairly quickly. 'We would go up there and I would pull records out, I was the master at pulling records out. Throwing shit in to make it fit.'

All the while, the youngsters in the crew were learning from the older members. Eric Sadler was teaching Juice and Keith how to programme drum machines and samplers. 'Eventually, Keith and I would just sit in that little room and just work on shit,' says Juice. 'We'd come up with records based on a little vibe that was happening. He'd come up with a little beat, I'd grab some records and start scratching them in. That was my introduction to Public Enemy.'

9

The Birth of Public Enemy

The demo version of 'Public Enemy Number One' was recorded in December 1984, a full two years before it became their debut twelve-inch release for Def Jam. Chuck took it up to WBAU and gave it to Dr Dre who played it on his show *The Operating Room*. Jam Master Jay was also in the studio, and he liked what he heard. 'It became a mainstay on WBAU, and it shut those guys up,' Chuck says of the Play Hard Crew who inspired the record when they challenged Chuck. 'Jay was like, "Yo, that shit is hot."' What happened next is subject to debate.

According to some Jam Master Jay was the first person to play the demo of 'Public Enemy Number One' to Rick Rubin, who co-founded Def Jam with Russell Simmons. But other insiders insist Dr Dre did the deed. It could quite easily have been either. They were both present when the song was brought to the studio after all. Jay, a big fan of their radio show, had such enthusiasm for hip-hop that he was constantly playing the newest joints to any and everyone he came across. Naturally, Chuck still has mad love for Jam Master Jay after all these years. 'Jay would tape every show and then take it back on tour and all that so of course it got around and "Public Enemy Number One" would be the hot song.' It's also entirely possible that Dre – who would himself enjoy a hit with 'Can You Feel It' as part of Original Concept – played it for Rick when trying to hustle his way through the door. Original Concept would go on to release their debut album *Straight from the Basement of Cooley High* on Def Jam.

According to Dre, he played it for Run DMC and The Beastie Boys on a tour bus while he was DJing for The Beasties. 'I was playing them a bunch of stuff that we had from the station and this one tape stuck out. They were going, 'This "Public

Enemy Number One" record is crazy Dre, you gotta take it to Rick, you gotta take it to Rick.' At the time I was doing the Original Concept stuff so I said, "Let me take it up there."'

He duly passed it on to both Def Jam head honchos, but didn't receive the response he'd hoped for. 'I gave it to Rick Rubin and Russell Simmons. Russell threw it out the window. I put it in the deck, played it, and Russell got it and just threw it out the window. I said, "Yo man, why you throw my tape out the window?"' While Russell obviously didn't like it, Rick called Dre back in two days. 'He was like, "We're gonna sign 'em, we're gonna sign 'em!"' Bill Stephney, who by this time had graduated from working in promotions to become vice-president at Def Jam, insists that this is how it went down. But regardless of who played it for him first, Rubin was determined that he would sign whoever was responsible for such a groundbreaking song. Bill Stephney was in no doubt of Rick's seriousness.

'Rick said, "We gotta sign Chuckie D. If you don't sign Chuckie D you're fired!" In a typical Rick Rubin sort of way. So I'm like, "Is he gonna fire me with all this success that's happening?" They only have like one employee: me. What kind of sense does that make?' Despite his tactics and personal quirks, Rubin proved how ahead of his time he was. He caught on to how special 'Public Enemy Number One' was despite its sonic strangeness. In fact, he probably liked it more because of this quality. After all, as Chuck says, 'You gotta understand, that shit was noise in 1987. So you can imagine like 1984–85. It was like, "What the fuck?"' he says before recreating the sample from the JBs' 'Blow Your Head' with his mouth to emphasise the point.

If you've heard it, it's easy to imagine. If not, the noise is not completely dissimilar to the prolonged wail of a crying baby, albeit one with an unnaturally deep voice. But this baby has decided to hold his crying note like Bill Withers at the end of 'Lovely Day'. Chuck had been a fan of 'Blow Your Head' for a long time. He originally heard the song when he attended Roosevelt Roller Rink as a teenager. 'Let me tell you I was a rollerskating motherfucker,' he confirms with a laugh.

The idea to loop the song came from DJs who couldn't mix the record properly. Many DJs couldn't extend the groove properly and weren't mixing and blending (or back-to-backing if you prefer that term) the two copies of the same record in time anyway. There would always be the tiniest gap between the old 'waaaaaaaaaaah' and the new one. And as Rakim would insist in a year or two there 'ain't no mistakes allowed'.

At this time the term loop didn't exist, there still weren't any machines a producer could load a beat into. All Chuck knew was that it didn't sound right. 'I was like, "They need to hold that shit".' Determined to get it just right, the Public Enemy camp happily used the (now super old-school method) of twin cassette decks. Just as it had done with the turntable, hip-hop revolutionised the way cassette decks were used. 'When cassette decks first came out black people took them cassette decks and made pause tapes,' Chuck says. 'And pause tapes was the first remix tapes.'

Significantly, 'Public Enemy Number One', which went through many incarnations, was the first song to feature Flavor Flav and Chuck D on a song together. Flavor opens up the song by rehashing the real conversation he had with Chuck about the Play Hard Crew coming for his neck. Then, at the end of the song, Flav praises Chuck for a job well done on some 'that's right, you showed 'em'-type shit. It marked the beginning of a great musical partnership, one of the greatest in music history.

However, it didn't really matter how anxious Rick Rubin was to sign Chuckie D (he still hadn't shaved the 'ie' from his rap moniker) and Spectrum (despite recording 'Public Enemy Number One' they were also yet to change their name). They still didn't want to sign to Def Jam, or any label for that matter. The Spectrum massive were still very interested in emulating the success of radio personality Frankie Crocker. But they were having a hard time. 'This is before there was an Oprah, this is before Spike Lee's big, before Denzel's big, no one's really big yet,' observes Bill Stephney. 'The big people in the community were the radio stars.'

Not even Jam Master Jay, who stayed on their case about releasing the song, could change Chuck's mind. Flavor remembers picking up Jay and DMC to take them to the studio one day. 'I remember Jay telling Chuck, "Yo come on, man, why don't you put that record out, man". They were telling Chuck that shit for some months. Chuck was like, "Man, fuck that". It was really Jam Master Jay and DMC that talked Chuck into doing that Def Jam shit. So right now my hat goes off to Jam Master Jay 'cos he's really part of the start of PE. Of us being a recording group.'

But while DMC, and Jay in particular, never stopped trying to persuade Chuck that a career as a professional rapper was a good idea, it was obviously going to take something uniquely powerful to change his mind when it came to taking that leap of faith. 'I knew it would automatically just change my whole life,' Chuck explains. Def Jam tried to diversify their offer, giving Chuck the opportunity to write for other groups like The Beastie Boys, but Chuck wasn't keen on that either.

A variety of factors combined to eventually change his mind. The historic show that Run DMC played at Madison Square Garden as part of their Raising Hell tour set things in motion. Once again Bill Stephney was the main link between the Rush and Spectrum camps, but Jam Master Jay also made sure his homies were invited. Rick Rubin was hopeful that they would attend the show. Unlike the show Run DMC played in Long Beach, California, soon afterwards, the show at the Garden would be legendary for all the right reasons. This was the concert where Run famously told the 20,000-strong crowd to hold their Adidas trainers in the air prior to their performance of their historic song 'My Adidas'. Chuck, like everyone who saw or heard about this feat, was greatly impressed. (Wily old Russell Simmons also made sure that Adidas representatives saw the breathtaking response.)

But, despite the raw power of this spectacle, the media response to the Long Beach concert may have been even more crucial. Where Run DMC's show at the Garden had been an unqualified success, the show at the Long Beach Arena was nothing short of disastrous. Not only did the Crips and Bloods fight each other with scant regard for the concert that was supposed to be taking place, they also decided to rob and assault some concert-goers. Forty people were badly injured. The predictably hysterical media response which sought to blame Run DMC, and hip-hop by association, greatly vexed Chuck (as it did all hip-hop fans).

Away from all things Run DMC, the cold hard realities regarding the lack of opportunities open to young black men at the time also reared their ugly head. The people who would form PE had to reluctantly admit to themselves that the job in syndicated radio they hoped to win was just not realistic. Chuck realised their choices were severely limited. 'It was sorta like the only direction that was left because they wasn't gonna give us any shot on the radio, on professional radio in New York City. It just wasn't that time. Regardless of our skills in that field.' That's when Bill Stephney, Chuck and Hank all sat down and decided that instead of just doing another single they should try to come up with a concept. 'One of the concepts that I had obsessed about personally,' says Bill, 'was that we didn't have any political rap groups at that time.' Bill was a big fan of 'Sandinista' by The Clash. He wondered, 'Can we do something like that with a rap group?'

The mid eighties was a volatile time to be a young black man in New York. Black America as a whole was feeling the effects of the Reagan administration's 'trickle down' theory. It was a good lie. They promoted the always false idea that if the rich got richer, the wealth would eventually trickle down to the masses. The citizens of New York were hit harder than most. The fast-developing crack trade that would be dissected in 'Night of the Living Baseheads' wasn't helping anyone.

Caught up in the middle of all the madness, and directly affected by it, the crew would spend hours discussing these issues. 'Other young men of our time were hanging out smoking and drinking or doing drugs, or dealing drugs,' Bill reflects. 'All we did was talk about music and politics till 4 or 5 o'clock in the morning.' The idea was to direct that energy into their musical output. In this respect, they would have more in common with the punk rock movement than they would with the majority of mid-eighties rappers. This notion was irresistible to the people who would soon become PE and was the reason they eventually signed on the dotted line with Def Jam. The prospect of being able to put their politics into practice proved to be too enticing. Not even their deep-seated suspicion of the music business could deter them.

It was around this time that the graphic designer in Chuck surfaced to design the infamous PE logo. The image of a black man in the middle of a target is perhaps the most iconic logo in hip-hop history. It is certainly one of the most enduring and easily recognisable. Bill Adler, who, like everyone else, hadn't witnessed anything like it before at Def Jam was totally nonplussed. 'It was completely astonishing,' the former press officer recalls. 'Here was a group that said, "We're going to change the consciousness of an entire culture." Which is titanically ambitious to begin with. And they succeeded.'

PE stepped on to the scene at a time when the whole idea of black leadership was a thing of the past for America's black youth. J Edgar Hoover's tactics had worked: in the late sixties, soon after declaring the Black Panther Party for Self-Defense 'Public Enemy Number One' he famously proclaimed, 'There will be no more black leaders, unless we create one.' 'Chuck's voice sort of became that black leadership that everyone was looking for,' claims Bill Stephney. 'It's almost like when you heard Chuck's voice on record, you heard our version of Malcolm X and Martin Luther King, even though he's a rapper and it's a rap group.'

However, once Chuck was on board, he then had to convince Def Jam that signing Flavor Flav, who had no clear role within the group, was an equally good move. Eventually, Flav recorded enough vocals on the Strong Island crew's first album to be signed to a contract as a vocalist. But there was uncertainty about Flav at Def Jam. While some members of PE have spoken about how Russell and Rick in particular were unsure about what it was that Flavor actually did, Bill Stephney admits that he also objected. 'I'm the one who actually thought Flavor didn't make any sense,' he says laughing. 'I don't know if Chuck or Hank speak to this, but I don't recall Rick or Russell ever making any declaration that they didn't want Flavor to be part of the group. I know I did. I remember having a meeting, and I'm thinking, well, "We want to do some serious political rap group, we wanna be like The Clash you know, we can't have Flavor in the group! Are you out of your mind?"' This point of view would dog Flav at various points of his career.

Bill Adler confirms there was considerable disquiet over Flavor's membership in some quarters. 'You kinda had to scratch your head even at that time and wonder, "What is he doing in this group? What does he have to do with this kind of righteous solidarity?" Political solidarity. He was a brother on the corner, you know?' Hindsight, naturally, allows everyone to easily see how vital Flav was to proceedings. 'And yet he was a key element in the group,' Bill continues. 'He was brought in by Chuck as a comic relief to Chuck himself. It was really brilliant and rather self-effacing of Chuck to do that. It demonstrated a lot of knowledge on his part. Chuck D had the sense to build a counterpart to himself and build some comic relief in the form of Flavor.'

Thankfully, it didn't take long for the combined force of Chuck and Hank to bring Bill round. 'Chuck explains to me, "You gotta have Flavor," and then Hank explains it too: "You gotta have Flavor, 'cos Chuck might be too serious, so you need a balance there." At a certain point I said, "Okay, why not, it makes sense to me, let's just go with it."' Flav himself never suffered from these misgivings and was rightly confident from the jump. 'They were getting ready to make a big mistake,' he states on the subject. 'But I did end up getting signed, and I became one of their biggest voices, their biggest entities. I became their most sampled voice.'

Simultaneously, with the birth of PE, Unity Force became the S1Ws. The S1s incorporated the discipline of the Nation of Islam with some of the influences of the Panther party, and sought to rid the world of the pejorative phrase 'Third World'.

'How can someone else can define us, and call us third class?' asks James Bomb. 'We are the original people of this planet, so if we don't see ourselves as First World people, then someone else is going to define us and we can't let anyone else define who we are and what we mean to the planet earth. It's our resources that's fuelling the planet earth right now. You go to Africa, you'll find the most gold, silver and diamonds. All the precious metals that make society work as it works.'

The last piece of the puzzle to slot into place was Norman Rogers, aka DJ Mellow D. Mellow D used to fill in for Spectrum gigs as and when he was needed. Keith was the original and seemingly natural choice for the group's DJ, but quiet, dependable Norman was chosen by Chuck and Hank, probably because of those qualities.

Chuck and Hank were also responsible for creating Mellow D's Terminator X persona. Eric Sadler describes Norman as 'a big teddy bear, he's really like Yogi Bear, the most lovable, naive, goofy kid that you could ever have.' Such a personality would never fit in with PE. 'They decided, "You know what?"' Eric continues. '"Don't speak. You'll speak with your hands." And that's what he basically kinda stuck to.' This marked the only time someone's persona was significantly changed to fit the group. Of course, all performers perform. But this doesn't mean they're pretending.

Chuck and Flavor were the only people actually signed to contracts at Def Jam. Everybody else was a hired employee on a wage. Although it wasn't a great situation, nobody was starving. And once they started gigging things gradually improved. Some years later, Terminator X got his own contract.

For his part Eric sorted a deal that was different from everyone else's. When he was approached about working on the album he confirmed he was definitely interested but that he didn't want to work for a pittance. But that didn't change the fact that there wasn't much money to go round. 'I said, "Aiight it's near Christmas time so I won't charge that much, but I need to get a hundred dollars a jam,"' he remembers telling Chuck and Hank. His work on PE's debut album would amount to $1,200.

10

Work to Do

Once work on the album was properly underway in the second half of 1986, the group was focused. 'You're talking about a process where myself and Hank especially were involved 1,000 per cent in every second of the album,' Chuck remembers.

Public Enemy's debut album was called *Yo! Bum Rush the Show* because it was designed as the first installment of what was only meant to be a two-year programme. The first album's purpose was to kick in and bum rush the industry's door. No one ever thought the group's fortunes would skyrocket in the way they subsequently did. 'When Public Enemy happened, it was really beyond our wildest dreams,' says Harry Allen. PE have managed to last more than ten times longer than their initially planned lifespan.

The recording process proceeded fairly quickly. INS studios in Lower Manhattan – which is not too far from where the World Trade Centre once stood – became their home for four to five weeks. Sports-mad Chuck recalls that they were right down the street from the New York Mets when they were winning the '86 World Series.

For the first couple of weeks Eric, Chuck and Hank got together and laid down the basic backing tracks. Studio expert Eric used about five or six different drum machines. Once the skeletal backing tracks were down Chuck would rap over the beat so Eric could take it back and see how vocals would alter the soundbed, and what additional changes needed to be made. 'Once Chuck liked something we'd get him on it, and then I could tell where the track should head,' he says. 'Now I can put the drum rolls where they're supposed to go. I can take away stuff, add stuff.'

After that the next few days were devoted to Flavor. He

went back and forth with Chuck about how and where he should contribute. Once that was decided he went in and did his thing. Flavor was already prepared for what he had to do with 'Too Much Posse', the first in a long line of classic Flavor Flav solo songs. Every PE album contains one or two Flavor songs. It would be easy to compile a respectable Flavor Flav Greatest Hits set.

Bill Stephney is credited as the album's producer. In 1987, a producer was someone who oversaw a project and took care of its overall direction. These days, that's the role of an executive producer. Nowadays, a producer is a person who comes up with the beats and the music. Eventually, Bill Stephney wasn't required in any production capacity. 'People ask me, "How come you stopped producing on Public Enemy?"' reveals Bill, 'and I say, well, "More than anything I thought Chuck and Hank did a fantastic job musically with getting everything together and they can handle it within the studio."' There were also practical reasons, extraneous to the group. When Def Jam's sales started to go through the roof with the success of LL Cool J, The Beasties and Oran Juice Jones, Bill had begun 'essentially running the label for Rick and Russell'.

One of the key things about *Yo! Bum Rush the Show* that has been rarely touched on was the use of live instruments, which were essential to the album's overall sound. At the time, Stetsasonic and Run DMC were probably the only other hip-hop groups who didn't fully rely on samplers. In years to come, when PE incorporated the baNNed into their live shows the usual suspects – the self appointed 'real hip-hop heads' who hate anything even slightly leftfield – began complaining about how much their favourite rap group had changed. These critics probably never realised that PE were one of the first groups to use a combination of the 'old' (live instruments) and the 'new' (samplers). Bill, Eric and Flavor were the main musicians. The trio had been playing together for a minute. In addition to his less serious contributions like 'Claustrophobia Attack', Flav also penned some heartfelt love songs. Bill would play bass and guitar, Eric would also play the axe as well as keyboards and Flavor took care of the drums. There was no set pattern that determined whether a live instrument or a sample would be used. They simply went with the flow and did what worked best for each song.

'It was an incredible combination,' Bill recalls. 'We took advantage of the fact that we were part of that generation of folks who also played in bands on Long Island. We're the last generation, before the DJs took over.' All those who insisted PE's work wasn't real music probably never knew or cared that the ear and skills of a 'real musician' were brought to bear on their debut album. The combination of an old-school musicianship and the fact that Hank and Keith made music from the DJ's perspective is what has made PE so uniquely powerful through the years.

Instead of having the same uncomplicated drumbeat run through a song like far too many of his contemporaries, Eric would add subtle little changes that he imagined a real live drummer would incorporate. The hi-hat rhythm would change as the song progressed or here and there would be an extra kick drum or snare fill. He strove to break up a track a little bit and mix up the groove. He'd had very good practice. 'Before I did the PE stuff, I'd programme jazz drums, with thirty to forty patterns in a whole jazz song. As a musician I had friends who went to Berkeley. We're playing Crusaders and Tower of Power. I'm coming from that aspect. The combination of myself along with Hank and Keith and Chuck was a good combination, although Keith was kinda in and out from time to time. I was very technical. Keith and Hank especially brought to it what I would call a "musical ignorance". All they knew is, "Look, get funky motherfucker". It was the smartness and the ignorance that made the music really complicated and interesting.'

As time progressed they began to understand each other's quirks; where the other half was coming from musically. This allowed them to meet in the middle. Keith and Hank generally felt the songs didn't have to make sense musically, as long as they were banging. But Eric understood that while they could certainly bring the noise and make something new, at a certain point things did have to resolve themselves musically. Or as he puts it, 'It's fine if it's off a little, but somewhere it has to come on.'

Naturally, there was a degree of Spectrum City flavour in the mix. It wasn't just 'Public Enemy Number One' that was a product of WBAU. 'Timebomb' came about because Keith knew that Chuck had always jammed hard when he used to drop joints by The Meters when they were playing out. The sample from 'Just Kissed My Baby' is so good that ten years later EPMD would use it for their comeback single 'Never Seen Before'. So despite the fact that, by his own admission, Keith was kinda in and out, his fingerprints were still all over the album. He wasn't only responsible for putting together the song that won them the deal in the first place.

Once Chuck had laid his practice vocal and the songs had been Flavor-ised, it was time to bring the DJs in. For *Bum Rush* this largely meant Johnny Juice, but Keith also got busy and Terminator X played his part. Even Chuck got busy on the ones and twos. 'Chuck would call me and go, "I got these parts",' Eric says, 'and he would come in and do some old fucked-up scratching but what was brilliant about it was it was fucked-up, like really kind of off, but once you repeat that offness it creates another rhythm, which no one in life would've ever figured out or thought of.'

Sometimes The Bomb Squad would juxtapose all the different scratching styles. But for the most part it was The Johnny Juice Show: 'Johnny Juice would come in and just tear it up,' Eric continues. 'Cos he's a technician, he would do the majority, but then we'd bring in Terminator who would do the kind of rubbing, kind of scratching slow style. And that would add a whole 'nother dimension to the fast stuff cos it was a different style.'

Of all the scratching he did on the album, 'Raise the Roof' is probably most personal to Johnny Juice. It was the first PE song he ever performed on. Being an ex-graffiti writer from The Bronx, he wanted his first studio session to involve the *Wild Style* soundtrack. Charlie Ahearn's 1982 movie *Wild Style* was the first film to feature all the four elements of hip-hop – emceeing, breakdancing, DJing and graffiti – being practised under one roof. The title referred to a style of graffiti popular in The Bronx as the seventies became the eighties. Juice trawled the album for something to scratch. 'Wild Style was a big thing for me back in '79, I was totally ingrained in that shit,' he reminisces. Back when it was all so simple, his aunt used to take him and his other cousins to the local park jams. But as he had only just reached double figures, he was told in no uncertain terms to 'hang out over there by the swings and stay the fuck outta trouble'.

'I threw in that 10, 9, 8, and I scratched it in, just like that.' Sometimes, when the other guys weren't fully on point 'they'd be like, "Can you fix it?"' says Juice, 'and I would go back and go over the track that they did and do it tighter. I did almost all the records.' This is obviously why Johnny Juice is credited with rhythm scratching in *Yo! Bum Rush the Show*'s liner notes. Although he scratched live, Terminator X didn't perform a lot of the scratches that appeared on the records. Lack of time was the main factor. There were also financial concerns. As he himself would assert years later on the popular single from his second solo album, 'It All Comes Down to the Money'; the second line in that song's chorus lays it out clear: 'Whether it's rainy, or snowy or sunny'.

PE's meagre budget of $17,000 meant they had to record in a hurry. 'A lot of times me and Terminator would be there at the same time,' Juice recalls. 'We didn't have a lot of opportunities to keep going over and going over to get it right. They'd give Norman two tries, and if Norman couldn't do it on the third try, they'd be like, "Juice, see what you can do",' and I'd normally knock that out on the first take. I was superhyper man. My hands would be moving even if I wasn't touching a record.'

While the self-contained unit didn't have to worry about

interference from producers, in the late eighties hip-hop acts definitely had to worry about incompetent engineers. Like most at the time, the engineers felt that because they were rappers, these guys must be idiots. Eric was particularly pissed off. 'I'm like, "You know what guys, I've been in the studio a million times, we don't even need this guy".' As they knew nothing about hip-hop, the engineers would shoot down most of PE's suggestions. It's a good job The Bomb Squad never listened to these fools. 'They were basically telling us, "Well you can't do that, you can't put that much reverb on it, you can't push up that channel. You'll just have noise."'

Years later, Eric still sounds vexed about the situation. 'I was like, "I know what we can do and what we can't do. It's a new form of music, we're gonna do what feels good and what we want." They would be like, "You know what? It's gonna take a little time for us to get the sound." I'm like, "No it's not, 'cos I know how to work this stuff, don't give us this bullshit."'

Def Jam kept their word and gave PE the complete creative control they had promised. Rick Rubin visited the studio just once, said, 'Wassup', and bounced soon after. The only other person to get involved was a pre-Living Colour Vernon Reid, who was brought in by Bill Stephney to play the solo on 'Sophisticated Bitch'.

The only other people present at INS studios were Joeski Love, and occasionally his manager Vincent Davis. Keith Sweat was also recording an album at the time and once or twice the PE crew would glimpse him emerging from his jaguar in his mink coat. Was he aware of the sonic maelstrom PE were whipping up just down the corridor?

11

Yo! Bum Rush the Show

While recording proceeded without any major problems, actually getting the record out on the street proved more difficult. The Public Enemy crew felt (and still feel) their debut effort was hampered by that oldest of hip-hop record troubles: the dreaded release-date delay. Nowadays, it's pretty much the norm for hip-hop records to be pushed back for a month and often much longer. New albums will be delayed for as long as it takes to generate a buzz for the record and artist in question. Because the industry pays so much attention to an artist's first-week sales numbers, release dates have become one more weapon to market an upcoming release.

But as *Yo! Bum Rush the Show*'s release date was pushed back from late 1986 to early 1987 Chuck and Hank felt this made the record sound dated. Not so dated that the hip-hop community didn't embrace the group and their debut album. But dated enough for them to feel as if they were no longer at the forefront of new developments within the genre. Hip-hop has always moved at the speed of light. It has always produced new variations on its tried and tested sounds. Every now and again, something comes along that completely changes the game. Never was this more true than between 1986 and 1989.

The rate of progress was similar to that of Stevie Wonder's development in the early seventies. He'd paid his dues in the Motown trenches, and released classic songs like 'For Once in My Life' and 'Uptight'. But the music he produced from 1970 to 1975 was simply on another level. As an adult, he was able to offer more seasoned insights into society ('Living for the City'), politics ('Big Brother') and love ('All in Love Is Fair').

In the last four years of the eighties sampling techniques improved greatly, enhancing the production on many rap records. Admittedly, it wasn't unusual for some lazy producers to lift a whole record for their latest song – it still happens today – but the best producers in hip-hop had long since moved on. Rhyme styles became tighter yet looser and rappers in general were becoming a lot better than they had been in previous years. In accordance with this trend, DJs stepped their game up. Not only did scratching techniques improve, the mid eighties would see DJs like Jazzy Jeff popularise new techniques like transforming.

Three songs in particular represented this new generation of hip-hop artists: 'South Bronx' by KRS-One's Boogie Down Productions and two songs by Eric B and Rakim, 'My Melody' and 'I Know You Got Soul'. These joints raised the bar for hip-hop and gave Chuck and Hank food for thought. It also meant that PE would have to wait until album number two to establish themselves at the forefront of the genre. And all because The Boss was releasing a live album.

Bruce Springsteen was about to release *Live/1975–85*. And when the big heavy hitter of a major label comes out everything else gets pushed back. Springsteen was probably CBS's most successful and famous artist. PE were a new group on Def Jam, one of CBS's boutique labels. Springsteen's album also affected the release dates of other Def Jam albums. The Beastie Boys debut *Licensed to Ill* and LL Cool J's *Bigger And*

Deffer also appeared later than planned. Chuck explains their frustration at the time: 'Cos we had the vibe and the feel of what was going on in '85 or '86, we felt that we had an outdated situation. In '86 we designed our album sorta like in the pattern and the cadence of *Raising Hell* . . . They pushed our twelve inches back to 1987 when it was made for early '86. I remember hearing "I Know You Got Soul" and just saying to myself, "Man, this is the greatest thing in hip-hop ever."'

One reason posited why Def Jam records were pushed back more than usual was because the boutique label was largely an experiment for CBS. Hip-hop culture was definitely still a novelty to most. The success of *Licensed to Ill*, which eventually went quadruple platinum, and the fortunes of groups like PE changed this perception. 'Seriously, if it wasn't for The Beastie Boys Def Jam really would have been on a little bit more of an edgier ground and might not have pushed us through,' Chuck admits. They had to wait until March 1987 for *Yo! Bum Rush the Show* to hit record stores. The record didn't contain too much of the black power rhetoric that PE would become famous for in the years that followed. There were only flashes of militancy, most notably on 'Rightstarter (Message to a Black Man)' where Chuck spits lines like:

If you're blind about your past then I'll point behind
Kings, Queens, warriors, lovers
People proud – sisters and brothers.

It's telling that *Yo! Bum Rush the Show* is the only PE album with a song that has the word 'bitch' in the title. This never happened again: as time went on they laid off the lazy misogyny.

But this doesn't mean they weren't interested in presenting a side of blackness that the mainstream was less comfortable with. 'At the time our r'n'b guys is Freddie Jackson and all of that,' says Keith. 'The way we looked at it you had a bunch of ultra-soft black men representing the black race. It was like, "We're not like that", we're not that soft. In the seventies you had real strong black men representing black men. Not to diss any of the guys from the eighties. You had the Rick James, you had a few of them that was still holding out and still representing but you also had the Bobby McFerrin. That was why Chuck made that rhyme, "Don't worry be happy was a number one jam". You know, "You ain't in the hood!"'

While this point of view is valid, it does seem to be the reason that PE made some homophobic and sexist remarks in their earliest interviews. The very real music business practice of clearly favouring effeminate black men because they were somehow 'safer' does not excuse this.

Despite the setbacks with the release date, Chuck was already hustling real hard and showing his foresight. He had already begun introducing PE to the press in the UK and Europe, something that differentiated him from many other rappers of the time who, for the most part, only bothered with American journalists, if they bothered at all. At this stage of their career, things were going well for PE press-wise. Hank Shocklee had taken over as Def Jam's press officer while Bill Adler took a break to write Run DMC's brilliant biography, *Tougher Than Leather*. This meant that PE had two guys on the inside of the company to help orchestrate their moves.

Not unexpectedly, one of the few people writing about PE in the United States was Harry Allen, who had been close to the group ever since he met Chuck in Adelphi University's animation class. His first article on the group, which appeared in the *Brooklyn City Sun*, would only underscore just how much more than America England loved PE at the beginning of their careers. 'The very first article I ever wrote as a professional journalist was about Public Enemy and begins with me talking about a letter Chuck got from a girl in Bristol. A lot begins for us with Public Enemy and the UK at that time. People there are catching on. But people here haven't yet.' It was only during the earliest stages of PE that Harry could write about them. 'It wasn't that I didn't let on that I knew them, but I was really trying to avoid writing about Public Enemy 'cos I didn't want to be a booster for them, I didn't want to be their cheerleader and I didn't think it was really ethical in a way to keep writing about them. I wrote about them the first time 'cos it was such a good story and I wanted to declare that I thought they could do a good job.' He corresponded by letter with the fan in Bristol for a short while. She was talking about Bristol's trife life and how disheartening it was to see black men wasting their lives. She blamed the usual combination of unemployment, crime and drugs. 'Two things were striking to me. Firstly, my familiarity with the UK was virtually zero. So even the idea of black people in the UK was news to me. I can't say I didn't have any idea whatsoever that they were there. But certainly I had no idea what percentage of the UK was made up of black people or what their lives were like.' So to get a letter from a person there describing her life and a life he could relate to was something. 'For her to describe it so picturesquely and with such poignancy, it really touched me. This was someone who got it extremely early, who wasn't waiting for *A Nation of Millions*. She got *Yo! Bum Rush the Show*. Being at 510 South Franklin in Hempstead and seeing the mail come in from all over the world, that was . . . The idea that PE was affecting people in that way was totally crazy.'

Up to that point, PE's world had been extremely local. 'These were guys that I hung around with. We went to White Castle, snapped on each other and then went home or threw parties on the weekend. So this immediate global shift was like whiplash. It was very, very striking to me.' Harry stayed true to his word. After that initial article he only mentioned PE sparingly, in the *Village Voice* as well as the *Brooklyn City Sun*.

While PE were slowly but surely immersing themselves in the rap life, they weren't always welcomed with open arms. Even one or two of their heroes had it in for them. Chuck remembers being dissed by Melle Mel. 'In our first performances in '87 at the Latin Quarter Melle Mel was very rough on us. We would hear Melle Mel in the back yelling from the crowd with his big-ass voice, "Get them clowns off the stage", and Mel's voice, like I said, it would talk over the crowd so you couldn't help but hear him.

But I chalked it up as being this thing of "These are the ropes we gotta go through to prove that we belong." I was like James Brown, we don't want nothing, but open the door, let us get it ourselves.' After years of paying their dues, PE were more than ready to earn whatever accolades were going to come their way.

The great Melle Mel still remembers the incident. 'What happened was they were onstage at the Latin Quarter – I think it was around the time of the New Music Seminar – and they came out and performed a showcase, like nobody really knew who they were or whatever. And they pulled the music down and I think they were just talking. Anyway they had said something negative about Mr Magic and Mr Magic was a good friend of mine. I waited for them to kinda come down off the stage and I said, "Fuck Public Enemy!" I don't think I said too much more than that, that was basically it. And only 'cos they dissed my friend, you know. They were cool about it, I seen Chuck on the streets a little bit after that and we shook hands.'

This incident stemmed from a misunderstanding with New York radio DJ Mr Magic, who hosted a show on WBLS FM (his main competition was DJ Red Alert, who had a show on WRKS FM). Magic had been making noise for a few years on New York radio by then and had been brought to prominence by Whodini who recorded the tribute 'Magic's Wand'. Nineties rappers like Nas and Biggie also namechecked him on songs like 'Halftime' and 'Juicy' respectively.

Mr Magic had dissed 'Public Enemy No. 1' after KRS-One and Scott La Rock had gone onto Dr. Dre's show on WBAU and taunted him at the outset of the long-running Queensbridge-South Bronx beef. Magic had considered the Long Island camp to be in league with his abusers. As a result he had stated that the beat of 'Public Enemy Number One' was dope but the rap was wack. Flavor Flav would later immortalise his sentiments on one of PE's best known tracks, 'Cold Lampin' with Flavor'.

12

You're Gonna Get Yours

Chuck and Hank were determined to match the greatness of the newer-school rap songs. BDP's 'Poetry' only made them more determined. Chuck recalls how: 'I said, "These guys have taken the rhyme to another planet and we better get on that rhythm." We definitely felt that we were behind and we had to compensate.' Their plan was to make an undeniable B-side for their next single 'You're Gonna Get Yours', and a remix for the A-side. Johnny Juice was called up for the latter.

'They were like, "Yo, we gotta do a remix for 'You're Gonna Get Yours'," and when that was said Public Enemy were actually on tour.' This is another reason why Juice did a good deal of the scratching on these records. 'They were on tour a lot and we would finish and start a lot of these records while they were on tour. That's how we got shit done so fast.' Hank drove him and Keith out to the famous Greene Street studios to crank out what would later be dubbed 'You're Gonna Get Yours' (Terminator X Getaway Version). Left on their own they got down to business. They got to Greene Street and Hank disappeared. 'Hank said, "I want something real hot. Keith, you guys come up with something," and he leaves. Me and Keith are there, we had the original two-inch reel up so I'm like, "Just play the instrumental", he kept playing it and I just pulled out the actual vinyl of 'You're Gonna Get Yours', the album version, and I EQed it on the mixer so you can't hear too much of the bass, so it wouldn't clash with whatever was happening on the instrumental, and I just started scratching.' Keith liked what he heard, rewound the tape and Juice did a take. 'The whole thing was done in one take. "Great, let's go get some nuggets", and we were out.'

This is where things took a turn for the worse. 'To tell you the truth that was the beginning of the end for me actually,' Juice admits. 'When the single came out and I saw it said "Terminator X Getaway Version" I was fucking pissed. I said, "Terminator wasn't even in the fucking building yo. That's ridiculous."' Despite the circumstances, there wasn't tension between him and X. 'No, and the reason why is 'cos Terminator really didn't want to be in that position. Terminator wasn't a scratch DJ like that, he was a party DJ. Keep in mind these guys were Spectrum City, they would go to do gigs.' Juice was already unhappy with his credit on the debut album. 'I saw the way it said "rhythm scratching" and I got pissed off, like, "What the fuck is this rhythm scratch shit?" They were like, "You know, like guitar, rhythm guitar, lead guitar." And I'm like, "Yeah, but I did lead scratching." I thought, "Whatever". I was young at the time, I was only a teenager at the time, everybody else was in their twenties.'

Eric Sadler had similar issues. When he read the album liner notes and saw he had been credited with 'minimal synthesizer programming' it didn't feel good. 'I was like, "You know what I did: every single sound on this damn record apart from 'Public Enemy Number One' which I still had to reprogram and re-do." I did the whole thing along with the guys, and when I read the album credits it said "minimal", the word "minimal" was used. Then it gave me songwriting on, like, one song. I was mad for about a day but I didn't care. My boys on the other hand they were like, "This ain't right!" Nobody could even literally, and I do mean literally, a lot of them couldn't even turn on the equipment. They didn't even know where the off–on button was. It just was what it was.'

Even though the first seeds of discontent were being sown in the PE camp, Chuck and Hank's ambitions were satisfied when, not too much later, they recorded 'Rebel Without a Pause'. 'That was the B-side winning for the first time,' Chuck says happily. But before they could turn their attention to creating this new song they wanted and needed so badly, they had to go on their first major tours. These tours were the first example of PE's willingness to walk the path less travelled – to join The Beastie Boys' Licensed to Ill tour and the Def Jam live outing – while remaining true to their roots. This ethos has defined the PE live experience throughout their career.

13

The Show Goes on the Road

Public Enemy's suspicion of the music industry, and their natural disposition towards self-determination, led them to form their own management company, Rhythm Method Enterprises. To make sure the new company ran as smoothly as possible PE acquired the services of Ed Chalpin, who had previously managed Jimi Hendrix and Jimmy Cliff, and their former lawyer Ronald Skoler.

Because Russell Simmons' Rush Communications wanted to manage PE's latest project it had to buy half of the new company. They then had to try and figure out how to make the investment back. As a result, PE experienced high-profile touring for the first time as the support act for The Beastie Boys' Licensed to Ill tour. It made good sense to put them on tour to promote their recently released debut album. PE replaced LA-based funk rock group Fishbone and joined punk band Murphy's Law on the bill of the Beasties' tour.

It may seem strange to some that their first tour proper was with a rock band and a rap group who used to be a punk band. PE toured with punk rock acts before they joined other hip-hop groups on the Def Jam tour. In years to come, when they toured with groups like Anthrax and The Sisters of Mercy, they would have to remind fickle rap fans of the fact that they were one of the first rap groups to cross over to a white audience.

They discovered first-hand what they had let themselves in for during March '87 when Chuck, Hank and Flav travelled out to Detroit venue The Fox to check out the tour they would be joining. This tour would be slightly different to what they had been used to as Spectrum City.

While PE had witnessed Run DMC's high profile Raising

Hell tour, albeit from behind the scenes, the Licensed to Ill tour was the first tour with a rap act to reach 'really, really suburban white towns', says Chuck. 'The tour just blew my mind,' he continues. 'Especially the Beastie Boys' performance. The magnitude, the size, the rebelliousness, the difference.' Chuck, Flav and Hank decided they would have to step their game up. 'It wasn't like performing round town at the local neighbourhood centre that we used to rent and throw gigs at and stuff,' Flav remembers thinking. 'This was the real shit now.'

But, while they were certainly nervous, there was a more pressing problem. The fledgling group had to work out what they were going to do with the $1,000 they would receive each night. It might have been less of a problem if they were actually getting the full grand. Firstly, there were two management companies taking fifteen per cent each. Ron Skoler and Ed Chalpin had to take their cut, and Chuck and Hank, as joint heads of the company, must have received something too. Unfortunately, booking commission meant they had to kiss a further 10 per cent goodbye. So at the end of it all PE only had $600 to distribute among themselves.

Fortunately, Chuck had a van at his disposal which saved on costs. He used it to take the six-man crew – Chuck, Flav, Griff, Terminator X and two S1Ws – around the country, assuming driving responsibilities himself for the most part. His place of work owned the van, so Chuck exercised extreme caution when it came to taking care of the vehicle. Chuck's then girlfriend also allowed him to use her credit card. Together PE drove to fifteen cities in the north-east of America.

The first show took place in Passaic, New Jersey, on April 1, 1987. There was still the odd teething problem. As PE eased into their first show the one thing that should never, ever occur during a hip-hop set happened right in front of Russell Simmons – the record skipped. Years later, Chuck can laugh about it easily. 'Flavor remembers quite clearly that he saw Russell smiling and then when the record skipped he saw the smile disappear instantly.'

Despite that initial setback Chuck remembers it as a 'great twenty-five-minute set'. They were loved by the alternative crowd. Now 'alternative' can mean many different things to many different people. Broadly speaking, those who follow alternative music like to think and/or be perceived to think outside the box. PE have always had love in the hood, the inner city or the ghetto (or whatever term you might use). But as they have never been one of those groups who wallow in and pander to the worst aspects of disadvantaged neighbourhoods, they will never attract significant numbers of those who, for one reason or another, have succumbed to the various traps of the ghetto – self-made or not.

Indeed, this is one of the greatest attributes of PE. Their shows have always had a diverse mix of ghetto dwellers, rock fans and a smattering of more bourgeois middle-class heads of whatever race. In their own small way, they have done more for race relations than may be initially supposed. None of the above means that they didn't know how to act in the hood. It just means that they weren't completely defined by where they came from. They considered things a bit more. They were, after all, the Black Panthers of Rap.

In the Beasties, PE had the perfect companions with whom to ease themselves into the world of high-profile touring. This alternative crowd suited them just fine because their music firmly cast itself as different and alternative to the hip-hop mainstream. Bill Adler had long since realised that, unlike Run DMC and especially LL Cool J, they didn't fit the sensibilities of mainstream black pop magazines like *Right On!* and *Black Beat*. The lack of publications geared specifically towards hip-hop – *The Source* didn't exist until 1988 and would take a couple of years to build a readership – meant they were still often relying on the 'alternative press' for publicity. '*Right On!* and *Black Beat* wrote about Public Enemy a little bit although there was really nothing cute and cuddly about Public Enemy. LL, I mean LL, forget it! He was tailor-made for *Right On!*,' Bill laughs. 'He was so cute, he had dimples, he was built, he was young, he was beautiful. Public Enemy on the other hand were these kind of scowling thugs. Very deliberately, not cuddly.'

The Beasties had been long-time fans of the Strong Island crew. At a time when they were the biggest phenomenon in pop music (*Licensed to Ill* would eventually sell four million copies), their unbridled enthusiasm prompted the first important white boys in the rap game to sing PE's praises whenever possible. So, while Run DMC co-signed them for the hip-hop community, the never-ending props from The Beasties ensured PE were adopted by the alternative crowd for good. Bill Adler recalls that when Run DMC and The Beasties were about to go on tour together they would rap the lyrics from *Bum Rush* back and forth to each other. 'DMC in particular was completely enamoured. Within a week of the release of the album DMC had memorised every lyric. Everything. And he went around the office rapping Chuck's lyrics. He was very,

very much on Chuck's dick. Our little Rush Productions/Def Jam crew was very enthused about these guys.' All these years later, Chuck D is still DMC's favourite rapper. Which is indeed an honour for the hard rhymer. 'Don't talk about Biggie Smalls to DMC,' Bill chuckles, ''cos he's gonna get mad and he'll tell you flat out, "Nobody was ever better than Chuck D."'

It is a testament to PE's onstage prowess that they were just as comfortable on the Def Jam tour as they were with The Beasties and Murphy's Law. The Def Jam tour also took place in 1987 and was a different matter altogether. These were the days when the harsh truth is that many white people were extremely wary about going to a hip-hop show (the media hysteria that greeted Run DMC's show in LA undoubtedly contributed to this). Chuck notes, 'To see 17,000 all black kids in an arena was not rare back at that time for all hip-hop.' On the Def Jam tour, for which they were joined by Eric B and Rakim, Whodini, Doug E Fresh, Stetsasonic, and the headliner LL Cool J, PE had an early slot of approximately fifteen minutes.

PE shared a bus with Stetsasonic all summer. This meant two big crews, thirteen to fourteen people in total, on one regular bus. The extravagant tour buses that are the norm these days were just not an option for two rap crews in the late eighties. Luckily, they got on well and formed a lasting bond. PE also forged a friendship with Doug E Fresh, the legendary rapper and beatboxer from Harlem who had enjoyed massive success alongside Slick Rick with the double A-side 'The Show', and hip-hop staple 'La-Di-Da-Di', which is still being sampled to this day.

Doug E Fresh was to play a big part in helping to form what would become the legendary PE live show while it was still in its infancy. But before he did that the Greatest Entertainer Alive simply impressed them all by proving just how well he could cope without Rick. 'I had wondered what the hell he was gonna do without his partner,' Chuck admits. 'I was quickly thrown the first day because he went in and totally blew my stove off. He totally wore this arena out and I had never seen one man in hip-hop just totally wear it out.'

For a crew as large as PE, Doug Fresh's solo stage-skills must have been impressive. Furthermore, despite his stage prowess, Chuck remembers him being 'humble and genuinely sincere'. During the soundcheck for the second show of the tour, which took place in Norfolk, Virginia, Doug made a suggestion that changed the PE show and gave it one of its most enduring characteristics: the drills performed by the S1Ws. Doug made the simple but effective suggestion that the S1s should move around rhythmically onstage instead of being stationary. 'Doug E Fresh is a showman, as far as I'm concerned he's in the top five showmen in entertainment. He was like, "Move y'all! Do something to excite the people." So we started drilling,' says James Bomb. The situation with only two S1Ws going out on the road was still in effect. 'That's how we did it when we started out, we alternated,' James recalls. 'Only two people could go at a time.' This continued until 1988. As students of hip-hop PE were not afraid to learn from the other acts around them, and especially those who had made noise before them. There were suggestions throughout that whole summer. 'I used to ask Doug Fresh for tips, and also Ecstacy from Whodini,' says Chuck. 'Ecstacy from Whodini was a tremendous asset to learn from. I would stand out and watch everybody's show.'

In the liner notes of *It Takes a Nation of Millions to Hold Us Back*, Doug E Fresh and Ecstacy of Whodini are thanked and credited as 'show inspiration'. PE's humility was one of the things that allowed their show to become as great as it has. Unlike rappers whose egos are forever running wild, PE acknowledged they weren't going to be great in their first year. Chuck accepted that they had to deal with setbacks and improve regularly. 'The problem with hip-hop today is everybody thinks that they can make a record and all of a sudden automatically they're gonna be great. There's a learning curve and I took that learning curve seriously.'

Not afraid to learn, some members of PE took things further, and matters into their own hands when they saw a solution to a problem. It was on this tour that Brother Drew evolved from an S1W into PE's soundman. During the southern leg of the tour, 'Kentucky, or somewhere in North Carolina', Drew decided to save the day, the bass, and how low it could go. 'I was onstage doing the S1W thing and I was wondering, "Why aren't the people moving?" So I was like, "Yo Griff, I'm going out there to do the soundboard."' When he reached the soundboard it became immediately clear what the problem was. 'Public Enemy got a certain sound, it's like a lot of low end, and black people, if they ain't feeling it they ain't moving, and they wasn't feeling it.' Drew knew what he was talking about. He'd been in a band with his brothers since high school and is yet another example of the PE camp belonging to the last generation that was involved with bands before the DJs took over. Occasionally, the band had played with Spectrum at their parties. Drew immediately became PE's soundman, and had found an important niche in PE. It also had a knock-on effect for hip-hop in general. How many rappers have expressed (the admittedly negative) need to 'beat down the soundman'? PE were never the type to express such sentiments. Thanks to Drew, it was never an issue they had to concern themselves with.

'I started doing the sound thing and I was one of the first black soundmen for rap music.' Amen to that. The tour was so significant that Chuck credits the experience of the groups rolling together for three groundbreaking albums: PE's *It Takes a Nation of Millions to Hold Us Back*, Stetsasonic's *In Full Gear* and De La Soul's *3 Feet High and Rising* (on which Stetsasonic's Prince Paul was producer).

14

Rebel Without a Pause

With their touring swagger intensifying daily, Hank and Chuck could turn their attention to cutting the track that would push them to the forefront of hip-hop. It's impossible to underestimate the importance they placed on, first, satisfying themselves and the fans of hip-hop music. They were finally satisfied when they recorded 'Rebel Without a Pause' on the Def Jam tour, as spring became summer in 1987.

'Rebel Without a Pause' ticked three important boxes. It matched 'I Know You Got Soul' in terms of its innovation and its breathtaking quality. It increased the tempo for Public Enemy, something they would do repeatedly during their forthcoming masterpiece, *It Takes a Nation of Millions to Hold Us Back*. The faster tempo was important as it would heighten energy levels at their shows. Most important of all, it sounded fresh. It was some next level hip-hop. Chuck and Hank rightly felt it could stand alongside the best rap records of the time.

Whether they bettered Kris and Scott or Eric and Ra is a matter of opinion. If they didn't, they certainly equalled their greatness. But, like anything in life worth getting, it didn't come easy. The process was a long one. Once the basic backing track had been put together, Chuck locked himself in his house for a whole day to bang out the lyrics. He remembers Hank dropping by at midday to try and persuade him to take a break, play some ball, but Chuck wasn't on it.

Since the track had to be groundbreaking for hip-hop, the group of producers soon to be known as The Bomb Squad had to employ different production techniques. Instead of simply looping the eternally useful 'funky drummer' break (hip-hop's most widely used breakbeat), Flavor Flav's skills as a drummer came into play. Flavor played the beat on the drum machine continuously and perfectly for the whole five minutes and two seconds of it. 'Flavor's timing helped create almost like a band rhythm on "Rebel Without a Pause",' Chuck notes. Flavor Flav also made another important contribution. His stream of consciousness ad libs, which punctuated every twelve bars of Chuck's hard rhyming, allowed the song to forgo the traditional verse/chorus, verse/chorus structure.

Another important element of the song that made it so unforgettable is Terminator X's classic 'rock'n'roll' transformer scratch that occurs towards the end of the song. It's fair to say that this is one of the most famous scratching routines in hip-hop music. It's like Chuck Berry's solo in 'Johnny B Goode' or Eddie Van Halen's guest turn towards the end of Michael Jackson's 'Beat It'.

Eric remembers it gave Terminator X an opportunity to step up and prove himself. 'Norman was there but we were like, "Oh, we gotta give Juice a call," and Norman was like, "Nah, fuck that man, what are you talking about? I got some parts for this, I got some ideas for this." We're like, "You're sure, Norm?" and he's like, "Yeah man, I got some stuff for this . . . " We're like, "Aiight, here you go," so we set up the turntables for him and all of a sudden here he goes. We're like, "Where the hell did you learn that?" and he's like, "Yo, I've been out on the road, man." So he learned some tricks from those guys on the road. He didn't want Johnny Juice to be the main scratcher.'

On tour, Terminator had perfected his take on the transformer scratch that DJ Spinbad had first invented, and that Jazzy Jeff and Cash Money had popularised. The scratch took its name from the *Transformers* cartoon as it sounded like the noise made when the Autobots morphed from a car into a robot and vice versa. But after repeated takes that had seemed more than adequate it just wasn't sounding right when they listened to the playback. It was left to Hank Shocklee to suggest that they take the bass out of Terminator's section of the song. With the bass gone the scratch fitted perfectly.

Similarly, Chuck needed more than a couple of attempts to satisfy himself that he had given the song the right passion and commitment. There were many, many takes, a trend that would endure throughout his career. 'I was so mad 'cos I said, "This close,"' he recalls of his first day of trying. 'The next day I went back and for some reason I just was thinking, "Rap through your diaphragm", or something like that, and I nailed it. Once I nailed it I was like, "Oh Lord, I nailed my part!"'

Finally, Hank had to mix all that noise down. 'Only someone with Hank's talent could mix all the different elements of a record like "Rebel",' Chuck insists. 'Hank made that mix with the engineer Steve Ett. When he brought it by I said, "Yo man, I could die man, tomorrow, 'cos that one record right there? Nothing could fucking go nowhere near it."'

Not wanting to waste any time, they took the record straight to radio. Kiss FM's Chuck Chillout received a copy as did Red Alert. Chuck Chillout played it immediately and 'Rebel' quickly became the biggest rap tune in New York.

'When "Rebel" came out all you could hear from the cars going by our house was eeeeeeeeeeeeeeeehhhhhhhhhh,' says Harry Allen with a very adequate impression of the famous break. 'Nobody was playing anything else that summer, I remember MC Lyte saying, "When I hear that song I wanna punch someone in the mouth." It was that kind of deep feeling. It's really under-documented how that record affected people.'

After the record became a hit in New York, it began to spread around the rest of the East Coast. Lady B, a DJ from Philadelphia, already knew PE from their Spectrum days. As she was one of the first to get behind their new hit in the city of brotherly love her support was priceless. 'From that point on it was bananas,' Chuck smiles. However, because records took a lot longer to travel in those days, the situation was very different in the southern states. A show in Kansas City featured a slightly bemused crowd staring at PE when they performed their first undeniable smash. They didn't know the record so they couldn't catch the groove.

Things were better in the motor city, Detroit. Chuck remembers it as 'our first real, real genuine response that was just to us'. As 1987 progressed and PE swung back east on the tour, the crowds began wilding out more and more when they played their new masterpiece. Around August the tour hit the East Coast and the crowd response intensified accordingly. For the first time the other acts on the tour began to notice that PE were getting a better response than expected. Soon after, a show at Madison Square Garden when 'Rebel Without a Pause' was the hottest record of the summer was a particularly live-wire affair. Chuck remembers it fondly: 'The Garden went absolutely fuckin' nuts, it was pandemonium.'

That was only for starters. PE were to spend the next two nights rocking Philadelphia, where Lady B had been hyping 'Rebel Without a Pause' for a minute. Philadelphia would prove so supportive of PE that it would be one of two cities that received a special dedication on *It Takes a Nation of Millions to Hold Us Back*. London was the other. Even at this early stage of their career, PE were proving themselves different to their contemporaries who, for the most part, stuck to the script. Most groups only concentrated on New York and LA, as they were the only cities that at that time had produced a respectable amount of successful hip-hop artists. But being from Long Island, the members of PE knew what it felt like to be overlooked and disrespected.

It didn't hurt that Philadelphia was always going to be more receptive to PE's politics than other East Coast American cities. Philly had always been progressive, and Islam was very popular among the black community in the seventies. Music producer Kenny Gamble, of Gamble and Huff, may have been the city's most famous convert, but he wasn't alone. The city provided a springboard for PE's politics. 'Our whole black power, black recognition movement really sparked from there, it travelled out from Philly.'

The way in which PE conducted themselves when they first played in Philly (before the Def Jam tour) also played its part in the group's love affair with the city that spawned Jazzy Jeff and The Fresh Prince, Steady B and, in time, The Roots. Their experiences of dealing with rap stars during their Spectrum days had not been forgotten. These experiences determined the way the Black Panthers of Rap behaved in May 1987 when they were invited by Lady B to perform at her club night. Chuck speaks of Lady B affectionately as a 'good friend to this day'.

Every weekend she hosted a night co-run by Power 99, the radio station she worked for, at After Midnight, a club in the middle of Philadelphia's Seventh City. It was one of the city's most popular nights. Chuck was adamant that when they arrived PE would be approachable. 'I told my guys, "We're gonna be a different group, we're gonna be the anti-stars."'

To that end, there were no limos, or other ostentatious displays of wealth that they could ill-afford. In addition, PE approached the line of rap fans that stretched around the club and made a point of shaking everyone's hand. This was most definitely not the norm, and Philadelphia's rap fans were more than slightly surprised. Pleasantly surprised, but surprised nonetheless. Even if they had wanted to cause trouble for whatever reason, it wouldn't have been a good idea: 'The 98 Posse followed us, they were across the street at a bus terminal. So they saw like twelve 98s in the van and when we pulled out and shook everybody's hand on the line they were looking at us like . . . ' Chuck contorts his face into the look of aghast shock they were greeted with in late eighties Philadelphia. This was the first time hip-hop fans in Philadelphia had been treated this well by rap artists from New York. Most New York rappers acted all high and mighty and standoffish. And while they had the 98s there just in case, PE broke the ice.

As soon as they arrived onstage and performed 'Public Enemy Number One' the place went crazy because the crowd had already been won over by PE's social skills and, ultimately, their knowledge of street politics. The After Midnight show made a gigantic impact in Illadelph. Word got round the street that not only do PE have a hot record, but these dudes are the coolest guys ever.

The good vibes were still very much in the air when PE and the Def Jam tour arrived in Philly on September 2 to play a venue called (funnily enough) The Spectrum, for two nights. Once again, their new masterpiece was the biggest tune of the evening. 'When it got to "Rebel Without a Pause" I swear to God, man, I thought the building was gonna come down. The whole of the next day I was floating on air,' Chuck recalls. 'That was the first time I was like, "We got some powerful shit going on."'

The next day was just as crazy. Ironically, PE weren't even supposed to be on tour by that time. Boogie Down Productions were supposed to have replaced PE on the tour by September. But that, of course, had changed when BDP's DJ Scott La Rock was tragically murdered in The Bronx on August 27, 1987. PE received the news while playing in Rockford, Illinois. Chuck got a knock on his door from Eric B. As a tribute, when PE played the Garden, they invited KRS-One to perform with Kool DJ Red Alert filling in for Scott. To display their grief further, Terminator X's DJ stand was adorned with lights and a coffin. A poster of Scott hung from behind. Chuck admits, 'It looked kind of eerie.'

Eventually, BDP did replace PE on the tour. This gave PE a short break to prepare for what the rest of September and October would bring. These months would see the Def Jam tour go to Europe and before that PE were about to tape a performance on *Soul Train*, the music programme that has long been an outlet for Black American performers. The black music institution would eventually cement 'Rebel' as a national hit when PE's appearance was broadcast in December 1987. It was the perfect way to cap what had been by far the busiest year of their lives. But before they got to see themselves on TV with Don Cornelius they were anxious to make their first trip to Europe a success.

15

The Enemy in Europe

Eric B and Rakim and LL Cool J joined Public Enemy on the European leg of the Def Jam tour. PE had a good relationship with LL, but still felt like they had to prove themselves to Eric and Ra. For a time, Eric and his brother Ant Barrier were, as Chuck tells it, 'very hard on us as Public Enemy because they thought that we were like a favoured child coming out of the CBS system while they came out with twelve-inches and earned the streets before we did'. They were yet to learn about PE's radio and mobile gig background.

Chuck has always insisted that if there was ever a union leader in hip-hop – something KRS-One has been calling for more frequently in recent years – it would be Eric Barrier. 'Eric B is always an underrated guy. People always talk about Eric B but they try to treat him as an afterthought. Eric B was the dude that demanded respect and you had to respect him. He's a serious dude.'

With LL it was another story. He was another rapper who knew PE from their Spectrum days. James Todd Smith was, after all, from Queens. Additionally, he had saved the day for Chuck years before they embarked on the Def Jam tour together. On the night in question, Spectrum were promoting a gig for a group called Masterdon Committee in Long Island, but the Committee decided not to turn up. Luckily for Chuck, he was thrown a lifeline when Dre gave him LL's home number. When he called him from WBAU, he happened to be home with his grandma. 'I said, "Would you mind coming out?" and LL Cool J came out to the roller rink to judge the emcee contest and got down on the mic acapella for like ten minutes with Dre on the wheels. He saved my life. I always thank LL for that.' So LL was more than familiar with PE's personnel and their extended crew. The two entities became closer when Chuck and Hank stepped in to help L finish the album that would become *Bigger And Deffer*.

Rick Rubin was otherwise engaged so the album's production was entrusted to West Coast producers the LA Posse (not to be confused with Mikey D's LA Posse who represented Laurelton, Queens) and PE, when they were still very much rookies in the game. This was another reason *Yo! Bum Rush the Show* came out in March 1987. For a while, Def Jam had intended to release LL's album in the spring, and PE's in the summer. But as his project hadn't been dealt with properly, L swapped places with PE and waited until the summer. (It's worth wondering how PE would've felt about their debut album if they'd had to wait even those few more months. Chuck and Hank felt it was dated in early – let alone mid – 1987.) The mixture of camaraderie and competition led to some cherished memories. 'We had some special times looking at young Rakim and young LL,' Chuck recalls.

At around the same time that PE rocked Philly and Madison Square Garden to the core, Rick Rubin was putting together the soundtrack to *Less Than Zero*, the movie of Brett Easton Ellis's novel which starred Robert Downey Jr.

As they were the newest group on Def Jam, it was a no-brainer for him to ask PE to contribute a track. In their quest to stay up to the times, the group decided not to use any of the songs they had worked on while on the road. They decided to come up with something fresh. The first new song they came up with was called 'Don't Believe the Hype' and its target was John Leland who, at the time, was a writer for the *Village Voice*. Like most rock critics, he failed to fully understand. The group judged him to be responsible for some serious hype.

PE had already decided they weren't particularly enamoured with how mainstream journalists dealt with hip-hop. The problem still exists today and things are only marginally better than they were in the late eighties. They especially didn't like the one-sided, ill-informed way that much of the press had reported on the incident that had occurred at Run DMC's Long Beach concert. 'They were being dogged by the media for something that they didn't start,' Chuck says, still visibly vexed years later.

'Don't Believe the Hype' was the first song they had completed after 'Rebel Without a Pause' (that's why Chuck's first line of verse two is 'Yes was the start of my last jam'). However, after recording an uptempo masterpiece like 'Rebel' the PE camp decided that 'Don't Believe the Hype' was too slow. As unbelievable as it may seem now, PE were not overly impressed with 'Don't Believe the Hype'. At least at first. They felt it was lacking something. So, for the time being, the song was shelved.

Following that decision, work began on what would become 'Bring the Noise'. This beat was more in tune with the rhythm and intensity of 'Rebel' rather than the funk – albeit an aggressive kind of funk – of 'Don't Believe the Hype'. The beat was so crazy it left Chuck wondering how he was going to attack it. As a dope emcee, he had many styles to choose from. Furthermore, they had just been on tour so that adrenaline was still buzzing inside him.

'People cut their best shit after getting off the road,' he observes. But there were still difficulties. Harry Allen recalls one occasion where Chuck's frustration boiled over: 'I remember the first time he played the track for me, 'cos he was having a hard time making it work. We were in Atlanta and he threw the tape recorder against the wall 'cos he was so frustrated.' Hank produced the killer suggestion that made all the difference. 'Hank said, "Why don't you come up and put all of these different styles on 'Bring the Noise'?" That happened to be the thing that worked.'

So, as keen listeners will notice, Chuck deployed three different styles of rhyming in each of the three verses in 'Bring the Noise'. He starts the first verse with a lot of room between his words. 'Bass . . . how low can you go/ Death Row . . . What a brother know'. The second verse is a lot more hectic: 'Never badder than bad 'cos the brother is madder than mad/ At the facts that corrupt like a senator.' The third verse is somewhere in the middle of the other two. 'Get from in front of me . . .

the crowd runs to me/ My DJ is warm, he's X, I call him Norm, you know'. After Chuck cut his vocals the crew remained in the studio while Terminator finished his scratches.

Once the song was completed, PE returned their attention to their impending European tour, which began on November 1, 1987. It's an understatement to say that, overseas, heads weren't ready. Firstly, England's hip-hop fans were surprised that they had made the trip across the Atlantic in the first place. It was still very rare for hip-hop fans in the UK to see their American heroes in the flesh. The most enthusiastic fans had read interviews (by this time Professor Griff as well as Chuck was taking care of interview duty) and, on isolated occasions, seen them on TV. The wider public were still largely uninitiated. Even in today's multimedia world – where cultural developments travel the globe almost as they happen – PE live in the flesh is a different affair. In the late eighties yet more so.

Perhaps unsurprisingly, PE's pro-black politics was the big reason that they shocked England during their first visit. They were certainly the first hip-hop group ever to walk on a British stage and urge the crowd to say, 'Fuck Thatcher, Fuck Reagan and Fuck Bush'.

This was a time when most rap groups just told the crowd to put their hands in the air. 'People were like, "Huh",' recalls Chuck with his best impression of a stupefied, surprised expression. 'They were like, "You can't say fuck the Queen!" We was like, "Yo, fuck Thatcher, fuck that dog-faced bitch." They were like, "Can you say this? Can it be right?" We had something that was happening in the streets that had people saying, "They the new shit. This is some new shit coming from something that we ain't never ever seen before. What the fuck is behind it?"'

They repeated the efforts they had made in Philadelphia and made a special attempt to reach out to the local hip-hop community. As well as being the first rappers to disparage Thatcher publicly, PE were more than likely the first hip-hop group to urge UK rappers to quit using American accents. Seeing as it didn't make much sense to go back to their tiny, crowded hotel rooms, the crew often found themselves 'damn near on the tube' hanging out with London's hip-hop crowd after their shows.

Just as it had done in Philly a few months earlier, this made a big impression. 'They'd never seen nothing like that before,' Chuck says. 'They were like, "Yo, these guys come from the United States and these guys are just the coolest dudes. They're not on no star shit."' Importantly, PE understood the Caribbean origin of many English-born black people (this didn't mean the African heritage was ignored, it just means that the especial Caribbean influence on urban communities and British immigrant experience since the fifties was duly recognised).

Eric B and Rakim and LL Cool J, meanwhile, were as unprepared for England as the English were for PE. Not only was it cold and grimy in their eyes, with a lack of nice food and hot women, they soon had to come to terms with the fact that the opening act, the rookies, had gradually become the hottest thing, not only in New York, but across the Atlantic as well. 'Rebel Without a Pause' had exploded across London as news of PE's American tour dates gradually filtered overseas. 'Timebomb' and 'Public Enemy Number One' had already been in Tim Westwood's rap chart before this happened. Mike Allen, who hosted the *Capital Rap Show* before Westwood and Dave Pearce's tenures, had supported the group as well.

Dave Pearce's introduction of PE at the Hammersmith Odeon in November 1987 would famously be sampled for the introduction to *It Takes a Nation of Millions to Hold Us Back*. Chuck remembers their first night well. 'The first thirty seconds of the first night are like Dave Pearce. Dave Pearce comes out and says, "Welcome to the Def Jam tour."' But Dave would soon be drowned out. 'Then he says, "Ladies and Gentlemen, give it up for Public Enemy." When we came on it was the whistles, that's the first thing I remember, the whistles.'

Visually, PE were not like anything else ever. Seeing them for the first time must have been mind-blowing. 'The first thing they see is our gigantic banner 'cos the only thing we had was our visuals,' Chuck recalls. 'The banner was gigantic so the logo meant something and it was looming, just towered over everything.' As their set was twenty-five minutes long, PE certainly had long enough onstage to make theirs a very hard act to follow. 'It got to the stage where the other two acts was just like, "What the fuck?"'

The show kicked off with Griff conducting the scene. The S1Ws broke into the military-minded moves Doug E Fresh had rightly suggested, and Terminator X began scratching to suggest the show was imminent. Lastly, Chuck and Flav raced onstage, and pandemonium ensued. The sheer number of people onstage acting as one was unlike anything hip-hop had produced before. Granted, some of their fans decided that the whole thing was punk to the nth degree. But the majority were simply too taken aback by PE's live show to know what to think.

Nothing proved PE's dominance on the tour more than the audience reaction to LL Cool J performing 'I Need Love'. Across America, LL's elaborate performance of the song, where he came out onstage on a big double bed, playing up his loverman status to the fullest, had gone down a storm. When he tried a similar routine in London, however, it just wasn't to be. During the first night of the Def Jam show the crowd forgot he was a hip-hop icon and that he helped to build Def Jam in the first place. L's performance was cut short when the crowd began to throw things at the stage. 'The people had kinda like totally flipped overnight,' Chuck explains. 'Their thing was like, "We don't really want him to be on no star shit", so that's what made them throw the coins at him and boo him and stuff like that.'

But PE weren't the type to rub salt into the wound or even lord it over Cool James. 'Of course we were backstage to console LL. He was still our champion, but you gotta give guidance 'cos this atmosphere is not like Atlanta. And he's a young guy so he doesn't know, this is traumatic to him. Me, I'm old and personally it doesn't matter. It's cool.'

Despite their understanding and good relationship, PE didn't disrespect LL by bullshitting him. 'We were consoling LL but we were saying seriously, "You better have your hard hat on! Because you talking about some hungry mother-fuckers."' Over the course of the second and third dates, PE made more contacts in London and 'really sunk into the

London psyche'. The twin efforts of making sure they had the best, most energetic show and their unprecedented social skills have meant that PE can still tour the country at will to this day and will continue to do so for many years to come. Witness their triumphant return in May 2008 to perform *It Takes a Nation of Millions to Hold Us Back* at Brixton Academy.

After those three, very energetic, live shows, the Def Jam tour personnel made the short trip to Amsterdam, where the tour continued. For Eric B and Rakim, however, this would be their last stop on the tour. It's difficult to pinpoint exactly why, but they left Amsterdam and returned to the United States. Chuck uses an interesting analogy to outline the differences between the groups, and the discord that was created during the shows up to that point.

'It wasn't that Eric B and Rakim couldn't resonate, it's just that after our speed and intensity it's hard. Eric B and Rakim was laid-back with just two guys on the stage. Compared to us it was like you got a race truck going on and then you got some nice convertible after that. But the race truck created havoc.'

Perhaps they weren't overly impressed that the group who had been the underdogs for so long were now winning every night. It could be that they were among the first to realise just how truly powerful the PE live show could be.

Chuck seems to think so: 'Eric was kinda like, "I'm not gonna get my ass whooped by the guys we've been with all year long." At the Amsterdam jam, the fourth day of whoop-ass, Eric and Rakim, their whole crew, said, "We're getting the fuck off this tour." It just wasn't the same as the United States, where they was winning every night.' Of course, it could have had absolutely nothing to do with that. Let us remind ourselves once again that like many American rappers on tour, they didn't like the food, women or the weather.

Needless to say, it turned out okay for Eric and Ra. In the following year they released *Follow the Leader*, which like its predecessor *Paid in Full* set new standards for hip-hop. But

PE's unquestionable dominance almost caused the tour to cease altogether. LL wanted to follow Eric and Ra back to America, but as the headliner, contractual complications would have left him facing lawsuits. As the main attraction, he had to hold it down.

So for the end of November and the early part of December 1987 the tour continued with just LL and PE. Along the way they took in Germany, Norway, Sweden and Denmark. They were not only among the first Def Jam artists to play in such countries, they were among the first hip-hop groups full stop. Today, many hip-hop groups tour Scandinavia regularly.

It was definitely not the glamorous life. During the whole tour, the only time the crew ate properly was at the venues. They claim their time in the venues was also the only time they were warm as well. Despite this lack of luxury, some of the characteristics that would define PE as a group emerged on their first European tour. Firstly, they proved that they were more open-minded to different environments and willing to adapt than a lot of their contemporaries. This would serve them well when they toured with groups like Anthrax and U2 in the early nineties. Secondly, they began the development of their superlative live show. By now they were extremely confident. 'Once we really got our stage thing under us,' Chuck says, 'we started saying to people, "Yo, you better come right, man", 'cos you might have better records, you might have records where people be like "aaaaaaaah", but we're gonna fucking try and take your head off. That was our thing.'

16

It Takes a Nation of Millions to Hold Us Back

Despite the unprecedented and hectic nature of 1987, Public Enemy didn't waste any time resting on their laurels. They spent the first few months of 1988 recording their trailblazing second album, *It Takes a Nation of Millions to Hold Us Back*. But before work could begin in earnest, there were a few matters to deal with. After being disappointed with his credit on *Yo! Bum Rush the Show* Eric Sadler had gone back to his habit of just writing jam after jam, while hanging with his boys and playing cards. When he heard they were beginning to work on the second album he decided the time was right to get his business together.

When he was approached about working on the album that would become *Nation of Millions* he was very clear on what he wanted. 'I said, "This is what I want. I want $5,000" – which is still kind of a joke – "but I'm not trying to cause problems with the guys for their deal." I said, "I want five grand, one point and my proper credit as a producer." I told Hank and I told Chuck and they talked it over.'

At first, he received a less than favourable response. 'Hank basically said, "Nah, fuck you, man, that's too much," and I said, "Okay, no problem." I went downstairs to hang with my crew and told them they're not gonna use me and they all started laughing. I knew there was no choice. There was no way they weren't gonna come back to me. Two days later I got the call.'

Initially, they worked at Chung King studios, but, similarly to when they were at INS studios, the engineers there talked down to them because they were a hip-hop group. Eric still sounds pissed off about it years later: 'For a while at Chung King they were still treating us as step-children.

There was this one engineer, I almost tried to kill him. He was like, "If you want to be an engineer there are plenty of schools you can go to, don't touch the board." I'm like, "Oh those guys gotta be kidding me."'

Before long, they upped sticks to Greene Street where they were more comfortable. The guys at Greene Street were still slightly apprehensive about a rap group coming through their doors, but they soon became impressed with PE's work ethic. When those guys went there, they went there to record. There was no drinking, no smoking and no women.

With their second album, PE consistently achieved the perfection they'd been striving for since the release of *Yo! Bum Rush the Show*. *Bum Rush* is a brilliant album but as a first statement it was a little hard to digest for some rap fans. Its harsh sound, typified by 'Public Enemy Number One', was very different. PE never experienced those problems with their second record. It is, simply put, the best hip hop album of all time.

When *Hip-Hop Connection*, the world's longest running rap monthly, held a poll to decide the top hundred hip-hop albums of all time, *Nation of Millions* was voted number one. A few years ago when *Spin* magazine ran a poll to decide the most influential albums between 1985 and 2005, *Nation of Millions* was voted number two. Both those inside and outside of the hip-hop community recognised the importance of PE's second album to the musical output of the last twenty years.

Nation of Millions changed hip-hop for ever. It made hip-hop synonymous with black consciousness and forced the culture to grow up. And it wasn't an accident either. The crew very specifically set out to make a hip-hop version of Marvin Gaye's seminal *What's Going On*. 'The shit had to mean something,' Chuck says. 'Our mission was to kill the "Cold Gettin' Dumb" stuff and really address some situations.' The record wasn't only responsible for advancing hip-hop lyrically. The revolutionary production techniques used on

Nation of Millions forced the rest of the hip-hop world to advance sonically in the same way that 'I Know You Got Soul' and 'South Bronx' had inspired PE.

The record boasts one of the most confident and confrontational album titles ever. It was inspired from a lyric in the third verse of *Yo! Bum Rush the Show*'s tenth song 'Raise the Roof'. Chuck starts his last verse with this couplet: 'And for real it's the deal and the actual fact/ Takes a nation of millions to hold me back.'

In March 1988, while PE were still searching for the title of their second album, Hank and Chuck were reading a Canadian magazine while on a small tour and, to their surprise, the statement that would become their album title was used as the headline of an article. When they saw it in print they felt its power and knew immediately that it was the album title. 'We looked at it,' Chuck says. 'And said, "That's it."'

The length of the title is almost as impressive as its confidence. 'That title is so fucking long it was unheard of. *It Takes a Nation of Millions to Hold Us Back*. It's nine miles long.'

'Security of the First World' (which was later sampled by Madonna and her producer Lenny Kravitz for her hit 'Justify My Love'), 'Mind Terrorist' and 'Show 'Em Whatcha Got' made it the first rap album to have instrumental interludes. 'Instead of having the cut, the cut, the cut, the cut, the cut. We said, "Well, we want to have this as a sonic offering and terrain."' This was something that Keith Shocklee had been doing for years on his mixtapes. 'It was something that we always did,' he says. 'We just got to do it on a record. We liked to have certain things to play with. You know, snatches of a little piece of a record. When I used to DJ I was playing little short snatches of records and before anyone knew what it was it was off, and I was off to the next.'

The producers who would soon be dubbed The Bomb Squad by Chuck would jam together for hours, listen to the results and then unearth a groove from the collage of sound. But once a groove was found, extracted and expanded upon, finding the final pieces of the puzzle could be an extremely laborious task. They would spend hours sifting through records to find the elements that fitted properly. 'Chuck would sit there, Hank would sit there, Eric would sit there, we used to sit there with the headphones on and just look for parts: "Aiight, this is a part",' Keith recalls. This became particularly difficult when they needed a new sample to fit a change in the record. As PE's joints changed up fairly regularly, this was a recurrent challenge that had to be met.

'That's some work there whether people realise that or not,' Keith says. 'Say we want to go to another D section. We're not a band, 'cos with a band if they say, "Go to the D section", you just go. A band can just change on the fly. Trying to find another record that didn't have nothing to do with it? It becomes, "What do you hear to make that on the fly change?"'

It was decided that the album should be exactly one hour long, thirty minutes on each side. These were the days of cassettes; if one side was longer than the other the listener was faced with a whole heap of dead air once the music finished. Seeing as they came from a radio background, dead air was anathema to PE: 'Dead air means you're giving someone time to think about something else,' is how Chuck looks at it. 'We don't want to give them a second.' Virtually every aspect of the album was fresh and new in some way. Instead of simply having side A and side B, The LA Raiders inspired the Black Panthers of Rap to have the silver side and the black side. Originally, the silver side and black side were meant to be the other way around. The album was meant to start with 'Show 'Em Watcha Got'. 'She Watch Channel Zero?!', a vicious attack on 'tell-lie-vision', was then supposed to be the first track proper. It was Hank's idea to start the record with Dave Pearce introducing PE during their first tour of England.

The cover of *Nation of Millions*, which was shot by Glen Friedman, showed Chuck D wearing a matching LA Raiders hat and jacket a year or so before NWA's *Straight Outta Compton*. This predictably led to some confusion as to where PE were from. Some fans would be surprised to find out Chuck was a New Yorker. But Chuck liked the way that the Raiders represented rebellion and that they were founded in Oakland, home of the Black Panthers. Chuck was actually the first high profile emcee to wear baseball caps on a regular basis. Before this, most rappers rocked a trilby or a bowler *à la* Run DMC, or the fisherman hats that were favoured by LL and EPMD. But a year later Run DMC sported baseball caps in publicity shots. Flavor Flav was even more about his fashion than Chuck. The cover shows him wearing a clock around his neck and his hat to the side for the first time on a PE album cover. The clock has always symbolised the fact that Flav, and by extension his crew, 'know what time it is'. The hat was just some old fly shit. You know how Flavor does.

When PE began to plan their second album, three songs – 'Don't Believe The Hype', 'Rebel Without a Pause' and 'Bring the Noise' – were already completed. By the time they left for their second UK tour in March 1988 the album as a whole was completed. Those three songs caused the first of many disagreements with Def Jam. Rick Rubin didn't want to include them on the album, perhaps because they'd already been in the marketplace. Chuck was adamant that they did. 'We were like, "We have to do this, we had people go out and buy *Yo! Bum Rush the Show* expecting to find 'Rebel' and 'Bring the Noise' on the cassette and it wasn't there. So we got to do this dawg."' After a little bit of back and forth, Rick relented.

The fourth song to be finished was the anthemic 'Night of the Living Baseheads'. In order to ensure that their live shows remained as exciting as those they played in Philadelphia and London, the crew decided they had to make the songs on their second album faster than those on *Yo! Bum Rush the Show*. 'Night of the Living Baseheads' certainly fits this criterion. An almost hypnotic horn sample from The JB's 'The Grunt' underpins Chuck's harrowing assessment of the crack epidemic that was devastating black America at the time. PE also revisited the multitude of half-finished songs they had first started on tour.

'Black Steel in the Hour of Chaos' was one of those records. If it hadn't been for a strange twist of fate, the song wouldn't have even made it on to the album. The mesmerising beat for 'Black Steel in the Hour of Chaos' was originally meant for another member of PE's camp. An artist called True Mathematics, who later made a memorable appearance as Sergeant Hawks on 'Get the Fuck Outta Dodge' on *Apocalypse '91 . . . The Enemy Strikes Black* (he played the same character on Terminator X's solo record *Valley of the Jeep Beats*), had to give up the famous piano loops to Chuck, 'I used to be like, "You can have whatever track you want,"' he recalls. '"But if you fuck it up and can't handle it I'm gonna take it."' Even without the beat that became 'Black Steel' True Mathematics still made noise with his album *True Mathematics' Greatest Hits*.

Another song that was lying around was 'She Watch Channel Zero?!', the album's only song built around heavy guitars. Rick Rubin, the album's executive producer, had been doing some production work with the metal group Slayer and the beat for 'Channel Zero' was originally created as part of his work for them. Kerry King's guitar parts were sampled and incorporated into the track.

'Prophets of Rage' was the last song recorded for the album. Like a lot of PE tunes, it was conceived in traffic. Chuck's moment of inspiration came as he was driving over the Kosciuszko Bridge. 'Don't Believe the Hype', which had originally been rejected because of its tempo, was plucked from obscurity thanks to DMC.

In late March, after they had finished recording, Chuck and Hank were in Lower Manhattan. They received a shock when they heard DMC playing the rejected 'Don't Believe the Hype' in his gigantic Bronco. Hearing the song at high volume made them realise just how powerful it was. They not only decided to keep the record but, thanks to DMC, they made it the first single from their album. It dropped in May 1988, and set the album up perfectly. 'Don't Believe the Hype' was memorable for many reasons – Chuck's relentless and articulate attack of clueless critics who denigrated PE and hip-hop in general without a full grasp of the facts, and the brilliant vocal interplay between Chuck and Flav – but Harry Allen's shout-out in the final verse is one of the most unforgettable few seconds in hip-hop history. Towards the end of the extra-long third verse, Chuck gets so exasperated he spits, 'Some writers I know are damn devils . . . Their pens and pads I'll snatch 'cos I've had it'. A few lines later Chuck and Flav decide to ask their long-term friend to clarify things for them. Chuck raps: 'I'm going to my Media Assassin, Harry Allen, I gotta ask him,' before Flav chimes in with, 'Yo Harry, you're a writer, are we that type?' Harry confirms their suspicions by repeating the song's title slowly but surely in a deep drawling voice.

'Putting me on that record was a gift that keeps giving, even twenty years later,' he says. 'It was like a ten-second advertisement on one of the most popular hip-hop records anywhere, certainly the best-loved hip-hop record anywhere, and it just keeps giving. I run into people all the time and they're like, "Have we met?" and it's not that we've met, it's just that they've heard the name somewhere but they can't place where. It was a pretty wonderful gift of Chuck to honour me that way.'

It was with their second album that PE achieved their aim to politicise hip-hop and become the Black Panthers of Rap. Thanks to PE, a lot of former Black Panthers, and freedom fighters in general, were able to realise that, as Chuck puts it, 'their movement was still alive somewhere'. But, despite politicising hip-hop, *Nation of Millions* is also lauded because of Flavor Flav, whose presence has always leavened Chuck's political message. Flavor Flav came into his own on the second album. While *Yo! Bum Rush the Show*'s 'Too Much Posse' was definitely very dope it was 'Cold Lampin' with Flavor' that really announced Flav's presence. 'Too Much Posse' is without doubt worthy of attention. Apart from having a heavy beat and a wicked intro before Flav starts rhyming, it is a concise description of how things were shaping up in American ghettoes in the Reagan years. It is like one of their late night discussions manifested on record. During the half-rhymed, half-spoken word intro, Flav mentions how,

There's a lot of posses out there
Trying to take over posses
And trying to turn those posses
Into their posse.

The third and fourth lines are similarly telling: 'You may as well join them – you know you can't beat them,' Flavor raps. 'Pack a hundred people – ya know ya gonna need 'em.' The hostile takeover has always been a feature of business of any kind. A decade and a half later the Roc-A-Fella film *State Property* would feature thugs ordering rival crews to 'get down or lay down'.

'Cold Lampin'' is more memorable. The first talking point is the vocal sample that starts off the record. The voice saying 'no more music by the suckers' at various speeds is that of DJ Mr Magic. When 'Public Enemy Number One' was released he played it on his show alongside all the other hot joints of the time. However, after playing PE's debut single he had dissed the group, having mistakenly embroiled the group in the WBAU-WBLS radio war, and was blissfully unaware that Flavor Flav was not only listening, but taping his ill-chosen words.

'He was like, "Yo, we don't know who these guys are, we don't know who the hell they think they is, but we will have no more music by these suckers, they sound like suckers, so there will be no more music by these suckers".' Unluckily for Magic, Flav was always chilling by his radio, waiting for his crew's first record to be played. As is to be expected, the thrill of hearing themselves on the air as artists was huge. 'I always had the pause button ready,' Flav insists enthusiastically. 'If I heard the first snare of "Public Enemy Number One" I was letting that shit go.'

'Cold Lampin'' is also important for showcasing Flav's now ubiquitous 'yeeeaaaaaaaah boyeeeeeee' catchphrase. True, his brilliant spoken word intro to 'Bring the Noise' (the type that only Flav can pull off) features the catchphrase right before Chuck hollers 'bass', but as 'Cold Lampin'' is a solo track, and the third track of the album, it made more of an impression.

While the vast majority of those who heard *Nation of Millions* before its release realised that the record was pretty special, not everybody was convinced. Even at this early stage of their career there were those who doubted PE's street smarts and weren't afraid to run their mouths accordingly. Even some of those close to PE doubted.

'I can remember one of our friends, who's sadly no longer alive, had one of the first plain copies of *It Takes a Nation of Millions*,' recalls Harry Allen. 'He was an emcee very connected to the streets and to hip-hop and what was happening and I remember him listening to it and afterwards saying, "It's really good but I don't hear anything for the streets." We didn't realise that PE was going to change the streets.'

It Takes a Nation of Millions to Hold Us Back was released in July 1988. 'New York was electric,' Chuck reminisces wistfully. 'Electric.' Unlike with their first album, Chuck and Hank now felt like they had something that not only could easily hang with the best of the best, but had redefined what the best could be.

Unfortunately, when the record hit stores it caused more problems with Johnny Juice. 'When I saw the *Nations* album with my name just saying I did "Baseheads", I was like, "You know what? Peace." And I left.' Perhaps it hurt the most that he contributed scratches to the song that followed 'Cold Lampin''. '"Terminator X to the Edge of Panic", that was me,' he confirms. 'I can't say if all the scratches were done by me or Norman 'cos a lot of times he would start them and it wouldn't work. Then it'd be like, "Juice, you finish it." But like I said a lot of those songs were done while Public Enemy were on the road . . . it wasn't like Norman sucks, he wasn't around. It wasn't a personal thing, it was like, "We gotta get these fucking songs done." "Don't Believe the Hype" was done by Norman. "Bring the Noise" was Norman. But I scratched on a lot of those records.'

Juice's styles created some of the most memorable parts of some classic songs. Juice had – and has – a habit of scratching with no crossfader. On 'Night of the Living

Baseheads' this technique was an important element in creating the cacophony of noise behind the loud sample of Chuck saying 'bass'. The lack of a fader means you can hear the backspin of the record, 'That was one of my styles back in those days. I did it on purpose to make it more abrasive, when they heard that they were like, "Yeah, just do that shit you do with no fader."' Still a very young man, Juice decided that he was a nevertheless a gifted student and, as he puts it, 'didn't want to stay around and deal with this bullshit'. He didn't see any money from Kings of Pressure (maybe Brown was right) and his financial rewards from the PE stuff were minimal. He earnt $300 for the 'You're Gonna Get Yours' remix, $300 more than he earned for his work on *Yo! Bum Rush the Show*.

There was one saving grace. The publicist at Rhythm Method, the great David 'Funken' Klein, regularly got him DJ gigs around town. Dave, who would go on to run Hollywood Basic Records – home to acts like Organized Konfusion – didn't even take a cut. 'That was my dog. He's dead now, he passed. He would call me up like, "Juice, I got a gig for you at the Milky Way, I got a gig for you at the Red Parrot". I was DJing at places I wasn't old enough to be in.'

While there's never a perfect way to do these things, when Juice left to join the Navy in California he didn't tell anybody. 'I just left. Chuck was very, very upset with me. Chuck was like the best dude in the world to do artist development with but he also happened to be the king of the rappers. He had no idea Public Enemy was going to blow up the way it did. And he had only planned on doing one album.'

Juice's contributions to hip-hop extend beyond his work with PE. Harry Allen documented this contribution in a hip-hop-themed issue of the *Village Voice*. 'On the cover there was Grandmaster Flash and The Furious Five, Run DMC, Doug E Fresh, Stetsasonic and Public Enemy,' Juice recalls. 'Inside they interviewed a lot of different people, they did a lot of things and they listed every radio show, and they had who did 'em and they had me in there and they said I was probably the best on-air DJ in rap.'

Juice and his friend Jeff Foss played on WRHU, Hofstra's college radio station. Their Saturday night show stretched from 10 p.m. to 2 a.m., but only the last two hours were dedicated to hip-hop. 'Nine to twelve was pretty much Mr Magic, Marley Marl and on another station was Red Alert and Chuck Chillout,' Juice admits, 'We knew we couldn't get the rap crowd for those hours. From twelve to two after Magic and them dudes were off the air, I would get down with the underground shit.'

Juice had a secret weapon that had even these rivals tuning in to his show. 'I was the first dude on radio – and this is what it said in the article in the *Village Voice* – to rock what they call blends now. I would take a hip-hop instrumental and rock an r'n'b a cappella over it. All them motherfuckers got that shit from me. I used to call that shit love-mixes. It was weird because sometimes Marley Marl and Kenny Ken would call up the station saying, "Yo Juice, that shit was hot", and then they would bite my fucking mixes.'

A couple of his favourite blends were Biz Markie's 'Make the Music with Your Mouth' instrumental with Anita Baker's 'Caught Up in the Rapture' vocal and BDP's 'Criminal Minded' instrumental with the a cappella from Janet Jackson's 'Let's Wait Awhile'.

'I would start it off with Janet: 'There's something I want,' and then the beat would come in. Motherfuckers would go crazy. I was the first motherfucker doing that.' Juice says, 'There's some conjecture as to who actually invented it, it's between me and this dude named Grandmaster Vic from Queens and that motherfucker was nice. Vic was dope. But I never heard Vic do that, I thought I invented it but it's quite possible more than one person can come up with the same technique. But I was definitely the first one to do it on the radio. Then next week I would hear someone doing my mix on BLS. I'm like, "Ain't this a bitch". Thank God Harry Allen wrote about it so it was like, "Thank you sir". Every weekend I had a new love-mix and motherfuckers went crazy. I had a girlfriend at the time, she used to call 'em pantywetters. Throw 'em on and the panties got wet. I called 'em love mixes, I couldn't have called them pantywetters at the time. Now I probably wouldn't get in trouble, but I would have back then.'

Harry Allen not only documented this back when it was new, he recognises that Juice should get further credit for pioneering what came to be known as 'mash-ups' by those outside of hip-hop culture.

'Johnny Juice is a great guy, a very lively guy, very intelligent and he has a big heart. I remember hearing his mixes over the air and just loving them to death. I did mention them in a piece I wrote in the *Voice* in the hip-hop issue. I think I wrote most of that issue in fact. It was a lot of pieces in there. I remember thinking it was just really, really imaginative. At the time I wasn't really hearing anyone putting things together. To force disparate records that don't even like each other together? It was almost like an antecedent to mash-ups.'

Eric Sadler was similarly upset after the second album. 'For *Nations* I was told I was gonna get my songwriters, I was gonna get my producing, and this, that or whatever.' When he looked at the album and saw he was credited as an 'associate producer' it was (to say the least) less than satisfactory. 'I'm like, okay, "What's an associate producer first of all when I was the only one there day and night?" Everybody else was there,' he clarifies, 'but I was still the main person booking every session, hiring all the musicians and producing all day along with everybody.' Who was writing these credits? It's almost impossible to work out conclusively who was responsible. Was it group members or record company personnel?

The fact that his money was straight helped him to look on the bright side of things. But he decided he was gonna re-learn the business to stop him getting jerked a third time.

He decided, 'I need to be there, I need to know everyone at the record company. After *Nations* I was there for everything, every aspect of every credit. When we get to the third album it was a whole 'nother different story.'

As they were already on the Run's House tour of autumn 1988, the truth of the matter is that PE had little time to dwell on these things. As well as Run DMC, this tour featured Jazzy Jeff and The Fresh Prince, EPMD and JJ Fad. Thanks to Doug E Fresh's advice and their incendiary concerts up to then PE made sure they secured the third slot on the bill. On this tour PE would enjoy more camaraderie with the other acts and really reap the rewards of being part of a united force in hip-hop.

17

Making the Video

Nation of Millions also marked the first time Public Enemy made videos. There was a simple reason that no videos appeared for 'Public Enemy Number One', 'Timebomb', 'You're Gonna Get Yours' or even 'Rebel Without a Pause'. PE's record contract stated quite clearly that they would be liable for half the costs. And what would be the point of paying half the costs of a video, when no one was going to play it anywhere? Why should they make a video just for the sake of it? Remember, these were the days when MTV only played videos by a handful of black artists. If you weren't Michael Jackson, Janet Jackson or Prince, you faced an uphill struggle. Luckily, 1988 was the year *Yo! MTV Raps* arrived on our TV screens. It was a niche outlet, but at least it was an outlet. Even more luckily, their former WBAU brethren Dr Dre and T-Money worked on the show.

When it is considered that PE's budget for their debut album was only $17,000, you can understand why they felt trying to tout a video to the network was an uphill struggle not worth negotiating. 'We always came under budget, man,' Chuck explains, 'so to have somebody come along and be like, "I can shoot a video for $50,000," it was like, "What the fuck?"' The first PE video wasn't really a PE video at all. When the UK division of CBS got around to promoting *It Takes a Nation of Millions to Hold Us Back* they were horrified that there was no video for the first single 'Don't Believe the Hype'. So they took it upon themselves to make their own promo clip which took snippets from PE's London concerts and, as Chuck puts it, 'the whole environment surrounding us'. They even employed a fake Flavor Flav to dance in a few scenes. To say the video misrepresented the group is an understatement. This situation helped PE to decide that the time was right to start making their own videos. Even though they weren't big fans of the whole process – Chuck is notorious for telling photographers they have exactly sixty seconds – they realised that if you were going to make music in the late eighties you'd better get photographed and filmed. And if it was worth doing, it was worth doing properly. 'We wanted to be able to set the stage and create a video that nobody had ever seen before,' Chuck says.

They achieved this and more with the video for 'Night of the Living Baseheads'. The concept came to life in a meeting in the Def Jam building attended by the group and various label reps. They weren't interested in having video treatments pitched to them, especially after the way the 'Don't Believe the Hype' video went down. Making music from the DJ's point of view helped them decide that – like the rationale behind the composition of *Nation of Millions* – there was no reason why a video just had to run through one song without stopping.

'We have two turntables to work with in hip-hop,' Chuck reasons, 'why can't you do it from a film perspective? If you come from hip-hop going in and out of a song is not unusual. We put together almost like a little playlet.' In order to make that playlet as real as possible, Flavor Flav went back to their old hood and got some real baseheads to put in front of the camera. But contrary to what some have been led to believe, Flavor Flav wasn't high himself during that video shoot.

'I was getting high around that time,' he admits. 'But I ain't come on camera high. I went and found real crackheads to get on that shit.' Yes, he was going through 'his nightmares', Flav was wilding out for sure. But he never went to sleep and woke up ragged and ruthless, messed-up and toothless with nothing but sneakers on his feet. 'I was never really a real live crackhead,' he confirms. 'I used to take a little crack and sprinkle it in the cigarette. But I was never a crackhead, I was never out there like that.' Whatever the case, PE certainly achieved their aim of making drugs look nasty to kids.

Chuck wanted to recreate the feeling of disgust he experienced when he first encountered heroin addicts in The Bronx during the early seventies. When he went to visit relatives, it would be impossible for the young Chuck to ignore the heroin addicts slumped over in front of tenement buildings. It's an image that put him off drugs for life. To this day he has never taken an illegal substance. 'I ain't want to look like this dude with green shit coming out of his eye,' he says, perhaps not unreasonably. If some nasty smelling, dishevelled and washed-out heroin addicts put him off drugs for life, couldn't it do the same for their ever growing number of fans?

PE were mindful of the fact that one song, however powerful, was not going to suddenly stop the crack epidemic there and then. They were aware that they were chipping away at the problem rather than stopping it dead. Despite this, an anti-drug song was very important to Chuck D. Between the early seventies and late eighties he had noticed, with considerable frustration, how cocaine evolved from being something that was mostly used by rich white people into a drug that was readily available in poor black communities.

'When they had the cocaine wars in the late seventies in New York, cocaine was viewed as a rich white person's drug that you get in Studio 54.' Bit by bit cocaine worked its way into the poorer communities where it wasn't even really the drug of choice. 'There was a lack of weed supply in the seventies because the cats that had moved in had tried to move coke into the black neighbourhoods. I remember clearly cats looking for weed, looking for nickel and dime bags, and then they'd go to the same cat and the cat would say, "Well, I ain't got no weed you know, but this is what I got". Cats would say, "Well I ain't trying no coke", and then it'd be, "Yeah, but take this shit, it's on me". Then all of a sudden cats would be like, "Well I love this coke but I ain't hooked".'

During their Spectrum days he would often observe

partygoers lacing their joints and normal everyday cigarettes with crack. 'Flavor came out of that environment, I got him out of that environment and said, "Let's do music."'

In a living room in Pittsburgh, Pennsylvania, a young C-Doc was among the many fans struck by the 'Baseheads' video. '"Night of the Living Baseheads" was the first Public Enemy song I ever heard,' he says. 'And I saw the video on *Yo! MTV Raps*.' About a decade later, he would begin building the relationships that would lead to him working with PE. 'When I heard Public Enemy I thought, "What the hell is this?" So for Christmas I asked for *It Takes a Nation of Millions*. My mom bought me the tape for Christmas and that was in my Walkman for a long time. I just became a huge Public Enemy fan.' Their other video, for 'Black Steel in the Hour of Chaos', got their point across just as clearly. The prison-based video is a lot less shocking but effectively illustrates the anti-authority message of the song.

These videos helped *It Takes a Nation of Millions to Hold Us Back* become one of the few rap albums released in the late eighties to sell more than a million copies. It may seem strange to some, especially in today's sales-driven climate, but record sales have never been the be all and end all for PE. While many other artists make similar claims, it's hard not to believe Chuck when he says he doesn't care about how many records they have sold.

'What it sold meant nothing to me,' he insists. 'It's always going to be someone selling a million records, whether it's good or not. If they can't get anybody else, it'll be like, "Yo man, we'll sell a million Pussycat Dolls". They need at least four or five situations to sell big units to feed everything in the company.' To offer a modern parallel, most hip-hop fans believe Nas when he says that sales are not everything. The remixes for 'Where Are They Now' – which featured a host of heroes from different hip-hop eras – is one example of him walking the walk. The *Street's Disciple* album – one of the most personal records in hip-hop history – is another. Ditto

Hip-Hop Is Dead and the album orginally intended to be titled *Nigger*. All of these records were put out not with commercial considerations in mind, but because they were what Nas wanted to explore artistically; in short, they have integrity. Actions speak louder than words.

Any group who had to be persuaded and cajoled into accepting a record company contract are not your typical fame-hungry star-gazers. It's also important to remember that *Yo! Bum Rush the Show* was only moderately successful – 300,000 copies sold at the most generous estimates – and Russell Simmons had already made clear his feelings on music that attempted to 'preach' to the masses rather than entertain. He came from the disco era and definitely preferred music that was about having a good time.

So making a record that was a million more times political than *Bum Rush*, with such a politically charged title, was just not the obvious move for a group trying to shift more units and become more famous. PE come from a time when platinum, gold and double-wood weren't terms widely associated with music. While the gold award for 500,000 copies sold was introduced by the Recording Industry Association of America in 1958 they didn't introduce the platinum award until 1976 and the multi-platinum award until 1984 when PE recorded 'Lies'. As with everything else, these new developments took time to seep into the consciousness of music fans. They must have passed PE by.

The following observation from Harry Allen, one of Chuck's oldest friends, speaks for itself. 'Chuck buys his cars used still,' he reveals. 'He doesn't believe in the idea that, "I should buy a car and it depreciates in value by thirty per cent by me taking it out of the lot and driving into the street." That doesn't make sense to him.' How many platinum rappers boast about buying cars straight off the lot? Does that sound like someone obsessed with the finer things in life?

Different events later on in their career, such as the way they left Def Jam records, would provide further proof that they were not making music just for the financial rewards. Chuck's attitude is that it's not PE's job to count records, it's their job to make them. It's the record company's job to sell those records. Then, if you're a performer, you go out into the big wide world and perform your art. Chuck accepts that some observers may label such an attitude naive.

'People could say, "Won't people cheat you out of royalty cheques and all that?" Yeah, all that's happened because we are a product of the eighties where contracts were one-sided. In the nineties where contracts were re-negotiated it set the template for people in the late nineties and the millennium like Jigga and Ludacris to actually make rock star money.'

While Chuck doesn't seem to care, and hates being quizzed on the subject, PE have sold around twenty million records during their career. 'When we made *Fear of a Black Planet*, they said it sold a million in less than a week,' he says. 'But that's Sony/CBS at that time. Polygram later on. Universal. Whether you live or die, man, they got things set up that will sell you dead or alive. Bob Marley, he's still selling big records right. You gotta make things work for you. You can't look at anyone else. So the counting . . . I've never understood it, I never have.' Despite this attitude, Chuck is no slouch when it comes to business and PE have stayed afloat and prospered for many years – and on their own terms too.

18

Fight the Power

So, 1988 had been even better, and busier, than 1987. Public Enemy had achieved everything they wanted to. They had succeeded, with *It Takes a Nation of Millions to Hold Us Back*, in making hip-hop's *What's Going On*. Additionally, their heartfelt record had resulted in the love and recognition they had wanted so badly since *Bum Rush*'s delayed release date had affected their perception of that record. As a live act, they had proved themselves as a force to be reckoned with across the world. They may not have cared, but their record sales definitely kept Def Jam and CBS happy.

But 1989 was going to be different. During 1989 PE experienced their greatest triumph and greatest disaster more or less simultaneously. At the same time that 'Fight the Power' was indisputably the biggest anthem in hip-hop, indeed, probably the biggest anthem hip-hop had ever seen, the group nearly self-destructed because of the maelstrom that erupted around Professor Griff.

'Fight the Power' is probably PE's best-known song. To this day, the group close their concerts with their biggest hit and it never fails to be a rowdy finale. Spike Lee first approached PE to do a song for his film *Do the Right Thing* in 1988, not long after *Nation of Millions* dropped. The crew were getting ready to join Run DMC on the European leg of the Run's House tour but figured this was worth their attention.

PE demonstrated their foresight and helped to create something memorable. At this time Spike Lee didn't have the stature he enjoys today. *Do the Right Thing* would cement his reputation, and 'Fight the Power' would play its part in this process. Of course, Spike has to be given similar credit for picking PE. At a meeting in Lower Manhattan, Spike told Chuck, Hank, and Bill Stephney that he needed an anthem for his movie. The trio representing the PE camp had no problem with this. But they wanted to do it themselves. Spike had drafted in a producer named Raymond Jones to do the beat, but after consideration he agreed to let The Bomb Squad make their own rhythm. It was a wise choice. With the first meeting a success, Spike went off to make his movie and PE went on tour.

One night, while flying over Italy, inspiration struck, and Chuck finished up the lion's share of what is probably his best song. 'I wanted to have sorta like the same theme as the original "Fight the Power" by The Isley Brothers' – he says of the extremely funky protest song which originally contained the line 'You gotta fight the powers that be' – 'and fill it in with some kind of modernist views of what our surroundings were at that particular time.'

'Fight the Power' became legendary for a number of reasons. Firstly, the beat that The Bomb Squad cooked up – by all accounts Keith Shocklee was responsible for the majority of the work – is simply amazing, the perfect beat. Like of all of PE's records, it is a protest record you can dance to.

The lyrical content takes everything PE stand for and places it under one easily understandable slogan. We've got to fight the powers that be. And those lyrics were dropped with the utmost style. On 'Fight the Power', the verbal interplay between Chuck and Flav is even more fluid than it was on records like 'Terminator X to the Edge of Panic' and 'Don't Believe the Hype'. Of course, the final verse got the most attention. And it's pretty easy to see why.

Chuck begins by stating, 'Elvis was a hero to most/ But he never meant shit to me'. He then hammers his point home by continuing: 'Straight up, racist the sucker was/ Simple and plain.' At this point Flavor Flav chimes in with: 'Muthafuck him and John Wayne!' In many ways this was more shocking and distasteful to some than songs like the self-explanatory 'Burn Hollywood Burn' or their support for Louis Farrakhan and the Nation of Islam.

The reaction to the song was similar to that which PE received when they first toured England and told the crowd to shout, 'Fuck the Queen' and 'Fuck Thatcher'. People in general, especially those old enough to have known Elvis in his heyday, wondered, 'Who are these young black guys saying, "Fuck Elvis"? Elvis was the king!'

Chuck was influenced to disparage the so-called king of rock'n'roll by Clarence Reid, aka Blowfly, a rather interesting poet who has recorded X-rated, Dolomite-style records since the mid sixties. Reid, a songwriter for many classic r'n'b acts like Betty Wright, Gwen McCrae and KC and the Sunshine Band is believed by many to have written the first ever rap song, 1965's 'Rap Dirty'.

Many years later, 'Blowfly Rapp' featured Blowfly engaged in an imagined battle of wits with the Ku Klux Klan. During this exchange Blowfly reels off a list of insults to his white (sheeted) adversary before facing a few of his own. After being told a few home truths the KKK dude responds by saying, 'Well I'm the grand wizard of the KKK, and muthafuck you and Muhammad Ali.'

Muhammad Ali had yet to become the undisputed inter-national hero he is today. His refusal to fight in the Vietnam War was still fresh in the memory. For further proof, take another look at the first *Rocky* film. Apollo Creed is a thinly disguised version of the greatest fighter of all time.

'It was just the part of the song I remember. I was saying, "Oh shit",' Chuck recalls. 'It was something that stuck in me so when I wrote the third verse of "Fight the Power" I reversed the charges.' Chuck, who is fascinated by black music history, was not happy with the false idea of Elvis as the undisputed king of rock'n'roll when the true pioneers, like Chuck Berry, Little Richard, Bo Diddley, Fats Domino and Ike Turner, had to settle for second-best and much worse. Consider how many black millionaires have been created by hip-hop. Imagine if this could have happened in the fifties or sixties. Many rock critics, especially those who like to gloss over or ignore the true history of rock'n'roll, hated this lyric when 'Fight the Power' dropped. Some still do all these years later. Some hate the fact that Elvis is called racist. But, let's face it, he certainly didn't seem to mind profiting from the overtly racist prac-tices of the music business. He didn't mind stealing songs, dance moves and vocal techniques from black artists and presenting them as his own. So people need to chill.

The line about John Wayne was inspired by Jim Brown's autobiography *Out of Bounds*. Brown was less than compli-mentary about the hero of the Old West and known racist. In 1971 Wayne famously told *Playboy* magazine, 'I believe in white supremacy until the blacks are educated to a point of responsibility. I don't believe in giving authority and positions of leadership and judgment to irresponsible people.' Who knows what John Wayne would've made of Barack Obama? Chuck decided to add the lyric on Brown's behalf. But those weren't the only lyrics that made the faithful proud. After rubbishing two icons of White America Chuck went on to ask why 'most of my heroes don't appear on no stamps'.

'It was a weird twist 'cos later on in America, you started

seeing more black stamps coming out,' Chuck says. It's worth considering that, as with 'Night of the Living Baseheads', no one thinks that it was all down to PE that things improved. It's far more likely to have occurred because 'younger people got into more established areas and younger black folks are moving up. It's just a viaduct on what's going on.' Nevertheless, PE brought these issues to public attention like never before.

The 'Fight the Power' video is easily in hip-hop's top five videos of all time. Shot in Brooklyn, it's half political rally, half PE performance. PE were so powerful that they didn't need to hire any extras. People just wanted to be involved. But when PE should have been enjoying the highest point of their career, they were faced with the fight of their life. Even before the Griff situation popped off, things in general were not going well. During 1989, Chuck had begun travelling from tour stop to tour stop on his own, rather than face the unbearable tension that now inhabited the official PE tour bus. This meant travelling on Greyhound buses. The sight of Chuck D, fast becoming one of the most famous faces in America, travelling between places like Detroit and Cleveland would arouse the interest of the other passengers. As he would always have with him a tape recorder, headphones, and, naturally, a pen and a pad, any lingering doubts as to whether or not it was the real Chuck would disappear pretty quickly.

It was a necessary evil as the open road once again proved to be the tonic Chuck needed to write some classic songs. As he wasn't driving himself, he obviously had more time to devote to songs like 'Welcome to the Terrordome', which became the first single from *Fear of a Black Planet*. When Chuck first mentioned *Fear of a Black Planet* in July of '89, only 'Terrordome' and 'Fight the Power' existed.

19

So Much Trouble

When Professor Griff was interviewed by David Mills in early 1989 it almost finished Public Enemy. The idea of something like anti-Semitism emanating from the PE camp, of all places, was unthinkable to many familiar with the group. As Chuck said while the controversy was raging, 'You can't talk about attacking racism and be racist [yourself]'. The David Mills interview was by no means the first time that Griff had made highly questionable comments about Jewish people, but it was the one that stuck. When the interview first appeared in the *Washington Times* towards the end of May it seemed to pass people by. This could be because few beyond its core audience took the daily newspaper too seriously. An ultra-conservative publication founded by one Reverend Sun Myung Moon, the leader of the Unification Church and the Family Federation, the paper was an early bastion of the right wing media that now seems to dominate America. Critics have dismissed the paper as a mouthpiece for Moon's ideas and sympathies.

It was a completely different situation when the *Village Voice* picked up the piece in June and reprinted it. All of a sudden, it was on. People (of all persuasions) take the *Village Voice* very seriously. The quote attributed to Griff was, 'Jews are responsible for the majority of wickedness that goes on across the globe.' Obviously a completely ridiculous idea. Anyone who makes a derogatory comment about another racial group can expect to be attacked for their views – unless they're powerful enough to suppress their critics. But Griff's alleged anti-Semitism stirred a particularly vehement reaction, as it was supposedly made by a member of an 'aggressive' black rap group towards a historically persecuted ethnic group.

'That was the thing that went out which was definitely, first of all, not true,' Griff insists. 'It's hard to believe that people would believe a quote like that, a misquote like that. "Responsible for the majority of wickedness." How do you know what's the majority of wickedness? How do you quantify that? How do you balance that? No man, you can't do that. So he took it way out of context. Like, right now you could chop this up and make it sound like I'm saying something that I'm not.'

PE's edition of VH1's famous documentary series *Behind the Music* shows Griff making a similar rebuttal. After they play back to him a snippet of the tape, the narrator remarks on how Griff insists the tape was doctored. He is asked whether he made the comment. 'No, definitely, not in that context,' he replies. 'To say the majority of Jews are wicked? That's crazy, really, really crazy.' Is he telling the truth? The fact is that he doesn't deny discussing issues surrounding Jewish people, and many will certainly be sceptical. On the other hand, it wouldn't be the first or the last time the press knowingly misquoted a hip-hop personality.

There are many different accounts of what happened. One version of events has it that Mills is in conversation with Griff when Griff allegedly asserts that the 'Jews are responsible' but fails to finish the sentence and explain what he supposedly thinks Jews are responsible for. Mills then prompts him by actually saying the infamous words 'the majority of wickedness that goes on across the globe?' According to this version of events, Griff then answered in the affirmative.

Chuck recalls the tense circumstances of the interview: 'David Mills was following up stories from the *Melody Maker* and *The Face*, where the interviews by the Stud Brothers opened a can of worms addressing the question of Palestinians' treatment by Israel. Griff supported the Palestinian side and from there the curiosity of anti-Semitic questioning arose in the interview during a Public Enemy gig in DC. I was tied up doing a meeting with promoter Darryl Brooks, thus Griff was delegated to pick up the slack. Both he and Mills were testy. Mills thinking I put him off, Griff having other things to do, having to handle it at an inappropriate time. It was fire on gasoline before the first word.'

Regardless of how it happened and what exactly was said the one indisputable fact is that the situation spread beyond the condemnation in the press: records were removed from shelves, concerts were cancelled and PE fans across the globe could not believe what was being reported.

Immediately, the tension between different factions within PE, chiefly those between Griff and Flavor, increased considerably. The two polar opposites had been bound to clash from day one, and often had – particularly when Griff's duties as tour manager meant he had to make sure Flav made it to shows on time and in a reasonable state. As a super-disciplined individual, he was not impressed with Flavor's flamboyance. But his authoritarian style was never going to be the best way to deal with a free spirit like Flav who didn't feel like being told what to do. On the other hand, as PE increased in stature and fame, the best hype-man in hip-hop began to feel himself a little too much. In a way you can't blame him. Flav was hot to death. The money and success seemed to push both these characters further into their respective extremes. As is often the case with successful bands, especially those that genuinely set new trends, the same things that help them become successful are the same things that end up tearing them apart. The situation meant a great deal of pressure was put on to Chuck's shoulders.

While not agreeing with the things Griff was credited with saying, Chuck, as the group's pre-eminent spokesman, did not want to fall victim to the pitfalls of the divide and conquer traps he had seen so many high profile black figures succumb to. At the very least he wanted PE to present a united front. For a short while he managed to walk a frayed tightrope where he didn't expressly support Griff but didn't ostracise him either. This stance was much criticised during the first months of the nineties. Many demanded, and expected, Chuck's outright condemnation of Griff. It was not forthcoming. A few years later, in the book he co-wrote with Yusuf Jah, *Fight the Power: Rap, Race and Reality*, Chuck himself admitted this stance wasn't the best one. He remarks how, 'This was some shit that was attached to me but I was looking for somebody else to fix a mistake I should have been fixing . . . we were letting a loose cannon go off and I wasn't displaying the proper leadership skills.'

There were also, predictably, knock-on effects throughout Def Jam, as well as its parent company, CBS. Russell Simmons and his right-hand man Lyor Cohen were put under immense pressure from executives who, for the time being at least, didn't want to associate themselves with the onslaught of negative publicity. As a Jewish man, Bill Adler decided he didn't want to work with the group any more. He decided not to make a big fuss about it. He just quietly told his superiors and let his colleagues pick up the slack.

'Russell and Lyor certainly didn't pressure me to keep working with the guys,' he notes. 'I think Chuck probably wasn't happy. But Chuck loves me and the feeling is mutual and this must have been distressing to him. You probably know at least as well as I that he was feeling this tremendous pressure.' Furthermore, as an insider who didn't have to rely on the media, Bill was able to make up his own mind. 'It was hard for me to see Griff as the embodiment of evil, as this terrible frothing anti-Semite, he didn't fit the bill.'

Adler had reached this conclusion after having a face-to-face meeting with Griff to see whether or not the media were making the public believe a lot of hype. The meeting confirmed Bill's worst fears: 'Griff was a soldier, looking for the marching orders. Even more than Chuck, Griff then was a "follower of Farrakhan". Unfortunately, at that time Farrakhan was promulgating the notion that the Jews were primarily responsible over a period of centuries for oppressing the black community. This kind of belief is classic anti-Semitism. It hardly constituted Farrakhan's whole message, but it was a distinct element of his worldview.'

The shadow of Farrakhan and the Nation of Islam had always loomed large in PE's background. But when the Griff situation went down the connection was scrutinised relentlessly. Chuck had famously namechecked Farrakhan on a couple of occasions. On 'Bring the Noise' he told fans, 'Farrakhan's a prophet and I think you wanna listen to/ What he can say to you'. During 'Don't Believe the Hype' he defiantly declared himself 'a follower of Farrakhan' and cautiously warned, 'Don't tell me that you understand/ Until you hear the man'. To put this into its proper perspective, songs like 'Rebel Without a Pause' and 'Prophets of Rage' would also give props to the likes of Joanne Chesimard (better known as Assata Shakur) and Nelson Mandela (who was still waiting for his long walk to freedom).

When considering the uproar, it's important to note the main reason for PE's endorsement of the Nation had nothing

to do with its anti-Semitic leanings or any of its other fail-
ings. The Nation of Islam, was (and, to a degree, still is) the
only institution that can turn a knuckle-head thug from the
school of hardknocks (who won't listen to reason from anyone)
into a disciplined, determined and ambitious individual. This
ability to make wayward young black men see the error of
their ways has always been the Nation's stated aim in black
communities across America, and, on a smaller scale, England.
Farrakhan's often repugnant comments about Jews which
surfaced before the Griff affair provided unnecessarily easy
ammunition for those who just wanted to attack an articulate black man. Farrakhan is in a strange position where
some of his critics attack this anti-Semitism but agree with
everything else he endorses.

But while Farrakhan wasn't the only black revolutionary
referenced by Chuck before Griff's interview with David Mills,
it's significant that on the blistering 'Buck Whylin'', Chuck
makes his position clear by opening his second verse with the
line, 'Ain't nuttin' changed, still down with Farrakhan'. Nothing
had changed because anti-Semitism was never the reason the
Nation of Islam was endorsed by PE. With hindsight, it seems
obvious that these are issues that should have been addressed
in a better way. But everything is easier with hindsight.

There was a Jewish writer named August Babel at the turn
of the last century who described anti-Semitism as 'the
socialism of fools'. As an intelligent and extremely personable
Jewish man in close contact with Griff, who had great relationships with many black people, Adler's perception of events
is invaluable. It is certainly not uncharitable. 'Let's grant that
Griff was a person of good faith, looking for an explanation
for the downtrodden status of African-Americans. As a young
black man with a lot of race pride, he surveys the landscape
in 1987 and 1988 and wonders: "Why are my people downtrodden? Why are we second class citizens in America? Why
are we still subject to discrimination? Why are so many of our
people impoverished and uneducated? What explains it?"

These are all legitimate questions. His answer then? "It's the Jews' fault." I'm sorry, but this is a defective analysis. In my opinion, it constitutes the socialism of a fool.'

The lack of proof beyond a reasonable doubt – of either derogatory comments or Griff being led into a trap – makes it difficult to come to a conclusion. It seems probable that Griff did make some sort of comment or comments about Jewish people, but at the same time, it's very possible that he was led into a trap, and it is easy to doctor tapes. It seems the situation will always retain a certain ambiguity.

Of all the Def Jam personnel, Lyor Cohen in particular was not going to feel, or express displeasure, at Bill's decision not to deal with PE any more. Cohen is Jewish, with a strong Israeli accent, and one of the most well-known figures in hip-hop. 'Because of his Judaism, he felt an extra conflict about this, as did I,' says Bill. This conflict compelled him to respond to Chuck's apparent solidarity with Griff by taking him to LA's Simon Wiesenthal Centre to enlighten him further about the history of Jews as victims of the Holocaust.

Higher up the corporate food chain, the repercussions were more brutal. CBS's CEO Walter Yetnikoff's comments in *Howling at the Moon* leave nothing to the imagination. He has just been told about the Griff affair by (his then second-in-command) Tommy Mottola: 'My first instinct was to can Public Enemy and throw Griff in the East River. But that wouldn't work. Their *It Takes a Nation of Millions to Hold Us Back*, a brilliant work, sold millions, and their new one . . . was poised to sell even more. I had a responsibility to CBS shareholders. I was a responsible guy. But this was Tommy's problem. "You handle it," I told him.' Yetnikoff was not wrong. The controversy helped PE to sell even more albums, to those curious to find out what all the fuss was about. Harry Allen for one recalls, 'Hank talking about being at Tower and seeing some guy who might have been about seventy with a copy of *Nation of Millions*.' If PE's second album had been a modest seller like its predecessor *Yo! Bum Rush the Show*, they would have most likely found themselves removed from the Def Jam roster very swiftly. We shouldn't be too surprised by the label's business-minded attitude. 'I'll say this as delicately as possible,' begins Bill Stephney. 'The folks who worked within the music business at that point are not for the most part the most politically active people on issues of ethnic pride.'

20

Even More Trouble

Bill is a central figure in another subplot of the Griff affair. It's no secret that ambition can put a strain on even the longest held, tightest friendships. Other record companies that were dealing with the Public Enemy family helped to make the situation more complex than is realised. Things were (literally) not as black and white as they may initially seem. Some insiders have asserted that it simply was not the case that there were a lot of white Jewish executives on one side begging Chuck to fire Griff, and all of Chuck's black friends on the other side saying, 'You gotta stand by him.' Allegedly, Bill Stephney and Hank Shocklee were just as anxious as anyone for Griff to be kicked out of the group (there are rumours that Chuck alone opposed it).

Before the madness, Hank, Bill and Chuck had been offered a label deal by MCA. They had dreamed of making such a move for a long time. A degree of self-determination had always been important to PE and it seemed that after years of waiting they were finally going to get it. However, according to some, the top brass at MCA were rightly concerned about the Griff controversy. The story goes that the rest of PE were told in no uncertain terms: get rid of Griff or the deal is off. This caused a split between Bill and Hank on one side, and Chuck on the other. When it became obvious Chuck was going to stand by Griff, Bill and Hank stopped messing with him, took the deal and went off to found SOUL records. If this is true, it caused a rift between the three of them which reverberates to this day. Chuck had to do something to ease the immense pressure he was under. Sadly, that something meant opting out of the SOUL deal. Of all the various things vying for his attention his business ties with Hank and Bill were the most delicate, and something had to give. It wasn't an easy decision.

'There was just so much pressure and I think the lyrics to "Terrordome" speak to it,' Bill recalls. 'There was just so much pressure on him that he just wanted to back out.' Hank, Bill and Chuck came to the conclusion that either they had to handle the whole of everything as a team – such things as PE's internal problems, SOUL records, and all that entailed – or Chuck had to take the PE reins on his own. The latter took place, but there are also some very simple and practical reasons why the deal was worked out the way it was.

The SOUL records deal was a long time in the making, and there were a few options on the table. MCA chairman Irving Azoff was planning to leave his post and start a big new company with a very popular, very successful record producer called Jimmy Iovine. Throughout 1989 and some of 1990 Chuck, Hank and Bill met fairly regularly with Jimmy Iovine until they grew weary with waiting and impatient to seal some sort of favourable deal. Bill had just given up his spot as vice-president of Def Jam, so time was of the essence.

Jimmy Iovine, who would go on to oversee the careers of 50 Cent and Eminem, urged them to sign to MCA. He was planning to do a deal with either MCA or Warners and this would clear the way for them to forge business links in the future. Unfortunately, as is often the way in the music business, things didn't occur as planned. Irving Azoff did a deal on the side with Warners for Giant Records and left Jimmy out in the cold. That left the PE three at MCA without either of their main conspirators. They decided it was a case of 'better the devil you know' and to stay at MCA. Jimmy Iovine formed Interscope Records within a year and we all know what happened there – great success with Aftermath, Shady and G-Unit records.

'SOUL records was really supposed to be me, Hank and Bill Stephney,' Chuck says. 'But when the whole Griff thing came in Al Teller was the head guy at MCA and he was getting board pressure and stuff like that so I wasn't going to make any decision on Griff based on that situation so I opted out.'

Bill Stephney, however, completely contradicts this version

of events. 'Contrary to popular belief, with the whole SOUL records deal we were doing at MCA, no one ever called us and put any pressure on us at all about, "Oh, are you guys gonna deal with Griff?" At least to me, I don't recall it. Hank and Chuck didn't talk to Al Teller at that point, I did. I was the business guy who ran everything.'

Despite this stance, he doesn't attempt to gloss over the very real problems that were obviously engulfing the group: 'There was a lot of internal pressure,' he continues. 'I do recall one big gigantic meeting we had at 510 South Franklin, trying to solve all of this stuff that sort of became heated as I recall. One of the things that underscored Public Enemy is that we were trying not to be hypocrites. Being the naive young people that we were, we were trying not to be hypocrites. Political leaders and musicians were all hypocrites. You had musicians telling kids, "Say no to drugs", and they were coke addicts. Politicians black and white who would lie at the drop of a hat.'

There are also certain ironies about the situation. Many of PE's closest confidants were Jewish. PE were signed by Rick Rubin, their publicist was Bill Adler. Their main photographer, and the man who shot many of their album covers, is a Jewish man by the name of Glen Friedman. Lyor Cohen was an important figure at Def Jam. Their partners in Rhythm Method Enterprises were Ron Skoler and Ed Chalpin.

'There were so many people of Jewish background around them, more than black, by the way,' says Bill Stephney, 'that it would be pretty stupid to consider the group anti-Semitic. To talk about in the press or anywhere that Jews are responsible for this or that when essentially Public Enemy's whole support system was people of Jewish background was a big gigantic contradiction. It's not like the support system was a bunch of black folks. There was a famous line: "Public Enemy were not anti-Semites, they were filo-Semites."'

As someone who worked in the media and at the *Village Voice* (albeit as a freelancer), Harry Allen was in a unique position to comment on the greyer areas that presented themselves. Even though the popular newspaper was right to severely question the group in the wake of the David Mills interview, they were not big fans of PE to begin with.

'The *Village Voice* was certainly a very interesting place to be and a very interesting magazine to read,' he opines. Even before the Griff situation, 'There was a lot of indifference and hostility to their political message. It's not like they were saying, "This is the greatest thing since sliced bread." It was hostility and then greater hostility. So the *Village Voice*'s record is not a good one on Public Enemy. But certainly with the Griff offence they really had a good reason not to be friendly.'

While this is true of most of the white rock critics at the *Village Voice*, it must be said that Greg Tate, who has gone on to become one of the most prominent black critics in America, also felt it necessary to criticise PE even as he acknowledged their greatness. In a review of *It Takes a Nation of Millions to Hold Us Back* he opined that 'Since Public Enemy show sound reasoning when they focus on racism as a tool of the U.S. power structure, they should be intelligent enough to realize that dehumanizing gays, women and Jews isn't going to set black people free.' In turn it must be said that, at the time, both Chuck and Harry Allen were highly critical of Tate.

Incredible as it may seem, there wasn't an excessive amount of time to dwell on all of this. There was the immediate day-to-day business to be dealt with and no time for much brooding. And, despite the fact that Chuck was prepared to put himself through hell for Griff, it would be naive to expect him to do it with a happy heart. Chuck's devotion to Griff – remember they were childhood friends who were born on the same day – would not have stopped him from wondering why he went out on a limb to defend him.

Throughout the trouble and strife, it was clear that PE's future was very much in doubt. 'It was the darkest time in our history,' Harry says, recalling the tense atmosphere that invaded the dressing rooms backstage at PE shows. 'All those conversations were going on about "What are we going to do?"

and "How are we gonna handle this? Why did this happen?"'

On June 21, 1989, a couple of months after the interview with David Mills was published, Chuck held the press conference that put forward PE's true and official position regarding anti-Semitism. Chuck confirmed that an anti-racist group could never endorse racist philosophies. 'We are not anti-Jewish, we are not anti-anybody,' he told a modest audience, David Mills included, at New York's Sheraton Centre. 'We are pro-black, pro-black culture, pro-human race. Professor Griff's responsibility as Minister of Information for Public Enemy was to faithfully transmit those values . . . in practice he sabotaged those values.' The message of this conference was that PE were planning to continue *sans* Griff. But going further than that, the next day it was announced that PE were breaking up.

However, not only did PE reappear within days, but it appeared Griff was still rolling, despite the fact that he had supposedly been kicked out of the group. There were rumours he had been brought back in, but with a different title and instructions not to speak to the press. About a month or so after that, disaster struck again: The *Kansas City Jewish Chronicle*, who had apparently interviewed Griff in the city's Hyatt Regency hotel, ran a story on Griff where he stood by his comments as being '100 per cent pure'. Whether or not this was true, Griff was now out for good. On the *Behind the Music* documentary Griff claims he never said a word to the reporter. But he was still gone.

And that wasn't the end of the controversy. Rabbi Abraham Cooper of the Simon Wiesenthal Centre had taken out adverts in various media outlets denouncing PE which led to a live confrontation with Chuck on NBC's *Today* show. On October 5, 1989, a clearly riled Chuck D asserted that the comments attributed to Griff 'don't represent the views of Public Enemy, and Rabbi Cooper, you know so'. This exchange clearly inspired the lyric, 'Told the rab, get off the rag', in 'Welcome to the Terrordome', which would pour more fuel on the fire.

It was written as Chuck arrived in Pennsylvania late one night and it's one of his most autobiographical and defensive songs. The recent strife inspired the defiant first line of the song: 'I got so much trouble on my mind, refuse to lose.' 'When I first wrote that record I was thinking about it like, "I'm in the middle of a boxing arena." You're seeing inside the crowd, you're seeing politicians, you're seeing pundits, you're seeing adversaries all in the crowd, arguing and fighting as I'm going down to the ring. That's why you have such a long lead.'

Once Griff had truly left the group for good he hooked up with Luke from the 2 Live Crew and signed to his label. Albums like *Pawns in the Game* and *Kaos II Wiz-Dome* were moderately successful, but they didn't set the world alight. All in all, Griff released four albums in the nineties. 'To be honest with you without demonising anyone all of that was Chuck's doing, me hooking up with Luke. I wasn't a rapper. Fuck was I gonna make a record for? I wasn't a rapper. Chuck hooked that deal up, I didn't hook that up. I don't know how that shit came.' So how did he change from not being a rapper to being one? 'I was forced to,' is the immediate reply. 'Gotta eat . . . so yeah, man, it was one of those situations.'

Chuck remembers being in Florida and having 'a conversation with Luke and Luke said, "Yeah, [he'd] talk to Griff".' There is a school of thought that says that Griff's diminished role within the group frustrated him to the point where he lashed out. Chuck's recollections of his conversation with Luke seem to support the view that Griff felt underused in PE.

'I said, "Griff has always wanted to produce and always wanted to do some more and he feels he's not really allowed to in the camp."' He went on to tell the 2 Live Crew frontman, '"I don't have a problem with him becoming a member but it seems there's some reason for Hank not letting certain people get into the production aspect while also [the] being on the road aspect." At the same time I remember Hank telling him, "Be on the road or be in the production crew." That didn't sit too well. I always knew Griff had these abilities.'

Real-life situations outside of PE were always going to be affected. Under the pressure, Griff's marriage broke down and he had to move out of his house. He had no money, and he was definitely rolling strapped. But things got even realer than that. People were trying to take PE out. Seeing as the situation had caused a rift with their agents the William Morris 'talent and literary' Agency, they had more free time on their hands than they were used to – for the first time in a long time they weren't playing live shows at every available opportunity. It was around this time that Prinses Hemphill (who, in time, would play a major role in Flavor Flav's reality TV experiences) became PE's 'special events co-ordinator'.

'It was very incredible,' she recalls. 'I remember the first time Chuck called me and he said, "Prinses, did you set up a speaking engagement for us?" And I was like, "What?" And he explained it was meant to be like Ice Cube, Ice-T and all these people. They found out that the location had explosives in the basement.' Someone, somewhere, was trying to get a number of rappers in one location – and prominent figures like Chuck, Cube and Ice-T – so they could detonate explosives and do away with some troublesome hip-hoppers.

'You'll have to ask Chuck what was up that day,' she continues. 'There were a number of occasions when Chuck came to me and asked me if I set this engagement up and we found out . . . that that's what was going on. It was a very scary time. I was a young female watching this stuff going on.'

When the speaking engagements went according to plan, however, it was a beautiful thing. Prinses' job was to have them speak to kids in whatever city they happened to be in. As soon as they arrived at their latest destination Prinses would take them 'straight to the projects. There was always a good turnout.' The inevitable coverage from the local news media didn't hurt either. Occasionally, Prinses would use her status to persuade celebrity athletes to join PE in persuading 'the kids' that the trife life was definitely not their best option.

PE had always had security threats, and had received special attention from skinheads long before the Griff affair blew up. In the PE camp, Malik Farrakhan enjoys the same kind of

seniority that was the privilege of Eddie, Cedric the Entertainer's character in Ice Cube's *Barber Shop* franchise. PE's
head of security recalls situations in Germany and Greece. But
nothing too drastic ever came to pass.

'Those two places have been problems, we've had different
kinds of threats. But it's never happened to the point where
it's made us pack up and go. We got through it no problem.
I've never had to hurt anybody, never been hurt. I don't recall
any altercations where somebody's got stabbed, cut, been shot
or ended up dead. My record is clean. Music is good and what
we represent, what we put out there, will keep you from
fighting. They knew they had to have met their match. They
said what they had to say, and they had their little bald head
and their little bones and all of that but we'd spank that ass.
So that was over before it began. Nothing got out of hand.'

After the controversy had died down a little, some members
still saw Griff around here and there. Brother Drew, who was
always one of the peacemakers within the PE camp, ran into Griff
at industry showcase Jack the Rapper one year. He had attended
with his brother and their band. 'Prince was performing and
somebody said, "Yo, you know Griff is here with Luke," so you
know we kicked it. I always kept in touch with him, he was doing
his thing and we were doing ours. But it's a great thing that he
came back to the group.' Griff officially rejoined for the *He Got
Game* album, eight years after his interview with David Mills. He
is obviously pleased that he 'managed to kinda win the love of
my brothers back. To the point where we could at least get along.'

While everyone is seemingly cool with each other now, Griff
has clearly not forgotten his treatment by his bandmates at the
time. 'I'm a soldier man,' says Griff. 'And I think if you keep it
in its proper context and understand it from a military point
of view it's like, "This guy's a soldier but his troops went left
on him and left me out there to die." That's how you gotta
look at it. It's real, that's real talk, as we say in the hood.'

21

After the Storm

Unsurprisingly, the Griff controversy affected the music. In a sense the group did break up. The worst musical consequence of the whole situation was that the team that put together *It Takes a Nation of Millions to Hold Us Back* never worked together again. The credits of Public Enemy's third album reveal that Bill Stephney, credited as producer on *Yo! Bum Rush the Show* and production supervisor on *It Takes a Nation of Millions to Hold Us Back* was not present for *Fear of a Black Planet*.

Well, that's not strictly true. Below The Bomb Squad's credit for taking care of everything to do with the album's creation is the short message, 'Overseen in the 1990s: Fuck Dick Lewis – Mr Bill Stephney is watching!' This is a clear reference to the inlay of *Yo! Bum Rush the Show* where among the thank yous is the sentence: 'Producer's note: the 1990s are here, so take no shorts (particularly when we know that Dick Lewis is watching).' Back in those days, there was a commercial in the United States, and New York especially, for an electronic store called Numark and Lewis. Dick Lewis, the owner of the stores, hosted most of these commercials. His catchphrase was, 'Dick Lewis is watching.'

'That was a good thing,' Bill says, 'cos Chuck and I really hadn't been communicating that much. Since I was severed from the Public Enemy process that was Chuck saying no matter what, Bill Stephney is a part of this. It was a nice thing for Chuck to do.' Nevertheless, from that specific period onwards Bill was essentially separated from PE. He asserts that while the Griff affair indirectly caused this to happen, it was not the main catalyst.

When SOUL records finally did open for business, they

released some great records that failed to see much success. 'Change the Style' wasn't the only great record on Son of Bazerk's *Bazerk, Bazerk, Bazerk*. 'The Band Get Swivy on the Wheels' and 'J Dubs Theme', favourites of Bill Stephney's, are just two other joints that make the album memorable. If you see it, cop it.

'It was good stuff but it was too conceptual,' Bill decides of groups like the Young Black Teenagers and their debut album of the same name. The group of young white boys took their ironic name from the surprise that had resulted when it became obvious that white kids were getting down with hip-hop culture. Ice-T's 1993 album *Home Invasion* – whose cover featured a young white kid surrounded by symbols of black culture – trod similar ground. 'If not for the name they probably would have been one of the great white rap groups of all time. Their name was too much baggage.'

It definitely was. It must be said that YBT's biggest hit, 'Tap the Bottle', occurred after they left SOUL records and dropped their second album *Dead End Kidz Doin' Lifetime Bidz*. Gotta love that title.

But overly conceptual records weren't the biggest problem. Bill recalls, 'The business relationship between Hank and myself I think was unbalanced 'cos we needed Chuck as the third party. He was the glue between me and Hank. So in essence SOUL records never really worked 'cos our team had been broken up.'

22

The Bomb Squad Blows Up

The first few months of 1990 had probably been the most productive of The Bomb Squad's history. Between January and March 1990 they produced three very dope albums. Public Enemy's *Fear of a Black Planet*, Ice Cube's *AmeriKKKa's Most Wanted* and Bell Biv DeVoe's *Poison*. Those twelve weeks also sadly marked the last time all of the original members would work together. Relations were strained to say the least.

'All I know is at that particular time, when we were getting ready to work on *Fear*, nobody was talking,' Eric Sadler says. 'Hank wasn't talking to Griff, Griff wasn't talking to Chuck, Chuck wasn't talking to Hank, Hank wasn't talking to Keith. It was a little war going on.' Eric was the only person who was still speaking to everybody.

Right at the end of 1989, Chuck and Keith had begun working by themselves on the tracks that would form *Fear of a Black Planet*. Eric Sadler recalls going up to 510, where pre-production still took place, to check out the tune that eventually became 'Revolutionary Generation'. He fully acknowledges Keith's large contribution to a lot of memorable tracks and makes a point of mentioning, 'Keith wrote "Fight the Power" by himself, he really wrote "Terrordome" by himself. Keith was responsible for a lot of stuff that he'll never get the credit for. Keith came out with the main tracks for a bunch of stuff with all of our names on it.'

There was a lot of pressure. Instead of picking from the many, many basic backing tracks that Eric had accumulated, Chuck wanted them to come up with something on the spot. It wasn't easy, but they persevered. 'A lot of songs on that album were written right there and then,' says Eric.

Despite the distress, there were some days when things went well. The day 'Burn Hollywood Burn' was recorded was one of these days. Big Daddy Kane and Chuck D had been promising each other that they would do a record together for a long time. Eventually they hooked it up and Kane passed through Greene Street to make it happen. He has fond memories of the day: 'I liked the way I mentioned old black movies from the seventies,' he says. 'I said the little part about going to watch *Black Caesar*. It was cool. I thought the subject was heavy and I mean I liked the way it came out, you know, Chuck did his thing, Cube did his thing.'

While Chuck and Kane had been going over the finer points of the tune that lambasted Hollywood for decades of negative stereotyping, Cube was chilling in the studio just kicking it. He had been spending some time on the East Coast and it was no secret that he wanted The Bomb Squad to produce his debut solo album.

'Cube was sitting on the couch and he just said, "Hey, I wanna be down."' Chuck remembers. 'So me and Kane looked at each other like, "Fuck it, why not?"'

Later on Chuck realised that this marked one of the first times in rap music where he would have to figure out the legal issues that resulted from spontaneous creativity. Cube was with Priority, Kane was signed to Warners, part of the WEA system, and PE were ultimately signed to Sony. Chuck doesn't have fond memories of trying to sort through the red tape. 'Believe me, that was hell trying to get clearances from three different companies.' It was worth it though. 'Burn Hollywood Burn' also marked one of the first times when people from different rap crews collaborated together.

Fear of a Black Planet saw Flav continue to step his game up. It's difficult to decide which of his contributions is the best. Both 'Can't Do Nuttin' for Ya Man' and '911 Is a Joke' are definitely memorable and possibly the two best Flavor Flav solo tracks in existence. The beats are hot, his rhyming has again improved further and the subject matter extends beyond his considerable flyness. Despite the money and the fame it is no secret that Flav still knew many ghetto dwellers from the wrong side of the tracks. 'Can't Do Nuttin' for Ya Man' was born of the contradictions and contrasts that arose as a result of the now rich Flav still choosing to hang out in poor neighbourhoods.

'I remember when I was in my car. I was in my Corvette riding from Long Island going to The Bronx. I was slipping,' he admits. 'I was roasting. I mean I was smoked-out crazy. And everybody kept asking me for stuff and yet nobody wanted to give me stuff. So then if anybody ever asked me for something I would be like, "Yo, I can't do nothing for ya man."' It was that simple.

'Next thing you know I started to vibe on it: "I can't do nothing for ya man," um ahh um um ahh. So I went and told that to Chuck. Chuck was like, "Record that shit man." I spent the whole night coming up with that record.' 'Can't Do Nuttin' for Ya Man' was for ever etched into the consciousness of hip-hop fans when it was chosen to be played during some of the most memorable scenes in Kid 'n Play's seminal film *House Party*. The movie revolves around the duo plotting a house party when Play's parents leave town to visit relatives. They then have to deal with the consequences. 'Can't Do Nuttin' for Ya Man' was chosen to feature in the scene where the party was in full swing. 'That was big to me,' Flav decides. 'Yeah, that was big to me.'

'911 Is a Joke' is a more thoughtful and satirical song. Flav lampoons the emergency services for repeatedly failing to respond punctually to calls for help from the black community. 'If your life is on the line, then you're dead today,' was just one of many humorous lines that alluded to a very alarming reality. If you fell ill, or an accident occurred, you better get to the hospital your-damn-self. The video depicted a supposedly seriously ill Flav being roughly manhandled and generally mistreated by ambulance staff who had taken ages to turn up in the first place.

Flav has no problem admitting that the original idea and title came from Chuck. 'He gave me that as a project to do. Like, "Yeah, I'm a give you a project to do. Write about how 911 is a joke." So I said, "Aiight," and I went and wrote the record. I went and got high and wrote the record,' he laughs before comically raising his voice. 'I went and got ripped, I went and got out of my mind, and I started speaking all kinds of crazy shit 'cos usually back in the days when I used to smoke, it used to broaden my ideas and everything.'

However, 'I didn't like the record at first . . . 'cos I had did the track a certain way. Next thing you know, after I recorded the shit, Hank and Keith were like, "Yo, he think it's gonna stay like this. Wait till them motherfuckers leave and go out on the road." Public Enemy goes overseas, I come back and everyone's going crazy over this "911 Is a Joke". I'm like, "Wooow, my shit is a hit," and I heard the shit and it was to a different track. I was like, "Daamn, the shit is wack."' This point of view soon changed when he began performing the song regularly and saw the great reactions it was getting.

Flav recalls one occasion when, irony of ironies, the tune itself led to medical help being delayed. One time when

Flav was in New Orleans' Iberville Projects his presence was enough to cause the locals to harass some ambulance workers. 'When the ambulance came through there, everyone threw bricks at the ambulance, talking about "911 Is a Joke". The ambulance couldn't even come and pick up the patients. I was like, "Wooooow".'

Once all the tracks were done, sequencing the disjointed record caused more headaches. If The Bomb Squad had been working as one, perhaps it would have been different. But they weren't. 'A lot of people were like, "Wow, it's a brilliant album",' Eric says. 'But it really shoulda been much better. If we had more time and we didn't have to deal with the situation of nobody talking . . . ' he trails off.

Fear of a Black Planet was also an important album as far as the minefield that is sampling is concerned. Copyright laywers had a field day with it, to the extent that PE knew that they would never be able to make an album in the same way again. 'We got sued for everything,' laments Chuck. 'We knew that the door on sampling was gonna close.' Acts like PE weren't to blame for this. The hip-hop groups who would take whole songs and just put them on top of a beat were the ones who brought it to the attention of the money men. It was this type of sloppiness that prompted the sampling laws which meant an album like *Fear of a Black Planet* was never going to be cost effective.

'Welcome to the Terrordome' exemplifies the collision of samples in the record. There are many different elements vying for attention in its opening bars. Before the long lead into the first verse even commences there is a trumpet sample from 'Bom Bom Zee' by TS Monk. As the long lead draws to its close there are a number of vocal samples before Chuck begins his verse. Among them is a voice promising, 'This is a journey into sound', and an announcement from the 1966 Motown Revue concert where the compere asks, 'Would you join me please in all welcoming the tempting Temptations?' PE cut off the last three words.

PE didn't just sample things wholesale. They played them

and manipulated them, incorporating sounds and flavours into a new whole. Techniques like this paved the way for the likes of DJ Premier, Pete Rock and, in time, 'your favorite producer's favorite producer' J Dilla. There were even samples that never made it on to the record. Originally PE were going to sample Joe Quartermain's 1971 hit 'I Got So Much Trouble in My Mind', but Chuck decided he wanted to say the words with feeling instead. It was a decision that most likely saved the group a lot of money. Hip-hop groups weren't always the perpetrators. A year or so after 'Terrordome' was released Chad Jackson sampled Chuck's voice for his novelty pop dance hit 'Hear the Drummer (Get Wicked)'. Artistic concerns were not always paramount, but financial matters were. Corporate America was finally beginning to realise just how much money there was to be made from hip-hop. This meant the end for PE's approach to sampling. The more samples in a song, the more money you paid out. Simple as that. These laws were one of, if not the, main reason that producers in the late nineties like Swizz Beatz began to use keyboards to create their beats.

Fear of a Black Planet also marked the first time that Keith Shocklee was credited as being a member of The Bomb Squad. It's impossible to think that the Griff affair was not responsible for this outcome. The cabinet re-shuffle meant some received an internal promotion of sorts. Unfortunately, the whole mess also brought to a halt the work The Bomb Squad had been putting in for other artists. While the various members of the great production team had enjoyed success with the likes of Slick Rick, Vanessa Williams and more so with Bell Biv DeVoe it was their work on Ice Cube's debut solo album *AmeriKKKa's Most Wanted* that really cemented their rep as the greatest producers of their time.

23

AmeriKKKa's Most Wanted

AmeriKKKa's Most Wanted is a massive, momentous event in hip-hop's history. NWA were probably the only other music group in existence – never mind hip-hop – who could rival Public Enemy in the 'most dangerous band in the world' stakes. In the late eighties, *Straight Outta Compton* was the only other album that came close to equalling the shock and awe-impact of *It Takes a Nation of Millions to Hold Us Back*. So when Ice Cube began to fall out with Eazy-E, Dr Dre, Jerry Heller and the rest of NWA, and subsequently went to New York to work with The Bomb Squad, it was a big deal. They more than matched people's expectations by making an epoch-defining classic.

Cube and Chuck had met before Cube's departure from Eazy and Jerry's Ruthless Records. They first crossed paths in Las Vegas on the first night of a series of dates that NWA and PE had together. 'Me and Ren were the biggest fans,' Cube reminisces. 'Big fans. Chuck D is my favourite rapper. Of all times. You wanna talk about rappers? Chuck D to me is the most significant.' The Niggaz With Attitude had been influenced by the Black Panthers of Rap. 'If you really listen to the NWA album we used a lot of the same breaks that Public Enemy used. For example "Fuck Tha Police",' he continues before humming the intro: '"Jiggajigajiggaumum daa naa." That's "Bring The Noise".' Cube exchanged numbers and when it was time to record the solo album everyone was waiting for, he knew where to turn: 'When I ended up leaving the group I knew I couldn't get Dre so it was kinda simple. I was like, "Fuck, I can't have the best producer on the West Coast, let me get the best producers on the East Coast."' To this end, Cube got on the phone and began forging links with PE personnel.

'Ice Cube was calling me up during the summer of '89 and

also the fall of '89. Really the second half of '89,' Chuck recalls. Cube was not happy with his small payback after the massive success, and his huge contributions to albums like *Eazy Duz It* and the seminal *Straight Outta Compton*. Dre and Eazy had nice new cars and money to burn. He got a platinum plaque to take back to his mama's crib, where he still lived. He was not happy. But this was not a good time to be dealing with PE.

'I'd just got finished with the Griff situation so I was very tentative of telling another person what to do with their group,' admits Chuck. 'I was kinda like, "I don't know if you should even be bothering, I don't know if I'm the best person to ask".'

Even after Chuck demurred and suggested a few of the producers at the time who were making noise, guys like Sam Sever and Marley Marl, Cube still felt he was the person to ask and continued calling. 'He got a lot of demos from different people and he still said, "Nah, I want ya'll to do it. The Bomb Squad to do it." I held off, like I don't want to be involved in something that broke up another group, I already had problems with my own group, so I held off.'

The first person Cube built up a relationship with was Brother Drew. 'He used to call 510 a lot, but wasn't nobody picking up the phone,' the soundman says. 'Then I was like, "Yo Keith, this kid from NWA Ice Cube keep calling, wassup."' After flying to New York, Cube ran into Chuck at the Def Jam building and explained his new circumstances. 'I told him, "Yo, I'm solo now, here's what I'm trying to do."'

This was the same day that Chuck planned to hit the studio with Big Daddy Kane to record 'Burn Hollywood Burn'. It didn't take long for them to collectively decide Cube was gonna spit a verse on the song. He was with it. 'I said, "Shit yeah, that'd be perfect to kick off my solo thang."' Perhaps most important of all, Cube got to sit down face-to-face with Chuck, Eric, Hank and Keith. Chuck remembers Hank 'nodding his head and saying, "Alright yeah, we'll do it."' From there Cube scooped up Sir Jinx (noted West Coast producer, cousin of Dr Dre and member of CIA, Cube's first group) and it was on and popping.

Chuck remembers sitting in a car with Cube and telling him that it all starts with a notebook. 'I said, "Before you start working on the album you gotta talk about the theories of how you wanna be able to never repeat yourself twice. Choose some great topics, some great stories like I know you're gonna do but try to be diverse in your ideas."'

They talked about the theory of *AmeriKKKa's Most Wanted* for a few days before they got into the practicalities. They were up against it. PE were about to go off on tour again. This meant that while at the start Chuck was working heavily on *AmeriKKKa's Most Wanted*, Sir Jinx, Eric Sadler and Cube took up the reins and came up with the identity of the record.

While Chuck went off on tour, Ice Cube began to acquaint himself with the way The Bomb Squad put their thing together. When he and Sir Jinx first arrived in Strong Island they were directed towards a warehouse where Eric Sadler was waiting to help them pick their beats. 'This warehouse was full of records, I mean just rows and rows of records. Eric said, "Once you pick out your record I'll loop it up for you."' Before any recording took place, Cube and Jinx spent a fortnight picking beats and breaks. Once they had a crate-full they took it up to the big studio.

Cube recalls that it was Eric's job to sort out the bottom beat, the bedrock of the song. Once he'd laid it down everyone else would come up in there and, as Cube puts it, 'start adding all the breaks in there, give it all the personality'. But because PE were on tour this process took a little longer than planned. Once Ice Cube had put his scratch vocals on the rough versions of the tracks Eric let them mature for a while.

'Our process was, once I layed all the stuff, now Hank and Chuck come in and we all dissect it and take stuff out, put stuff in,' says Eric. 'We all work together. But what happened was he [Hank] wasn't around and Chuck was off and on the road.' This was something that didn't sit too well with Cube. So one day he paid Eric and Keith a visit at Greene Street to see what the hold-up was.

'Cube comes down and starts cursing me and Keith out: "You motherfuckers ain't shit. If Dr Dre and them are gonna come out with another album, I better get on my mutha-fuckin' job! You pussies laying around here doing bullshit, y'all ain't doing nothing." I was like, "Oh shit!"'

By this time Eric had moved to Manhattan and was only about a block away from their favourite studio. This meant he was there working nearly twenty-four hours a day. The gangsta pep-talk proved to be just what was needed to restart the process. 'He was right,' Eric admits. 'Because I was waiting for Hank and Chuck to come in. After he made that point me and Keith started killing it.'

They started doing everything they could to finish the record and Cube really immersed himself in the process. Eric told him that, while a lot of the songs they had recorded so far were nines and tens, there were still too many sevens. Cube agreed. 'He was like, "Fuck it, they're done, throw 'em away, those are off the album".' One thing The Bomb Squad liked to do was work on five or six songs for an album and then pick the best song from that initial bunch. Whatever they decided was the best song would then be earmarked to be the worst song on the finished album. Everything from that point on would have to be better.

This is one reason why *AmeriKKKa's Most Wanted* is such a brilliant album. Joints like 'A Gangsta's Fairytale', 'Turn Off the Radio' and the cautionary tale 'Once Upon a Time in the Projects' were always going to establish Ice Cube as a solo force to be reckoned with. Respectively, these songs showed off his sense of humour, his hatred of those who attack hip-hop culture (the tune features a radio presenter boasting about how his station doesn't play rap), and his street knowledge. Eric was over the moon. 'Every time I would listen to Cube I would be like, "This mu'fucka's brilliant. This is turning out really, really well." Not many albums or even many songs turn out how you hear them.'

It was inevitable that Cube and Chuck would collaborate on at least one song. When Chuck wasn't on tour he would be in the studio. 'When Chuck came into town? Chuck was brilliant,' Eric says. 'He would call me up at two in the morning like, "I'm back in town. Let's go down there and record." He had ideas and changes and all this stuff.' Together, they came up with 'Endangered Species', which referred to young black men in America.

'I'd always loved Public Enemy's high energy records,' Cube enthuses. 'I loved "Rebel Without a Pause", I loved "Who Stole the Soul", "Bring the Noise" of course. These were the songs I just loved to hear Chuck go off on. You know "Night of the Living Baseheads". "Here it is, bam and you say goddamn".' So when it came time for him to do a record with the hard rhymer he made sure it had the same qualities. 'I was like, when I do a record with Chuck, the shit's gonna be moving.'

Flavor Flav showed up on the less essential 'I'm Only Out for One Thang', a predictable, if at times humourous, ode to groupie love which is typical of the casual sexism that has always haunted hip-hop culture. PE's 1991 video *Tour of a Black Planet* features snippets of Cube performing his duet with Flav, as well as the far more righteous 'Burn Hollywood Burn'. It's a trip to observe the young Cube with Jheri curls poking out from under a baseball hat which bears the simple legend: 'Nigga'.

After a month or so the album was done. It was the first time the East Coast and West Coast had worked together. Chuck proudly remembers how PE brought a little bit of their style to the bravado Cube had honed as NWA's main lyricist. 'The don't-give-a-fuck-ness mixed with the consciousness was a potent mixture. It was almost like, you know, "Fight the police".'

Once again, however, there were credit issues. That same 'don't-give-a-fuck-ness' led to some differences in opinion. 'Cube was very good at sticking to his guns,' Eric says. 'So when we finished his album, he was one of the few people that when Hank submitted the credits to him he was like, "Fuck that! Nah, y'all weren't there." He was in control of his own thing.'

It's not always possible, especially when you're dealing with the music business, to ascertain whose version of events is correct when these issues crop up. However, this time the facts definitely support Eric's assertion. While his name is all over the credits, and Keith pops up every now and again, Hank's name doesn't appear on the credits for *AmeriKKKa's Most Wanted*. He is, of course, listed as a member of The Bomb Squad. But his name doesn't appear underneath any of the song titles. Eric remembers, 'I was there every single day and night. Keith was definitely there about fifteen to twenty days. Hank was there about four or five and Chuck was there sporadically, like maybe a week and a half, off-and-on but when he was there he worked.'

AmeriKKKa's Most Wanted was the first of many brilliant Ice Cube solo albums and set him on the path to the glittering Hollywood career he enjoys today. His most recent albums *Laugh Now, Cry Later* and *Raw Footage* prove he's still a microphone fiend. Cube stayed cool with the PE camp and even invited Brother Drew on tour with him so that his sound would be right.

During Cube's tour for his debut album, one of the most important stops was of course Harlem's Apollo Theater. Drew was planning to attend as a fan of Cube's music, but Cube had other ideas. 'He said, "Come down 'cos I need you to work,"' Drew says. 'They were the first West Coast group that turned the Apollo out. They had motherfuckers throwing money on the stage and I got it all on film.' Things went so well that after the show the tour bus drove straight from the Apollo to Drew's house, waited while he packed a bag, and headed off on tour with their new soundman. It was a good job that Drew could cancel whatever he had going on for the next three weeks. On the road, he became something like a bigger brother. Cube and Da Lench Mob were still in their early twenties, and the cases of St Ides malt liquor that regularly appeared on the tour bus – this is when Cube was doing the adverts for the drinks company – were not exactly a calming influence.

'There was a lot of shit they didn't know on the road . . . so I couldn't be Drew like Drew in Public Enemy, I had to be like, "This is bad, this is . . . you know". One cat had just robbed a bank and we're going across state lines and all that. I'm like, "Yo cousin, you can't do that".' An article in *The Source* magazine from mid 1990 quotes Ice Cube crediting 'Brother Drew from Public Enemy' with introducing him to the Nation of Islam, and therefore a more assured, disciplined way of life.

That is not to say that there were not times when Drew benefitted from the 'youthful exuberance' of Ice Cube and Da Lench Mob. As tends to happen while touring, Drew ran into a problem with one promoter. The situation was left with Drew promising to return at a later date. Cube had other ideas. 'Ice Cube said, "Fuck that. You're out here with us, we're gonna handle this shit now." Some motherfuckers got guns and went and broke into the office and said, "Yo, what the fuck is the problem, y'all got a problem with Drew, you got a problem with us and we can handle this shit now." I was like, "It ain't even that deep."' He was still playing the big brother. Cube even recommended 'Brother Drew, Public Enemy Number Two', as he became known, to other artists he was close to. That's how he ended up doing the sound for Ice-T. 'Ice-T was like, "I need you to do my sound," and he peeled money off right there and then.'

24

She's Driving Me Out of My Mind

Bell Biv DeVoe were a different kind of proposition. Initially The Bomb Squad were very wary of having anything to do with Ronnie, Rickie and Mike. 'I looked at it like, "What are we gonna do with them? They ain't no rappers! They're singers!"' Keith Shocklee says. '"That's New Edition, they're some singers. We do rap!"' It turned out that the trio didn't want to be known as those kids from New Edition any more. They had had quite enough of what they saw as kiddie music and wanted to step their game up. They even wanted to rap. This presented a challenge for The Bomb Squad. 'It was like, okay, "Let's see what we can do with 'em".'

Michael Bivins had been trying to track down Chuck for a long while. When he was finally successful Chuck put him in touch with Keith. Keith vividly remembers the first night they showed up to the studio. As they were straight from LA they had Jheri curls and were rocking cardigan sweaters. Keith and co were wearing 'classically baggy jeans, hoodies, Timberlands and all that stuff'. Keith was clowning.

'I'm like, "You want to be rappers? Look at the way y'all dress. Y'all ain't street. You better get some clothes man, wasssup!"' They went and changed their whole wardrobe.' They even came up with some styles of their own. 'When they came out with the BBD style one shoe one way, the other shoe the other way, looking wild, I was like, "Aiight y'all, go ahead".'

Working with The Bomb Squad enabled the r'n'b trio to see how music was made from the rap side of things. An important element of this – obvious to hip-hop fans – was getting them to write their own material. When they had worked with Jimmy Jam and Terry Lewis, one of the most successful partnerships in modern black music (their work spans from the late seventies through to the present day), everything was laid out for them. Janet Jackson's favourite producers wrote all of it. Keith wasn't feeling that. 'I said, "That's new to me. I'm here to deal with writers that write their own stuff because I'm still from the school of rap being personable." It's about your lifestyle, it's about what you do.'

Bell Biv DeVoe didn't disappoint. They loosened up and got busy. The Bomb Squad had again succeeded in creating a memorable work. Any r'n'b DJ worth his or her salt knows that their old-school section isn't complete until the crowd has heard 'Poison', the first single from the album of the same name. (Other notable tracks include Keith Sweat's 'I Want Her' and 'Feels Good' by Tony! Toni! Toné!) Any crowd at any r'n'b club will oblige any DJ by throwing their hands up and singing, 'She's driving me out of my mind. That's why it's hard for me to find.'

Bell Biv DeVoe were so happy with The Bomb Squad that they called them back to mix the album. Instead of the shoulder-pad soul that was popular throughout the eighties, they 'wanted more of a street vibe to it', Keith explains. 'Eric got in there, mixed that album, and yo, pow! Then after that they took what they learned from us and just took it to the next level.'

Unfortunately by now Eric really had had enough of having to put up with his close friends running each other into the ground all the time. He continued to work with The Bomb Squad on the remix tip. But, as far as Public Enemy went, that was it. 'It got really, really nasty,' he laments. 'And I'm not the type of person who can deal with friends of mine talking about other friends of mine behind their back. I can't do that. If this one is talking about this one, and that one is talking about the other one, I mean badly, behind each other's back? You know what, this isn't what you guys sold me on. They told me, "It's us against the world. It's Public Enemy, we stick together, it's our thing." I only did the first three albums.'

25

Talking MLK

Despite the fact they had taken a severe bruising, by the time the fourth Public Enemy record, *Apocalypse '91 . . . The Enemy Strikes Black*, was released PE were one of the most famous and biggest groups in the world. Their place in hip-hop's hall of fame was already guaranteed. Their influence hadn't waned. Who else was responsible for all the hip-hoppers who were rocking Africa medallions (which temporarily replaced gold chains), Malcolm X hats, and kente cloth as testimony to their (hopefully) heightened cultural awareness?

Chart success across the world was now par for the course. Singles like 'Can't Truss It' and a remake of 'Bring the Noise' with rock giants Anthrax were massive successes. PE's influence had long spread beyond hip-hop. When the makers of *Terminator 2* (released in July of 1991, a few months before *Apocalypse '91*) wanted to prove that protagonist John Connor was a 'problem child', someone who simply would not budge when told to jump, they decided the character should wear a PE T-shirt. This may not have been the best advert the group could have hoped for. After all, PE have never been about being a bad influence on youngsters. But the fact that actor Edward Furlong wore the T-shirt in such a high-profile film – at the time it was the highest grossing sequel in movie history and spawned infamous catchphrases (who can forget '*Hasta la vista*, baby') – aptly conveys PE's elevated level of fame.

Apocalypse '91's cover celebrates a lot that is great about PE. Chuck holds court in the middle holding a skull. 'Holding the skull means we have our heads in our own hands,' Chuck explains. 'War is not the answer; we were trying to come into the nineties not having it be the decade of apocalypse.' An animated Flav rocks a crisp Jordan tracksuit and, as is his wont from time to time, a top hat. He has a big smile on his face that shows off his gold fronts and his arms are raised in the classic 'What you talking 'bout Willis?' pose. Terminator chills to Chuck's left, but unlike Flavor's regular-sized shades, the oversized sunglasses seem to be there to mask the wearer's personality rather than accentuate it. His high top and kente cloth reminds us that this was the early nineties. Behind them stand the four S1Ws, literally watching their backs. It was shot by high profile hip-hop photographer Ernie Panniciolli.

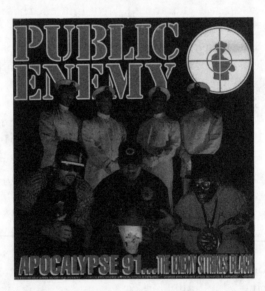

'We shot that in Hempstead, at a place Chuck used to work at actually,' recalls Brother Mike, who is stood second left directly in between Chuck and Terminator X. Mike is not only a good example of how self-contained a unit PE were, but of how there was more to the S1s than meets the eye. 'Those uniforms that you saw on there? I made them,' he reveals. 'I do that as well.'

Apocalypse '91 marked the official entry of Gary G-Wiz into The Bomb Squad. By that time, Gary had been working with Hank long enough for the elder Shocklee brother to trust him with the keys to 510 South Franklin. He had originally been earmarked to be a member of the Terminal Illness Crew and began slowly to immerse himself in the daily goings on at 510 soon after *Nation of Millions* dropped. 'I went up there and Chuck was like, "Eh, you didn't think we were gonna be able to do it, right?"' He recalls. 'I was like, "Yeah, you did it."' Over the next couple of years his visits became more frequent and he ended up playing some of the beats he was working on for Hank. 'He was feeling the stuff and he was putting together a new bunch of producers and he wanted me to work with him. It kinda then went that way.' After acquiring the keys, the hungry young producer was constantly up in the spot making beats. A lot of the time, Chuck would be in his office writing and working, and he couldn't help but hear Gary's work.

'One day Chuck comes through and says, "Yo man, I'm kinda liking what you doing out here, give me a tape."' But before Gary could submit some tracks to Chuck he had to clear things with Hank. Prior to the recording of PE's fourth album, the bad relations following the whole Griff situation still remained.

'Just to put it on the table Chuck and Hank were in beef at the time,' Gary says. 'I was working with Hank and I didn't want to cross any lines or anything. I wanted to check with Hank and make sure that he was cool with it 'cos I didn't want to be cutting Hank's throat. I'm very loyal. But Hank said it was cool and so I said, "Yo Chuck, here's your tape." Chuck was like, "Yo man, I could make an EP off this easy."'

While he was very careful not to step on anyone's toes, Gary was nevertheless very pleased with the opportunity to work with Chuck. Of all the producers with an axe to grind, Gary seems to grind his the hardest. His apprenticeship was not a happy one.

'I was doing remixes or whatever for Hank and all these producers started slowly falling off, one at a time. People would be upset, people wouldn't get paid or whatever. But I kinda stuck it out like, "Whatever, I'm here to make music."'

Did he go through any of that? 'Oh yeah, I probably did

three or four remixes for Hank where I didn't get any money and I was supposed to. But I just looked at it as part of paying dues. You come in the game and he's got the connections so I was like, "Whatever, I'll do these beats."'

Hank's studio was another appealing aspect of the PE gig for Gary. Hank had all the hot gear. SP-1200, S-950 samplers and all that good stuff. It was a lot better than 'the primitive stuff at my house that I was working on'.

Apocalypse '91 was originally meant to be an EP. Chuck wanted about four tracks to go around the new version of 'Bring the Noise' that was brought to him by Scott Ian and Charlie Benante, guitarist and drummer respectively for Anthrax. But once they started recording, it quickly turned into an album. The collaboration with Anthrax was another defining moment of PE's career. It was the first time a rap record had been a hit twice. No one is trying to pretend it was the first rap/rock collaboration. Run DMC and Aerosmith's version of 'Walk this Way' had rehashed Aerosmith's mid seventies hit. But with 'Bring the Noise' it happened the other way around, with Anthrax reinventing the hip-hop track in their crunchy, post thrash style.

The seeds of the video and the subsequent tour were sown during an interview with *NME*. 'During the interview we talked about each other and how we did the song,' Chuck recalls. 'And then we was like, "If we're gonna do the song, we're gonna do the video, and then we're gonna do the tour."' PE toured with the metal giants during the same year their fourth album dropped. Earlier that year, they had toured the US with The Sisters of Mercy. Chuck was so busy it was not uncommon for him to leave the studio and go straight to whatever venue they were playing at.

Inevitably, these endeavours raised eyebrows. Some elements of the mainstream media promptly decided that a tour featuring black and white bands on the same bill was never going to work. People were so shocked that authorities in Detroit refused to allow a PE/Sisters of Mercy concert to take place. Flavor Flav famously declared, 'They said this tour would never happen,' while onstage with Anthrax. Of course, touring with rock groups was nothing new to PE. Many of those who had something to say conveniently forgot (or didn't know in the first place) that their very first tour had featured The Beastie Boys and Murphy's Law on the same bill. But this didn't stop narrow-minded folks running their mouths.

However, despite the naysayers, PE had yet again proved themselves innovative and at the forefront of change. The reborn 'Bring the Noise' proved a major influence on groups like Rage Against the Machine and the nu-metal genre that rose to prominence in the late nineties. Whereas 'Sophisticated Bitch' featured a solo from Vernon Reid, the fact that PE collaborated with a real live, respected, and white metal-band, as equals, defined their crossover reputation. Scott Ian's guest verses, and the chemistry between him and Chuck in the video (and onstage), further solidified the union of rap and rock. Other important milestones in rap and rock's relationship include the *Judgment Night* soundtrack and Cypress Hill's *Skull and Bones*. Nowadays, rappers regularly work with rock groups. When Jay-Z recorded *Collision Course* with Linkin

Park in 2004 at the height of his powers, nobody really batted an eyelid. It certainly didn't do his credibility any harm.

PE's third tour during 1991 was a straight-up rap affair with peeps like Queen Latifah, Naughty by Nature and the Geto Boys. So the accusation that PE were somehow moving away from hip-hop was immediately discredited. They had never been limited or confined by the genre. Those who accused the group of such things shut their mouths when the Pete Rock remixes of 'Shut 'Em Down' and then 'Nighttrain' were released as singles.

At the time, Mount Vernon's Pete Rock was on his way to becoming hip-hop's hottest producer. Released alongside partner in rhyme CL Smooth, the six song-strong debut EP *All Souled Out* was causing mad excitement among hip-hop fans. The title track and songs like 'Good Life' were definitely dope. But it was 'The Creator' that singled out the duo as something really special, and caused the most havoc on the dancefloor. Some hip-hop commentators judge 'The Creator' to be the first record that started the 'phat beats' sound that characterised East Coast hip-hop for much of the nineties and beyond.

But Pete was still having trouble realising his full potential. One day Chuck was up in the Columbia offices and their product manager, Angela Thomas, told him about a young dude called Peter Philips who was trying to make more of a name for himself. 'People were not giving him a shot to produce stuff like that. I said, "Yeah, I'll give him a shot," and it happened to be Pete Rock and CL Smooth. They had just come out, sitting there looking for an opportunity, and I told Pete, I said, "Well here's 'Shut 'Em Down'."' Many advised Chuck that this was a bad idea. But he did it anyway.

While the remix was a massive hit, in a strange sign of things to come in hip-hop, the New York-centric tune failed to cause a stir down South. 'When Pete Rock put that "duh duh duh duh" [on there],' Chuck says with an impression of the horn sample, 'it immediately became a New York and UK record. It was new and it was hot on the theme of New York and London. Down South and everywhere else they wanted the original version, that "boom boom boom". It really showed us for the first time, you know, "keep spreading our sound around".'

Without doubt, these remixes helped raise Pete Rock's stock in the game. It's just possible that they are the main reason 'the Pete Rock remix' became something worth having in the first place. After the release of the highly anticipated album *Mecca and the Soul Brother* Pete became a go-to producer, and enjoyed the status that The Bomb Squad would have enjoyed if they had stayed together. Other famous Pete Rock remixes include his take on House of Pain's 'Jump Around' and a brilliant reinterpretation of Jeru the Damaja's 'Can't Stop the Prophet'. PE showed they knew what time it was by working with him when he was still, to a degree, building his rep. This worked both ways. The new versions of 'Shut 'Em Down' and 'Nighttrain' helped endear PE to rap's new generation.

For the record, the original version of 'Shut 'Em Down' is crazy fly too, and was also a massive hit down South. It was indirectly inspired by Kool DJ Red Alert. One day, Chuck found himself talking to Red Alert's biggest fan. The kid couldn't stop bigging up one of hip-hop's greatest representatives. 'He just kept saying it,' Chuck smiles. '"Red, man, he's just shutting 'em down. He's shutting 'em down. They're not checking out Magic, they're not checking anyone else." He just kept saying, "Red Alert's shutting 'em down", and it just stuck in my head.'

There were other surprises on the fourth album. On *Apocalypse '91* Flav dispensed with the party raps and got personal. To some extent, he had no choice. Following a physical confrontation, in truth a fist fight, with the mother of his children, the *New York Post* ran a story with the headline 'Rap Star Beats Lover' which sensationalised the harmful and disturbing domestic events.

'A Letter to the New York Post' allowed him to retort. While the song didn't attempt to excuse or gloss over Flav's repugnant behaviour, it did allow him to question the *Post*'s motives and the way that they only focused on the negative aspects of hip-hop. It was during the early nineties that it became more and more apparent to PE fans that Flav had some pretty serious issues, particularly with drugs. Nevertheless, despite the emotive nature of the accusations, it is important to make the distinction between a two-way fist fight and straight-up domestic abuse, where one person is relentlessly beaten over time. No one is trying to defend domestic violence. In this case, both parties were acting as crazy as the proverbial bag of angel dust. Again, this doesn't for one second excuse what went on. It just provides a fuller picture of events, something that the vast majority of tabloid newspapers are seemingly incapable of.

'"A Letter to the New York Post" was written 'cos at that time the *New York Post* was definitely a real fucking bullshit newspaper. They put my address in the newspaper. They're not supposed to put my address in the newspaper!!' says a still-exasperated Flav. He fully admits his part in proceedings. 'I had a little confrontation with my children's mother so they put it on the front page. "Rap Star Beats Lover". Wooooww. Rap star beats lover. Wow boy, that's a crazy-ass title right there, man. Chuck gave me the idea to write about the *New York Post*. I said, "Aiight".'

The *New York Post* weren't the only ones to get berated by Flav. *Jet* magazine was also criticised for taking their info 'straight out the *Post*'. In some way the fact that a black publication was distorting the events made things worse. *Jet* reaches the 'barber shops and beauty salons' that are the unofficial grapevine of the black community. Even worse, Flav was in the belly of the beast when the article dropped.

'I was in jail for that shit,' he says of the incident. 'I was in there and that shit hit the next day, headline news. I'm sitting in jail reading about myself, about what happened yesterday.'

The bluesy 'I Don't Wanna be Called Yo Niga' discussed the suitability of black people using the 'n-word' with each other, even as a term of endearment. A Tribe Called Quest's 'Sucka Nigga' would have the same conversation a couple of years later. It has to be said that the following Q-Tip couplet does apply to Flav (as well as countless other black people). Tip's bridge into the chorus is as follows: 'I start to flinch as I try not to say it, but my lips is like a oowop as I start to spray it.'

But despite everything that was happening in front of and behind the music, PE were still finding ways to fight the good fight. In the early eighties Stevie Wonder was at the forefront of a successful campaign for a national holiday to celebrate the birthday of Dr Martin Luther King Jr. King Day has since become an institution in the States, and takes place on the third Monday in January.

Unfortunately, the more overtly racist political climate of the time – political correctness was just around the corner – and the political division of America allowed two states – New Hampshire and Arizona – to refuse to observe the national holiday. In 1990 Arizona voters upheld Governor Evan Mecham's late-eighties decision to abolish the King holiday. The highly powerful 'By the Time I Get to Arizona' (originally the lyrics were written to the beat that later became the album version of 'Shut 'Em Down') took issue with this in PE's usual forceful way.

PE's videos had always provided a valuable visual element to their songs and effectively accentuated the point of Chuck's lyrics. The videos for 'Black Steel in the Hour of Chaos', 'Fight the Power' and 'Can't Truss It' accurately bring to life the vibe within prison, the emotion and anger of a political rally and the horrors of the plantation respectively. If it is possible, the video for 'By the Time I Get to Arizona' (directed by Eric Meza) was just that little bit more in-your-face. It begins with a state governor – a thinly veiled version of Governor Mecham – telling a roomful of journalists why he isn't a racist KKK supporter just because he refused to endorse the King holiday.

From there the video flits between a re-enactment of the

shooting of Dr King and an imagined scenario where the S1Ws, armed to the teeth with M16s, pursue the Arizona governor until they dispose of him at the video's end. Both black and white conservatives hated it, and used their indignation for their own publicity. A video showing black radicals gunning down a white politician? It was bound to be a problem. The video (that was shot in California) also featured Ice-T and Sister Souljah (who introduced the song). They would both soon find themselves facing some very public trials and tribulations of their own. The controversy that raged over Ice-T's 'Cop Killer' is well documented. The shrill protests from the likes of Tipper Gore and Dan Quayle almost finished his career. Ironically, he now plays a policeman on *Law & Order*. Sister Souljah's back and forth with Bill Clinton is only marginally less documented. In a 1992 interview she was quoted in the *Washington Post* as saying, 'If black people kill black people every day, why not have a week and kill white people?' The remark was part of a much longer response to the LA riots. Clinton likened her to David Duke, the famous KKK member.

'We did the Arizona video knowing that it was probably going to be played only one time,' Chuck admits. 'It really tested the waters. But the minute they all tried to ask me some questions I was already in Hamburg, Germany.' Was he letting the situation defuse slightly so it could be addressed in a sober, less sensationalised fashion? Or was he just avoiding some hard questions at a time when they would be most difficult? Chuck makes the point that the fact that Arizona didn't have a King holiday was far worse than anything that happens in the video. 'I took it upon myself to be Steven Spielberg and come up with my own apocalyptic ending of taking out politicians and it was supposed to be that they were crooked politicians. But you know, at that particular time any of that coming out of the area of rap was bound to attract a hysterical response.' Hip-hop was, by now, very used to its bad reputation in the mainstream media. 'It was like, "The nerve of this guy talking about this! He's not totally wrong, but he's not totally right."' Once again, PE found themselves treading on very thin ice. And Chuck was right. The Arizona video was even banned on *Yo! MTV Raps*. After the Griff situation, the Arizona affair was probably PE's second most controversial episode.

When PE joined U2 on the groundbreaking Zoo TV tour it allowed them to take the fight right to the source. Instead of their usual blistering set PE played just two songs in Arizona. 'By the Time I Get to Arizona' transformed what should have been a routine tour stop into yet another memorable PE moment. The stage was swamped as Chuck, Flav, X and the S1Ws were joined onstage by a coterie of Native American brothers to show solidarity with the only other race of people who got a worse deal in America than blacks. While U2 and Bono were yet to become synonymous with protest across the globe, they supported PE to the hilt. It wasn't as if they were taken by surprise.

'U2 was in full unison with Public Enemy,' James Bomb confirms. 'Chuck and Bono had talked about what was going to take place. They protested with us, and then they went on with their show. Martin Luther King is a symbol not only to black people but to people all over the world.'

PE weren't the only ones vehemently to disagree with Arizona's stance on the King holiday. Before and after the Zoo TV stop a wave of protests prompted a lot of embarrassing media coverage for the state. The Super Bowl, which was meant to take place in Tempe, Arizona, was moved to California. There was also the small matter of the loss of business that the state of Arizona had to deal with. By November it had lost $300 million, principally in lost tourist revenue. But there's no denying the part played by 'By the Time I Get to Arizona'. On November 22, 1992, only a few weeks after the concert, Arizona reinstated the King holiday.

While PE's tours with The Sisters of Mercy and especially Anthrax allowed them to spread their wings, when they supported U2 on their Zoo TV outing they experienced a truly high-profile live experience for the first time. Flavor remembers it fondly.

'That was great, that was fun, I had a lot of fun touring with U2 and Bono and them. That's where I first saw enormous-size crowds every night. We performed in front of 33,000, and better, heads every night. Man, the stadium was so filled up when we went on. And we went on right before them.' For just over two weeks, PE presented an ultra-tight half-hour set. And thirty minutes meant thirty minutes exactly. PE learned a thing or two on tour with the world's biggest rock band.

'It was tight. When your time is up you gotta be out of the way,' chuckles Chief of Security Malik Farrakhan. ''Cos there's a speaker moving, there're drums moving. Metal moving. You learn from it.' But while the tour was timed by the second, away from the stage the atmosphere was generous and convivial. 'Bono gave my kid a first class seat on the plane when he was seven years old,' remembers a still-appreciative Malik. The tour would open PE up to completely new audiences. 'That's another reason why we were able to gain a large white following,' Flav states. 'A lot of the people who came to their concerts were seeing us for the first time, and ended up feeling us too.'

The outing confirmed once and for all that PE were extremely content to follow the path less travelled. Unfortunately, many of the same critics – the hip-hoppers who wish hip-hop had never left the hood – took the tour with Bono and co. as the final confirmation that PE had lost their way for ever.

It was around this time that PE's stock declined significantly in the more narrow-minded hip-hop circles. Some within the black and hip-hop communities viewed these tours as tantamount to selling out, or at the very least being 'soft'. Although the stakes were nowhere near as high, parallels can be found with PE's heroes, the Black Panthers. When Huey

Newton, Bobby Seale and the rest of the Black Panther Party for Self-Defense began to forge links with the hippie-esque, flower-power-loving, tree-hugging anti-Vietnam protestors – many of whom were obviously white – other black liberation groups used this as evidence that they were sell-outs and were no longer real.

However, as an enlightened person, Huey rightly decided that anyone struggling for peace and awareness was a friend of the Panthers. He hit back at his critics by saying they were only interested in keeping up appearances. What was the point of parading around in traditional African dress when their brothers and sisters were regularly (and brutally) beaten up by the police? Police brutality was the reason the Panthers formed in the first place. Huey opined further that these 'armchair revolutionaries' were scared to take their fight to the true institutions of power. They damn sure weren't about to start observing the police doing their duties. History has proven that the powers that be were far more scared of the Panthers and their ten-point programme than they were flowing African robes, beautiful though they are.

Similarly, rappers who would quite happily kill a million of their brothers on wax, but never dream of speaking truth to power in the way PE regularly did, were not really in a position to criticise. Were PE victims of their own forward-thinking nature? It seems that no one is above the 'particular particulars' that exist in the black community.

PE never really let these attitudes stop them from doing the right thing. 'Chuck became a lot more aware of a bigger audience,' Harry Allen states. 'There's an issue here of how groups outgrow their audience, especially the first one that got into them. What is the life cycle of a group?'

The *Tour of a Black Planet* video that was released soon after *Apocalypse '91* featured PE playing to hip-hoppers from literally all over the world. Did the naysayers miss this video? Or did they just want PE to remain in their nice cosy little hip-hop box? It's probably a bit of both. As well as featuring priceless tour footage, the ninety-minute-long look at life behind the scenes also boasts a plethora of interviews with the PE camp, music videos and various clips and excerpts from TV appearances and radio interviews.

It also gave Flav a chance once again to show off his unique brand of humour. During one segment he playfully asks Harry Allen, who filmed some of the video, 'why [his] lips cover the whole screen'. Harry takes the joke in the spirit it was intended: 'I love that guy. I mean, he's one of the warmest, most genuine people I've ever met in my life . . . and he is extremely talented and very funny, and I love my big full African lips, I love 'em and I'm proud of 'em. Even if he's picking on you, you sometimes have to just laugh along 'cos the stuff he says is so outrageous.'

Harry Allen brilliantly complemented Flav on the introduction and chorus to 'More News at 11'. His little speech which ends the record reminds those who failed to catch on that this was the same dude from 'Don't Believe the Hype'. 'I was kind of thrilled to be back on another PE record. I don't remember the session much, but I was a little happy to be invited back to do something in that style, in that newscaster style. I pop up every now and then.'

The other hilarious moment on *Tour of A Black Planet* is Terminator X's joke interview with T-Money. In the short, and very funny, segment, T-Money doesn't receive an answer to any of his questions. Every time he offers the microphone to the tall stocky DJ in order for him to respond, X simply stands motionless, clearly sending up the persona that had been created for him. By the time the fake interview is nearing its conclusion, both parties can hardly contain their laughter.

Terminator X's debut album *Terminator X and the Valley of the Jeep Beats* was released in 1991. While the album contained hits like the Juvenile Delinquintz' self-titled ode to why they hated school (the food is inferior to a canine diet, and they weren't patriotic so they didn't like having to pledge allegiance) and 'Homey Don't Play Dat' by Bonnie 'n' Clyde, the big hit from this album was the powerful 'Buck Whylin''.

'Buck Whylin'' is memorable chiefly because of Sister Souljah and her spine-tingling cry of 'We are at war'. Her voice is startling and impossible to ignore. It's not likely ever to be forgotten by anyone who has heard it, particularly those who have heard it at high volume. The video is equally memorable. After Sister Souljah introduces the song Chuck and Harry Allen make their way to a jeep taking them to a press conference so they can let the people know what time it is.

A famous and enduring image of hip-hop's jiggy era was undoubtedly Biggie and Puff steering the speedboat in the Florida Keys during the 'Hypnotize' video. Were they influenced by the 'Buck Whylin'' promo? It doesn't seem likely. But the similarities are there for all to see. The video shows Harry and Chuck riding atop a jeep engaging in some revolutionary flossing en route to the press conference. The comparison is insightful for a couple of reasons. Firstly, rather than a glass of champagne, Harry is holding a copy of Neely Fuller Jr.'s important tome *United Independent Compensatory Code/System/Concept*.

'It's a book on racism/white supremacy, very influential on my thinking and a very profound analysis,' Harry explains. In the video Harry reads the book during the press conference, while nodding his head to the wicked beat. 'We were trying to send a certain visual message, a certain kind of idea.' Also, the differences in comfort between a speedboat and a jeep, not to mention the lack of scantily clad ladies, speak volumes about the different priorities of the two eras of hip-hop.

One of the most memorable moments of *Apocalypse '91* arrives at the end of 'Lost At Birth', which is perhaps the best introduction of any PE album. The sample that runs throughout the track is hypnotic and provocative; lines like 'So many people is sleepin' while standing up' set the album off righteously. But right at the end of the song comes the noise which most hip-hop fans will easily recognise but few will be able to describe adequately. It goes a little something like: 'oh, oh, oh oh-aaah.'

The noise is so striking that it has been sampled fairly regularly in the years since. Looking back, Yvette Michelle's hit 'I'm Not Feeling You' is probably one of the least likely places a PE fan might expect it to crop up. But it kicks the tune off very nicely. DJs have always loved to scratch it to pieces.

Apocalypse '91 was the first PE album that wasn't produced by The Bomb Squad. They are only credited as 'executive producers'. Most PE fans wondered who the Imperial Grand Ministers of Funk were. Even if they could forgive the overly grandiose title, hip-hop fans had never heard of Stuart Robertz, Cerwin (C-Dawg) Depper and 'The JBL'. They were not that familiar with Gary G-Wiz either, but at least his name had appeared on other PE albums.

'Its all bullshit,' Gary insists. 'Looking back now I'd say it was a definite smokescreen. I would've been solely credited with producing that album, it would've been strange for people and people would've said, "Well, who the hell is this guy?" It worked for Hank's benefit to have several names show up there. Mine is the only real name on there.' As with Eric's account of the work on Ice Cube's *AmeriKKKa's Most Wanted*, simple facts back up Gary's version of events. He quite correctly states, 'You'll never see those guys produce anything else.' He's right. Those names have never been seen or heard from again, on PE records or anyone else's records for that matter. But there's even better proof.

'If you look at the publishing you'll see that they're not there 'cos they don't exist. The only people who are credited with any writing are myself, Chuck and Hank and Keith.' He acknowledges that Keith worked on 'Nighttrain' and '1 Million Bottlebags', but says this was mainly post-production, adding little elements here and there. It seems that he's been waiting years to tell the world: 'I did all the tracks on *Apocalypse* aside from "Get the Fuck Outta Dodge". I don't even know who did that track, and of course the Anthrax track.'

G-Wiz experienced similar frustrations with the *Juice* soundtrack. Of all the 'hip-hop films' of the early nineties, *Juice* is probably the one that engages with hip-hop culture the most. *New Jack City* was primarily concerned with Nino Brown and the drug trade. *Boyz n the Hood* was clearly about gang warfare in LA. Both these films are classics. But the hip-hop element took a back seat. Not so with *Juice*. Hip-hop was more intertwined with the main plot in the film that announced Tupac's arrival.

G-Wiz and Eric Sadler are far from bitter. They are very friendly, cool guys who have simply been waiting years and years to set the record straight. Gary makes a point of saying he doesn't want to be negative all the time. However, 'It's tough, man, because every time we did a project you're gonna find out something that's fucked up. I look back now and people don't know what the hell I did. If people knew what I did they'd probably be like, "Damn!"' What's a producer to do?

When dealing with this matter, it's perhaps best just to let Gary say his piece. 'Hank showed up one day with a three quarter machine and a BS tape and said, "Hey, we're scoring a movie."' says Gary. 'He dropped that stuff off and left. Hank would probably dispute this if he could, but I basically sat in the room and scored that entire movie and then when we went in to mix it Hank and Keith were there and were adding a little bit of salt and pepper here and there but we were fronting to the producers like we all did it because of the kind of programme I was on back then. I was new to the situation. I knew these guys had already broke it big and I was trying to play my part . . . and if my part was stepping up and making all the tracks and everything and then playing it back like it was a Bomb Squad thing then that's what I was doing.'

Gary felt the injustice after watching the film for the first time. 'When I sat in the theatre and saw the credit roll for the first time and it said scored by Hank Shocklee and The Bomb Squad?' It wasn't a good look for him. 'When you're sat in the room for, you know, months scoring a flick, fronting like the crew did it and see that you don't even see your name on the motherfucker? When shit like that happens? That's where a lot of people got beef with Hank 'cos you know you don't do that kind of thing to people. Especially if you're not the creative touch, if you're not the one putting stuff together.'

Now Gary isn't trying to front like, 'Hank had nothing to do with creativity.' But he's keen to be clear that 'Hank's role as far as creativity was, "Oh, move that vocal over here." Or he'd come in and it'd be an arrangement thing. He was big on pep talks, big on coming in before a project and telling me how he sees it. He was like a visionary in that realm. But when it came to putting together beats and stuff Hank just didn't do that.'

In contrast, Keith Shocklee claims, 'I did a good seventy-five per cent of the score myself.' This could be seen as another episode in the murky saga of PE production accreditation, and illustrative of the disputes that simmer throughout the music business. But when confronted with Keith's claim, Gary felt strongly enough to forward some of the publishing information for scenes like 'Bishop Behind Locker', 'Bishop in Shadow' and 'Boyz Run After Robbery'. The way things are broken down regarding songwriting and composing definitely supports Gary's version of events.

As well as scoring the film, The Bomb Squad were also responsible for putting the soundtrack together. According to Keith, 'We did stuff that made sense. EPMD had to do a record cos they were in the movie. Naughty by Nature did a joint because Treach also appeared on screen.' The best song on the soundtrack was undoubtedly Eric B and Rakim's 'Know the Ledge', which by all accounts was remixed by Hank and Gary. There are a couple of other Bomb Squad-produced joints on the set. The most popular at the time was probably Big Daddy Kane's 'Nuff Respect'.

However, knowing that something made sense did not mean that it was always going to happen. Cindy from En Vogue appears in *Juice* and so they requested a song from her. But Sylvia Rhone said no. 'She was like, "Nah",' Keith recalls. '"But she's in the movie!" "Nah. I'm not letting you have it."' Kam'ron from the Young Black Teenagers, who is a dope DJ as well as a rapper, did all the cut scenes at the famous DJ battle that is hosted by Queen Latifah. 'My man Kam still works with me now,' says Keith proudly. 'I know how to pick my talent.' Kam'ron also did a lot of the scratching on *Apocalypse '91*. Regardless of who did the score, Keith is right when he says that it 'was one of the reasons why *Juice* was such an underground cult flick. Everything was true to the streets.'

26

Greatest Misses

The *Greatest Misses* album which appeared in the autumn of 1992 saw Public Enemy at a crossroads. Even though they successfully turned the concept of a Greatest Hits album on its head – instead of just featuring a selection of some of their most memorable songs, PE placed remixes of six of their most renowned compositions (these included 'Who Stole the Soul?' and 'Louder Than a Bomb') next to six new songs – the end result was still underwhelming. Innovation is not always rewarded. All of the remixes seemed to confuse those who just wanted a new PE album.

Greatest Misses was the first PE album that wasn't completely essential. Unlike its predecessors, it wasn't an all-conquering event. For the first time, their vision and purpose was not immediately obvious. Many PE fans were placated with the brilliance of 'Hazy Shade of Criminal', which proved PE's ability continually to create the most imposing collages of sound. In this case the noise that sits on top of the beat lies somewhere in between the screech of a car brake and the sound made when someone runs their fingernails down a blackboard. Most important of all, it is a sound that, as usual, sticks in your head and refuses to leave. But despite the greatness of 'Hazy Shade of Criminal', some heads complained that they didn't want to hear Chuck flipping the tongue-twisting style made famous in England by the Demon Boyz and in the US by Das EFX.

The fans were used to Chuck setting trends, not following them. Ice Cube would face similar accusations when he flipped the same style on a few of the songs, most notably 'Check Yo Self', from his third album *The Predator*. This is despite the fact that the rest of the album is perhaps the best appraisal of the causes and consequences of the LA riots put to record.

Greatest Misses was PE's chance to put out the EP that *Apocalypse '91* was meant to be, before it grew into a full-length work. *Apocalypse '91* had been an extremely successful album, but they still wanted to drop a record in '92. Since the record company was hounding them to release a Greatest Hits set Chuck came up with the idea of having six remixes. It was a continuation of what Pete Rock had done so successfully with 'Shut 'Em Down' and 'Nighttrain'. However, where the Pete Rock remixes were praised by fans and critics alike, those on Greatest Misses were not bestowed with similar accolades. Was this because the songs that were remixed were old classics rather than new favourites? Or did people feel like these remixes were not on a par with Pete Rock's efforts?

'The attitude seemed to be, "How can somebody else come in and do a Public Enemy record?" This is how it was in the States,' says Chuck. 'A lot of people criticised the remixes terribly and they just tore them to pieces and I think they tore them to pieces because they didn't think remixing us was necessary and possible but it's like, "Why not?"'

The negative reception wasn't too much of a surprise to them. PE were always prepared for such eventualities. 'We always knew there was an up and a down. You're never always gonna be up.' This doesn't mean they were just going to give up quietly though. 'One thing we also knew,' Chuck continues, 'is that you can be up, go down and go up again. You gotta accept the down. We knew that after hitting the ball out of the park like da-da-da-da, we knew that we were gonna hit a down period and we were just ready for it. Very ready for it. Whether it was gonna come in the United States or whether it was gonna come in England.'

PE's 'down' period in the US and England coincided with their massive growth in stature in places like South America, Asia and Africa. In '92 and '93 the PE crew took their live show to all these places. It allowed them perspective on their sudden dip in popularity among some fans (although PE diehards dug their heels in even harder when the group began to face criticism).

'Africa changed my life around to saying, "I don't care what the world feels,"' says Chuck. 'We planted some seeds in Ghana and Brazil and parts of Asia and that became the mission in '92 and '93. Africa was a turning point in my life [in terms of] realising what we should be about and what we should be paying attention to.'

Furthermore, PE deserve props for taking risks at the height of their fame. Chuck argues, 'You can let the hype ride you out, but we're the ones that said "Don't Believe the Hype", so we're gonna keep taking shots.' How many established groups are prepared to do that? Not many. The vast majority of groups out there, irrespective of genre, would rather let their hype live for them instead of taking a chance of any kind.

Away from all this there were the usual complaints behind the scenes. 'I would make a track, Chuck would rhyme on it, we'd walk away and then people would come in and add to it,' Gary says. 'We'd end up going back in the spot and not even really recognising the record, like, "What the hell is this?"'

During this time, the large amounts of remixes that Hank was hooking up meant that Gary was regularly running out of beats, and frequently running from studio to studio. The situation was made worse by the fact that in the period immediately following *Apocalypse '91*, Gary unexpectedly had to contribute to the albums by SOUL records' acts Young Black Teenagers and Son of Bazerk. This hadn't been part of the plan. Eric Sadler was meant to produce those albums but his relationship with the other members of The Bomb Squad had been on the ropes for some time by then, and eventually he left.

Gary had been looking forward to working with Eric and was unhappy about with this turn of events. 'Eric and Hank just couldn't see eye to eye and it just ended up not happening. I was cool with Eric, I'd come hang out, but I never really got to get with Eric on that level which was probably a mistake.

But I would call and hang out with him and get some perspective 'cos he knew what was up. I ended up having to make the tracks for both of those albums when I was completely out of tracks from *Apocalypse* and all the other stuff we were doing.' He was just coming up with beat after beat after beat. 'It's one thing when you can sit down and make a hundred tracks and somebody will pick ten. It's another thing when you're having to make tracks on demand for people who are paying money. That's pretty much the situation I ended up in.'

Just before the PE album *Muse Sick-n-Hour Mess Age* went into production this prolific spree came to an abrupt end. One day Hank told Gary that he had to sign a new agreement or the two of them would never work together again. The elder Shocklee brother did compliment G-Wiz on being well-rounded and very capable of handling a huge workload. But he insisted they would never again work on another project if this new agreement wasn't signed. Needless to say, this presented a dilemma.

'I thought about it and the deal was wack. Like I said I was already doing one hundred per cent of the music and giving him fifty. He wanted to come back and get another half out of me. I didn't want to get twenty-five per cent of a song I wrote a hundred per cent of, so I was like, "You know what? I'm not doing it." And that was it. We never worked together again. Hank came to me a couple more times to get the situation back together but nothing ever came of it.'

27

Muse Sick-n-Hour Mess Age

While the criticism meted out to *Greatest Misses* was probably deserved, the critical mauling received by *Muse Sick-n-Hour Mess Age* when it was released in 1994 was as unjustified as it was extensive.

Greatest Misses was viewed by many as a temporary misstep by a great group who would regain their way and return to producing the quality work that had made them great in the first place. *Muse Sick*, however, was largely portrayed as the nail in Public Enemy's coffin, proof that they were past it. Fourteen years later, the album's quality makes this point of view seem even more astounding than it did at the time. In many ways the reception received by *Greatest Misses* made the reaction to *Muse Sick* inevitable. 'Give It Up', the first single from this, PE's fifth full-length work, demonstrated the new position that they occupied within the world of music. Even though it was an international chart hit, it was largely ignored by some hip-hoppers – especially the new jacks.

Is this because the music was changing and it is the nature of hip-hop, and black culture in general, to pay attention to whatever's new and dispense with what is perceived as old? It is certainly the norm, rather than the exception, for the perceived hottest artists in hip-hop to be among the newest. Sure, there are the select few elder statesmen. But their every move is relentlessly scrutinised by those who can't wait to find some sort of chink in their armour.

Contrary to popular opinion it wasn't relentlessly panned across the board. In England, there were favourable reviews in *Echoes*, *NME* and *Melody Maker*. In the States *Spin* magazine reviewed the album favourably. It was two terrible reviews in two crucial, popular publications that did the damage. At the time most hip-hop heads looked to *The Source*. But *The Source* and all the other hip-hop magazines that were steadily growing in stature were far more enamoured with the likes of Snoop, Biggie, Wu-Tang and Nas than they were PE. It's fair to assume that a sizeable majority of non-hip-hop heads who were PE fans would look to *Rolling Stone*, perhaps the world's most famous music magazine. Both these magazines gave *Muse Sick-n-Hour Mess Age* a very definite thumbs-down. More than anything, the perception that PE were past-it gradually began to be accepted as fact. Importantly, for a group like PE, none of the above factors stopped them from playing to packed houses across the globe. PE's recently acquired following among the rock fraternity, plus of course the continued support of those hip-hoppers who weren't so easily swayed by the music press, ensured that their fanbase remained exceptionally healthy.

While it's true that a lot of people were gunning for PE around this time, there was some significant record company pressure and upheaval that seems to have contributed to the album's poor reception. At the time Def Jam was being sold by Sony to Polygram. Russell and Lyor were something like $25 million in the hole and they wanted Polygram to resolve this and also give them some cash for a fresh beginning.

While all this was going down Russell passed by the studio to listen to PE's forthcoming fifth album. But Chuck was holding out.

'When he came up to the studio and said, "Well, what have you got?" I was saying, "What is this doing for me?" 'Cos I heard the only thing holding up the deal was like, "What do Public Enemy have?"' Soon after this, Chuck accompanied Russell and Lyor to a big board-meeting at Polygram's manufacturing plant in Indianapolis. A lot of important Polygram representatives were in attendance. But Chuck still wouldn't let Russell or Lyor hear the album until he had a guarantee on what the sale would mean for PE. He wanted a few things. He wanted the label deal he'd had to forsake with SOUL a few years earlier and he also wanted Polygram to do something about all of the different lawsuits, 'the James Brown stuff', the samples from their earlier albums.

On the advice of his lawyer Chuck ended up agreeing to play his part in the Polygram sale. 'He said it would be a good deal to go into the Polygram system and it ended up being the worst move ever.' Russell Simmons was so happy when Chuck turned in the masters for *Muse Sick* that he sent him a big bunch of flowers.

One of the main problems with all of this was the fact the 'Give It Up' twelve-inch was released through Sony, the marketing plan for the record was devised at Sony and the promos were sent out to radio stations by Sony while the album was still in limbo, caught between record companies. Then the video company who were working on the 'Give It Up' video called to complain that they hadn't been paid. Nobody was taking care of business. PE fans were wondering where the hell this new album was.

It was supposed to drop in the spring of 1994. But it was only after delivering the record that Chuck found out that it was going to be released through Polygram. The single wasn't officially released until June and the album followed soon after: 'At that particular time our stuff was all over the place and we never had a proper footing,' says Chuck.

While Chuck didn't predict all the record company politrix, he did predict, on a hidden track, the bad reception *Muse Sick* would receive. If you press rewind on track one before the album kicks off you will find a short jam called 'Ferocious Soul' which foresees the backlash PE experienced with astonishing accuracy.

'This gonna be some old different shit,' Chuck promises at the beginning of the song, which is no longer than ninety seconds. 'Motherfuckers are gonna be mad but so the fuck what.'

'This is how you would do it before it was outlawed,' Chuck recalls. 'The whole thing with "Ferocious Soul" was, "We're making a record for the future, we're not making a record for now." In the liner notes we're saying, "We're making a record for 1999 not '94." But the critics at that time were not gonna pay attention to that and I knew exactly what they were gonna do.'

Were PE covering their backs with this pre-emptive strike? This is possible, but, even if this was the case, Chuck was still on point with his predictions. After criticising MTV, Chuck goes on to anticipate:

> We'll probably only get about two mics in *The Source*
>   and shit but who gives a fuck?
> Motherfuckers are gonna be mad.
> I ain't with the forties and blunts shit.
> I ain't with calling my brothers and sisters niggers or
>   bitches.

The last point is especially pertinent since hip-hop had taken a very gangsterish turn by the time *Muse Sick* dropped. Of course, life on the gully side has always been a feature of hip-hop. It's been a feature of black music since the blues. If Elvis et al. had never come along and done what they did then perhaps the truths that hip-hop exposes wouldn't be so shocking. The world (and the media) would have become used to it. Hip-hop music and culture hails from the poorest neighbourhoods in America so this isn't too much of a revelation if you know what time it is. Ice-T, Schoolly D and Boogie Down Productions (remember their debut album was called *Criminal Minded*) were just a few acts who could inform a listener about life on the wrong side of the tracks. But things were different in the early nineties, mainly due to the success of Dre's *The Chronic* and Snoop's *Doggystyle*.

These records were so popular that most hip-hop fans 'weren't trying to hear all that black shit any more', according to Keith. 'When the gangsta music came in everybody was like, "Yo, we tryna get paid."' Keith makes the point that having self awareness is one of the ways you can accumulate wealth. Perhaps more important than this, after the situation with 'By the Time I Get to Arizona', it became obvious that '"people are actually listening to this group. Okay, we need to do something to stop them from listening to this group. So to undermine it let's promote negativity and let these black kids just think about getting money."' Keith says from the perspective of the powers that be. 'Now the lyrics are about, "Yo son, I've murdered everybody on the block. I got my Uzi and my tech and I walk the streets." Why? Why you gotta have a Uzi to walk the streets with your own people?'

There is an argument, not without foundation, that even if there wasn't a conspiracy the music industry and the powers that be chose to promote gangsta rhymes over anything politically conscious. Let's face it, it was just easier than having to deal with all this black righteousness stuff. Society's top tier is scared of gangsters, but they're a lot more wary of organised black men who want to change the status quo and are taking steps to do so. Conveniently, the vast majority of the more rowdy rappers are in less of a hurry to change the status quo in the music industry. Who cares if their music has a negative social impact as long as it has a positive effect on the bottom line, right?

Gangsta rap happened to become popular at a critical time in hip-hop's history. In the eighteen months before 'Nuthin' but a "G" Thang', the first single from *The Chronic*, blew up, both PE's *Apocalypse '91* and NWA's *Efil4Zaggin* were massive hits and big sellers. But '"G" Thang' was the first hip-hop record to reap the rewards of full rotation on MTV (and not just during *Yo! MTV Raps*), the development of BET, twenty-four-hour hip-hop radio, and *The Source* magazine.

This was in a climate in which MC Hammer and Vanilla Ice had taken the charts by storm only a couple of years earlier. For that type of real rap to get that type of massive exposure was unheard of, and record companies woke up fast. All of this happened after PE's first commercial strike. So, the money men decided to play it safe with records and artists that, to varying degrees, echoed the new West Coast gangsta success.

A few years later when Biggie and especially Tupac blew up, a new lucrative cycle began. This isn't to say that conscious hip-hop was shown the door. Nas, Wu-Tang Clan and A Tribe Called Quest were all massive forces in early to mid nineties hip-hop. Groups like The Pharcyde, Freestyle Fellowship, Souls of Mischief and Tha Alkaholiks proved that gangbanging wasn't the only hobby on the West Coast, even if it was probably the most popular. Outkast and the Goodie Mob opened up the phat beats generation to the Dirty South. So there was some balance. But the massive success of the Death Row camp – spurred by Snoop's strikingly laid-back style and Dre's peerless production – rendered many of the aforementioned acts second-best when it came to commercial viability. They were just too good.

There is one more crucial factor in the decline of PE's popularity – the outstanding issues with their personnel. 'I truly believe that if we [had] all stayed together working as a team, a lot of the sentiment from the West Coast that took over hip-hop would not have happened as strongly,' insists Bill Stephney. 'But since the strongest group doing the pro-political, pro-social stuff breaks up, if essentially the whole team behind it breaks up and diffuses, why can't the West Coast come up and start to go with the gangsta message, the shooting this and that, the killing of black people? Anyone can present their own reality but at the end of the day there's a destination from that reality.' Portraying very real, but equally very messed-up things is not always responsible, Bill is saying. It depends on the individual.

In a way all of the above factors should not count for anything because *Muse Sick* should be praised. It is vintage PE. Once a person is chilling listening to the album, all that matters is whether that individual appreciates what they are hearing.

'Bedlam' is just as powerful as 'Don't Believe the Hype', 'Brothers Gonna Work It Out' or the album version of 'Shut

'Em Down'. This energetic banger is given atmosphere by the eerie sample that runs underneath the track. The more laid-back 'What Kind of Power We Got?' is equally brilliant. The mid-tempo Flavor Flav solo track has one of the best call-and-response choruses in PE's history. PE did that hardest of things in 1994. They updated their sound without compromising the overall feel of their music. 'So Whatcha Gon' Do Now' is a fine example of mid nineties East Coast hip-hop. There's the lovely bassline, a horn sample and a wicked mid tempo beat. Chuck's criticisms of the new breed of rappers 'talking that gangsta talk' shows where he stood in regard to the emcees who, often at the behest of their record companies, were very content to wallow in the worst, most negative aspects of ghetto life. Behind this big tune is another story of the strife that continued to plague the group privately. Originally, Chuck and Gary G-Wiz had hoped that 'So Whatcha Gon' Do Now' was going to be *Muse Sick*'s second single. But that wasn't to be. There was even uncertainty over whether the Gary-produced 'Give It Up' was going to be the first cut from the album.

'You can imagine how much resistance there was for "Give It Up" to be the first single. Hank had also worked on that project and brought in people to work with him, and it was a concession that Chuck made [that] if Hank let us put "Give It Up" out we'd let him pick the second single. Hank didn't want "Give It Up" to be the first single probably 'cos of my involvement.'

So, after 'Give It Up' dropped, the very funky 'What Kind of Power We Got?' became the second single. Now Flav's joint is, of course, hot to death. But it's arguable that in '94 'So Whatcha Gon' Do Now' was a better fit.

Despite all the ructions behind the scenes, *Muse Sick-n-Hour Mess Age* saw Chuck continue to put forward the (often forgotten or ignored) black point of view on subjects and events, that, at first glance, may appear relatively innocuous. 'Hitler Day' attacked the insensitivity and offensive nature of

American public holidays such as Columbus Day and Thanksgiving. Chuck argued that for black and Native American people these holidays represented the beginning of genocide and suffering on a scale yet to be repeated. Looked at from that perspective, marking these public holidays and celebrating these days truly is 'as crazy as Hitler Day'.

Muse Sick also represented PE looking to the future. Towards the end of the album 'Harry Allen's Interactive Super Highway Phone Call to Chuck D' showed that PE were already thinking about the internet and the changes that would occur in the music business and beyond. During the voicemail that Harry leaves for Chuck he mentions how technology is transforming and how the ways that people get and use information is also changing. Overall, he's welcoming Chuck to the digital age. Harry is as happy about this phone call as is he is about the shout-out on 'Don't Believe the Hype'.

'I really appreciated Chuck using my phone call to him and I appreciated even more that he was an honorable enough man to make sure I got my publishing.' This kind of thing speaks volumes about Chuck, especially as, at the time at least, Harry wasn't completely familiar with publishing matters and was not really expecting payment.

'I would only have learned much, much later and started to put it together in pieces,' he realises. 'I wrote it, that's writing isn't it? But he was honourable enough to say, "I put the music together, here's yours and here's mine." I'm thankful.' The phone call prompted the usual dumbfounded response. 'I remember at the time somebody wrote some letter that I sounded like I'd taken a bottle of stupid pills or something like that,' he recalls. 'They didn't know what I was talking about. This is really before the internet became a popular medium. This is before anyone had a common idea of what people were doing with this.'

Harry has long since been vindicated: 'I was talking about what has since occurred, all this stuff that we're seeing now about music being sold this way . . . that's what I was talking about. I was saying to Chuck, "We've got to be on this, we've got to be aware of these changes. I feel satisfied and glad that Chuck put that on the record because now if he hadn't it would've just been a call I made to him that has long ago been forgotten, it's on a record and it's dated and time-stamped.'

1994 also saw the release of the second Terminator X album, *Super Bad*, which was released under the moniker 'Terminator X and the Godfathers of Threatt'. It must be said that Terminator succeeded in reaching the ears of the new generation with the track 'Under the Sun' featuring Joe Sinistr. DJs loved to cut up the chorus which sounded particularly futuristic back in '94.

But this does not mean he neglected the old-school heads. First off, he worked with Larry Smith, the veteran producer who is so old school he uses his government name, rather than a rap moniker, on the album's other big track, 'It All Comes Down to the Money'. It introduced Whodini to a generation that knew classic tracks like 'Freaks Come Out at Night' and 'Friends', but had not actually got to experience Jalil, Ecstacy and Grandmaster Dee in their heyday. The video, which was shot in Atlanta, received heavy rotation on *Yo! MTV Raps*.

'Whodini were such a tremendous influence on us,' says Chuck. 'They were guys who helped train us in our performance chops and stuff like that. They had gone through a little thing in their career and we wanted to bring them back up and we brought them back up enough so that they could get another record deal.'

On the strength of 'It All Comes Down to the Money' Whodini signed a deal with Jermaine Dupri's So So Def, an imprint of Columbia Records. Back in the early eighties Dupri had been a dancer for the trio from Brooklyn. The album *Six* wasn't a huge success, but it isn't a wack album either. Chuck recalls, 'Terminator was very pleased that he could get Whodini and a lot of other classic groups.'

The most classic and greatest guest of all was the one and only Kool Herc. Herc made his presence felt on a few of the album's tracks. Chuck remembers it being a very emotional experience for the founding father of hip-hop. 'It was the first time he had ever been in a studio and he had a tear in his eye 'cos nobody ever brought him to the studio before. And I paid him.'

The album was released through Chuck's Pro Division, an arrangement he hooked up with Def Jam and Rush Associated Labels. After wondering aloud in front of the hierarchy at his record company if he should try and do boutique label business with Atlantic Records, Lyor Cohen put that opportunity in his pathway. Unfortunately, however, Chuck was once again just too busy to focus fully on the label and it fell by the wayside. Chuck would have to leave the major label system before his labels achieved lasting and recurrent success.

28

Chuck Goes it Alone

Following *Muse Sick-n-Hour Mess Age* Chuck decided to put Public Enemy on hiatus. If the group was to re-energise they needed a change and a rest period. Chuck dedicated more time to his regular appearances on news programmes (a crucial part of his quest to present the black viewpoint on the topics of the day) and his lectures at various universities and colleges. It's telling that KRS-One is the only other rapper regularly to perform lectures. The hard rhymer also returned to radio where he remains, time-permitting, to this day. Over the years, Chuck's radio activities have included shows such as *Unfiltered* and *On the Real*, a show broadcast on progressive talk radio network Air America.

However he didn't leave music far behind. 1996 saw the release of his first official solo album, *Autobiography of Mistachuck*. The years in between *Muse Sick* and *Autobiography* saw some heavy touring, particularly in Europe (where *Muse Sick* met with a better reception than in America).

But for the first time in his music career, Chuck grew bored with life on the road. Over the years PE's live show had constantly evolved. Their early years were spent making the transition from being a mobile DJ outfit to a proper live act. As the eighties became the nineties they honed these skills into one of the tightest live shows in hip-hop. Taking a cue from Doug E Fresh and Whodini they advised the younger cats in the game on how to do their thing onstage. In the early nineties their tours with rock groups allowed them to see how the other half toured, and this too had its effect on their live performance. Anthrax in particular had made Chuck determined that PE would maintain their high-energy levels throughout a whole show. But for the first time, Chuck felt things stagnating. He wasn't feeling it.

'I was clear, I told everybody, "I want some time off from touring," 'cos I couldn't see no growth in it and something had to change. I had to be away from Public Enemy for a second as far as the touring thing. It was just becoming the same thing and I was trying to figure out, what did I need to do with Public Enemy to be different?'

This period also marked the beginning of the end for Chuck and Def Jam. The main crux of the disagreement was that many of the things he had been promised as part of the Polygram move failed to materialise. The poor reception received by *Muse Sick* stateside is most likely to blame for this. 'I felt that Lyor and Russell had given in to what critics or whatever were saying about the record and not giving me what they had promised to give me.'

Chuck's response was to spread his wings within the Polygram system, to see what he could do. He wrote letters to various execs explaining that he wanted to release a solo record. More importantly, he wanted a label deal. This is how the first incarnation of Chuck's SLAMjamz Records came to life. This endeavour too was riddled with many largely unforeseeable problems.

After forging a deal on a handshake with Donny Ienner, Chuck went looking for his lawyer Ron Sweeney, who had advised him to do the Polygram deal. However, just when he was needed the most, Sweeney was nowhere to be found. At the time, Sweeney was busy with the hip-hop master Eazy-E, who at the time was on his deathbed. In the seven or eight months that passed, Chuck could have quite easily got himself another lawyer, but he was trying to be loyal.

'Everybody found out at the last minute that Ron Sweeney also represented him,' Chuck recalls. 'Ron said, "I had to get busy with somebody, you know, for seven or eight months," that's why my deal didn't get closed during that time. Donny was looking at me all the time like, "What the fuck is up?"' After those frustrations and hold-ups the deal was finally closed.

Danny Goldberg at Mercury was another person who answered one of Chuck's letters and expressed strong interest in working with him. Both Ienner and Goldberg must be exceptional individuals. They belong to the small number of record company people who Chuck speaks highly of.

'I have great respect for Donny Ienner and Danny Goldberg like you wouldn't believe to this minute. 'Cos I [think] they had high moral integrity and that was rare.' He makes a point of mentioning, 'No black executives stepped up to the table except one guy, Hiram Hicks, who headed up Island at that time.'

Jeff Ayeroff at Virgin also gets props, but in the end Chuck decided to go with Danny Goldberg. In addition to the hiatus, there were also practical reasons why he chose to not use the

Public Enemy name. Def Jam didn't seem to like the fact that
Chuck was manoeuvring within the same building and did a
number of different things to stop him using the term 'Public
Enemy'.

'That's why you might have seen some things like 'Fuck Def
Jam' at that particular time, 'cos they were preventing me from
operating in the building. I knew that Polygram had bought
half of Def Jam. What's gonna stop me as a black guy from
using the building? What, you gonna kill me cos I'm smart?'

Autobiography's jump-off single 'No' features Chuck railing
against corny choruses, mainstream dreams, phoney-ass
friends, jail time, little kid rhymes and overpaid A & Rs. It
was another hit for Chuck, and was well received by those
members of the hip-hop nation that were still tuning in, plus
the many non-hip-hop fans who had been big fans of Chuck's
over the years. The question of whether Chuck and PE were
still relevant, and who they were relevant to, was one of the
themes of the solo disc. Due in part to the reception of *Muse
Sick-n-Hour Mess Age*, the album begins with an excerpt of
the opening conversation in Spike Lee's *Clockers*. If you've seen
the film, it's easy to picture Scientific, played by Sticky Fingaz
from Onyx, sitting on the project benches and having a heated
debate about whether or not they still mess with PE. They
decide that they don't. Scientific seems offended when his
friend remarks, 'Chuck D is the bomb.'

'Chuck D ain't shit. Get the fuck outta here,' he shouts back.
'That nigga Chuck D is assed out,' says Go (played by fellow
Onyx member Fredro Starr). Wu-Tang, Kool G Rap, Tupac
and Dr Dre are more their thing. This illustrates the strange
place that Chuck D occupied in the mid nineties. For the most
part, the question of whether or not he was still relevant was
either answered with a resounding 'yes' (those heads disillu-
sioned with the way hip-hop was going in the mid nineties),
or a very definite 'no' (the younger kids, anyone under twenty
who had embraced the newer sounds).

Those in the pro-Chuck camp were bolstered by 'Mistachuck',

the album's first song, which is a thorough run-down of his achievements in the rap game. At a time when many of rap's classic personalities were busy trying to figure out how they were going to adapt to the new climate Chuck made no secrets of his contempt for the 'Big Willie' ethos that prized commercial success above all else.

In particular, he poured scorn on those black executives who were more than happy to cater to the powers that be, even when they knew that the records they were promoting would be detrimental to the black community. Such execs would never mess with a guy like Chuck who had no problem speaking truth to power – that's why they never responded to his letters. They would never stand up and be counted. Worst of all, few would ever truly flourish in the music business. 'I never really believed in these black execs 'cos they were really powerless and all full of crap,' he says. 'I never really wanted to be them.'

'But Can You Kill the Nigger in You?' saw Chuck working with Isaac Hayes, one of his idols and a titan of black music history. In a 1996 interview conducted for *Props* magazine by the esteemed individual and long serving hip-hop head Davey D, Chuck enthused about how recording with Hayes 'was the recording joy of my career . . . Isaac Hayes was surprised I knew so much about him'. He went on to reveal how 'it was him and Eric Sadler. Isaac Hayes played the keys, the chords . . . and then I rapped on it. Soon as I did, I asked him to sing a little part in it. So he sang that section at the end. To be produced by Isaac Hayes, shit! I reached out to Isaac Hayes and I went to Ghana and built a bond. I also used people in the SLAMjamz situation that I tried to build with Sony.' The album was well received but the success wasn't on the scale of previous PE albums. *Autobiography* also marked the first tentative steps towards a permanent reunion with Professor Griff. The two collaborated on 'Horizontal Heroin', a short track about the evils of one of the most addictive drugs in the world.

In 1996 Chuck also published his first book, *Fight the Power: Rap, Race, and Reality*. A collection of his thoughts on subjects as diverse as LA gang culture, black and Jewish relationships, and the role of black athletes in mainstream America (with a little PE history thrown in), it was a solid success on both sides of the Atlantic and everywhere in between. In his foreword Spike Lee describes Chuck as 'one of the most politically and socially conscious artists of any generation . . . [someone] able to inspire other young people to redirect their energies and thoughts for more positive and constructive objectives'.

On the back of the book Cornel West, professor of African American studies and philosophy of religion at Harvard, and author of *Race Matters*, praised Chuck as 'a towering artist of hip-hop culture and a leading public intellectual of and for young America'.

Chuck also had a short part in the Hollywood satire *Burn Hollywood Burn* – which took its title from PE's controversial 1990 track – alongside Whoopi Goldberg and Eric Idle. Next to Compton rapper Coolio he played one half of the fictional film-makers the Brothers Brothers. Chuck, who also contributed to the score, portrayed Leon Brothers.

It also transpired that the first incarnation of SLAMjamz did not work out. Perhaps Chuck is just too much of a visionary. Could he be charged with having unrealistic expectations? He makes a point of saying that it wasn't Danny Goldberg's fault and that he had given the hard rhymer the utmost support. But his plan to build artists abroad in the first place just wasn't going to work, despite the worldwide presence of Sony (which owns Polygram). It didn't help that The Fugees had just blown up beyond everyone's wildest dreams and were on their way to selling around seventeen million copies of *The Score*. That was always going to be the company's priority, especially over Chuck's studied artist development proposal.

Chuck's initial plan had been to launch Kendo Of The Hyenas In The Desert and Cosmo in Belgium and Amsterdam and have Melquan represent the UK. But the US wing of a record company just wasn't going to fund an overseas project. On a worldwide scale, there were factions of the company that were, to all intents and purposes, in competition with each other.

Due to the nature of the music business, there was even departmental competition between individuals who were meant to be working together for the good of the same company. And then there were differences in record company priorities. Chuck's third signing was his childhood friend, the extremely talented soulman Kyle Jason. Jason made a great soul record called *Generations* for $60,000 and all looked good. The only problem was that Columbia (another subsidiary of Sony) had just spent $800,000 on Kenny Lattimore's *From the Soul of Man* and they couldn't allow the $60,000 album to outshine the $800,000 album. They had a lot more money to make back, and Lattimore's album received all of their attention. Chuck concluded, 'You really couldn't do it as a major unit. So I removed SLAMjamz from Columbia amicably.'

29

Publicenemy.com

He Got Game, the soundtrack to the Spike Lee film of the same name, was Public Enemy's last album for Def Jam. That was not necessarily a bad thing. In a lot of ways that time period was positive for PE, perhaps even a rebirth of sorts. Chuck remarks, 'Enough things had healed and enough smoke had cleared in '97 to come up with a project and also to appear live in New York.'

All the things that had caused rifts within the PE camp – the Griff situation, the SOUL records episode and the personality clashes between band members – were all issues that were nearly ten years old. It would be hard for anyone to hold a grudge for that long.

PE rocked HOT 97's Hip-Hop Legends show at Madison Square Garden alongside KRS-One and Run DMC. But despite the renewed energy generated by the crew coming back together after Chuck's solo project, there was still the music industry to deal with. In 1997 the *Bring The Noise 2000* album, a compilation of PE remixes, came to life. It tapped into the *fin de siècle* fever that gripped the last few years of the twentieth century, when excitement and uncertainty about the new millennium reached fever pitch. Hip-hop mainstay Grand Puba even released an album called *2000* as early as 1995.

Bobby Simonson, aka Spacey B, a member of the now sprawling PE production crew, was responsible for all the remixes. Unfortunately for him, Def Jam immediately put a stop to the record. It's no secret that the music industry was scared stiff of this new technology (MP3, downloads, etc.). The subsequent fall in CD sales has shown they were right to be scared. Needless to say Chuck was furious. 'That's what really prompted me to say, "I'm trying to get out of my fucking

Def Jam contract." But then the opportunity to do the record with Spike Lee presented itself. This obviously changed things a little for the better, but not a whole lot.

Flav was also becoming increasingly exasperated with Def Jam who, for years, had refused to release his solo album. Maybe they felt a Flavor Flav solo record wouldn't fit in with the likes of DMX, Ja Rule and Jay-Z, who were all making big money for the company at the time. 'Thanks I get/ I helped put the roof on top this bitch,' rails Chuck on *He Got Game*'s blistering opening track 'Resurrection'. The song proves beyond doubt that PE were thinking it was 'time for a label switch'.

'The *He Got Game* album was another pressure move on Flavor Flav,' the best hype-man in hip-hop says in an uncharacteristic outburst. 'Not only that, but that was the last fucking straw that broke the camel's back with me and Def Jam. So that was it.' Flavor very nearly removed himself from the album. It was a good old-fashioned case of Q-Tip's infamous industry rule number 4080. If you don't know it, it states that record company people are shady. 'I really didn't want to put the album together 'cos they wasn't giving me what I wanted,' he continues. 'All because they said if you don't give us X then you ain't getting Y. I gave them X but they didn't give me Y, but yet they still wanted Z anyway before I could still get my Y. So I really didn't have too much involvement with that. But I was there for whatever Chuck needed me to do.'

Despite their contempt for Def Jam, the opportunity to put together the soundtrack proved too enticing. Taking things a step further than he had with *Do the Right Thing* and 'Fight the Power', Spike had PE record an entire album to accompany his 1998 film, which starred Denzel Washington as Jake Shuttlesworth. For Chuck, the opportunity to take on the combination of basketball and rap was especially attractive. On a broader level, PE would become the first rap group to do an entire soundtrack, and it recalled the efforts of Isaac Hayes and Curtis Mayfield with iconic films like *Shaft* and *Super Fly* in the seventies.

In the film, Jake's son Jesus is a basketball prodigy who must decide which college best deserves his talents, or if he is going to bypass college altogether and go straight to the National Basketball Association (NBA). The latter is never really an option. Competition for Jesus' signature is so strong that his incarcerated father is temporarily released by a crooked prison governor in order to try and influence his decision.

The first single and title track proved PE could continue effortlessly to rack up worldwide hits. Many fans and critics would cite *He Got Game* as their best album since *Apocalypse '91* but their dedicated fanbase was so big that a degree of success was guaranteed with each record. Songs like 'House of the Rising Son' and 'Politics of the Sneaker Pimps' appear in the film. The latter is one of the songs that examines the lot of the young black sporting star. 'Super Agent' and 'What You Need Is Jesus' are other examples. The former examines the unscrupulous agents who will tell a young black athlete anything in order to get him to sign with them. 'What You Need Is Jesus' tackles the way the NBA is perceived to treat the black athletes that belong to the organisation as largely interchangeable cattle. Chuck refers to 'the new slave trade' and how there's a 'manchild, six feet five, but juvenile', and how this young buck will be sold 'to the highest bidder'.

He Got Game marked the official return of Professor Griff to the PE fold. He never completely lost touch with PE personnel (he'd literally known them all his life) and was involved with Chuck's solo album. But now it was official to the bone gristle. Most significantly, he closes the album with 'Sudden Death', a collection of revolutionary thoughts. 'All he had to do was just come back and be true to the game, that's all,' Flav says about it, eight years after the fact. 'And that's being the Professor Griff that he is. He's done that and he's proven that. He's been back for a minute, and it's good to have him back.'

Given the scale of the controversy caused when Griff departed PE his return to the group might seem relatively low

206 | Russell Myrie

key. While it is true that he simply began working for the group again, his return wasn't completely without friction. S1W's James Norman and Roger Chillous left PE to work in their local community, something they'd been involved in for years. Chuck acknowledges that Griff's return may have been a factor: 'I dunno if there was a chill that still remained between Griff and them,' he ponders, before deciding, 'There were always unfixed situations between people, so as Griff came in they moved out. Keith "Krunch" Godfrey also moved out on his own and went out into the real world.'

'He brought a fresh idea back to the group again,' says James Bomb. 'It was a good look to have him back on the stage again and it was painful too, for myself, it was painful for the group members like, "Are we going to go through the same thing again?" That crossed your mind. But you still move forward, we didn't want to stop the process of having Griff back.'

He Got Game was also Terminator X's last album as a member of PE. At the end of 1998 the group had just finished touring through Australia and, as usual, were preparing for another outing on the road. That year had also seen PE headline the Smokin' Grooves tour, which was the first major rap tour in a long while. They were joined by Cypress Hill, Busta Rhymes and the Flipmode Squad, The Black Eyed Peas and a newly solo Wyclef Jean. When Chuck first tried to get in touch with the gentle giant to embark on their latest trip he was initially unreachable. When he did manage to get through to him he wasn't told what he wanted to hear. 'He said he "kinda wanted to come on tour and kinda didn't",' Chuck recalls. 'And then he just said that was it, which left us kinda like, "Okay, now what do we do?"'

It's fitting that Terminator left the crew on the eve of a tour. He was never a big fan of life on the road. Many PE crew members remember their first ever tour, when Terminator was so nervous that he would sleep under the covers fully clothed, just in case something bad happened. Lately, the great DJ who always fancied the quiet life has had just what he wants. He now runs an ostrich farm in North Carolina.

He has hardly been in contact since: 'The last time I seen Terminator X?' Flav ponders. 'Wooooww, that's how long it's been. It's probably been over, man, about maybe ten. How long you been with us, Lord? I haven't seen Terminator in about seven years . . . That was '99. Well that was it. He didn't even say bye, man, he just . . . I always wanted to catch up to him because I want to bring him back out. I want him to resurface. That's one of my, I'm not gonna say a dream, but I have anticipated a comeback for him. I'm gonna bring him back.'

For *He Got Game*, PE tried to bring The Bomb Squad back. For the first time in a long time, both Hank and Keith Shocklee, Eric Sadler and Gary G-Wiz had a meeting. Chuck was also present, and he informed them that this was their last album for Polygram, which by then was beginning to merge into Universal. However, it seems that record company concerns took a back seat to the tensions that remained.

In this respect, Chuck recalls 'a project that was bittersweet. Sweet in the way it brought teams back together to handle a particular record and the record was definitely good. But not all the teams worked together with each other because there were factions that were apart from each other. During that project myself and Hank, we differed, and we agreed, which was good – we always did that. But when we differed it was the fact there were other people there like Gary G-Wiz and Eric Sadler and Keith that had to be figured into there as much as some of the new guys that Hank wanted to come to the table, and Hank realised he couldn't control some of the new guys that he brought to the table the way he had a hold on guys before.'

As the last member to join The Bomb Squad Gary had added pressures. 'It was supposed to be a reunion situation but Hank basically said up front, you know, "It's gonna go down this way and everyone's gonna . . . " I just don't think it went over well with everyone. Everyone's thinking something different and it ended up being more of a broken-up situation than an inclusive situation but the ideal was to team everybody back up and there were some meetings. Unfortunately when you get something like that, that works for a period of time, it's difficult to reunite 'cos all the old shit is still there.' It has to be said that more recent producers like Abnormal and Kerwin 'Sleek' Young, responsible for 'Is Your God a Dog' and 'House of the Rising Son' respectively, were not as immersed in all the politics.

This time around even Chuck experienced some frustrations. That said, he doesn't name names or even hint at who the culprits may be. Some things are probably best left unsaid. 'I was writing for these songs and in some situations co-writers would come in and try to fix my lyrics,' he reveals with a look that says, 'Can you believe that shit?' 'I remember recording "Resurrection", and that record was like hell. Things got taken apart, fixed and I'm like, "Nah."'

Perhaps most significantly, for a man who prides himself on always coming under budget, Chuck was dismayed with the amount of money spent. The money spent on *He Got Game* still affects PE's finances within the Universal system today. At the time, many *nouveau riche* rappers enjoyed spending far more than they needed to on promotion, producers, studios and hot sixteens from the guest star *du jour*. This was the era of the $2 million Hype Williams video, Cristal champagne and excess in general. It was around this time that BG from the Cash Money Millionaires coined and popularised the term 'bling bling'. So, despite *He Got Game* going gold, there were so many pay-outs that there wasn't much money left to go around. Throughout PE's whole career they never had a record budget that exceeded six figures. *He Got Game* exceeded seven figures.

Chuck still isn't happy about this. 'I wasn't in charge of that record and it still affects me today, it affects my royalties. If it was up to me, I'd have given Def Jam a record for $90,000. I wouldn't have given them a record with seven figures attached to it. I'm still unclear how and where that money was spent.'

While there was excess, there were also certain costs that couldn't be avoided. By now, corporate America knew exactly how much hip-hop was worth and they wanted their pound of flesh. For the first time in their career PE realised that they might have to give up 150 per cent of one of their records. Anyone who has ever heard *He Got Game* knows it is built around Buffalo Springfield's anthem 'For What It's Worth'. In order to sample the tune, PE had to give up 50 per cent of another song. But this was a worthwhile sacrifice.

'My whole immediate goal is not to disrespect the legacy of a classic – [it is to] add to it,' Chuck says. 'I said when we take on "For What It's Worth" and make it into *He Got Game* it should be something big. Stephen Stills and the choir and all of that, it made a brilliant rendition and I think my lyrics nailed it 'cos I wasn't haggled any more.' Unusually for Chuck he knocked it out in two takes. And when Spike Lee heard it he knew he'd made the right decision.

He Got Game is memorable for many reasons. It took Chuck D and KRS-One just over a decade to rhyme on the same track together. Gary G-Wiz made it happen. Like most hip-hop fans, it seemed strange to him that 'Chuck and KRS-One had never been on a cut together'. 'Unstoppable' changed this. Gary had decided, 'I'm gonna reach out to him somehow and I'm gonna find his manager.'

KRS was recording nearby so G-Wiz hooked up with him at his session, took the track and everything there, and recorded him in the middle of his own session. 'Kris was real live.'

PE didn't leave Def Jam on good terms. But as one door closes, another opens. PE didn't need Def Jam to remain at the forefront of new trends. At the end of 1998 when PE were still bound to their contract, Gary G-Wiz and Chuck built publicenemy.com. All hell broke loose when they proposed putting even just four of *Bring the Noise 2000*'s twenty-seven tracks on the website. Gary remembers how 'the lawyers came out and people were screaming. We had a crazy beef over that. But that kind of got us going and got Chuck notoriety online as being one of the early guys on the MP3 thing, and we pretty much stayed there.'

This short excerpt from a post on the new PE website made Chuck's position crystal-clear. 'It seems like the weasels have stepped into the fire . . . Today Polygram/Universal or whatever the fuck they're now called forced us to remove the MP3 version of *Bring the Noise 2000*. The execs, lawyers and accountants who lately have made most of the money in the music biz are now running scared from the technology that evens out the creative field and makes artists harder to pimp. Let 'em all die . . . I'm glad to be a contributor to the bomb.'

Today he smiles at the situation: 'I said, "Well you know what, man, if you don't let us go from this situation we'll put everythang from Universal on the web." We didn't know what the fuck we were talking about,' he admits. 'But I said, "I'll have everything in your whole catalogue downloadable." We worked out a deal and they let us go.'

Gary had been patiently waiting for the internet to arrive in earnest for a long time. He got his first modem in the early eighties.

'I started actually dialling in and doing all that PBS thing and all that back then so it was a pretty natural thing for me. No one even really understood the internet, especially in the music business, till around '95, '96.' They don't call him G-Wiz for nothing.

In addition to publicenemy.com, Gary and Chuck started rapstation.com and Bring The Noise radio, on which Chuck presented a show. Publicenemy.com provided an outlet for C-Doc to come into the fold and expand the PE production team further still. In *He Got Game*'s liner notes Chuck mentions publicenemy.com and rapstation.com and made himself available through email. C-Doc emailed him recommending Columbia imprint Ruffhouse as a new home for PE. At the time C-Doc had two different email addresses: one he used regularly, the other not so regularly.

But he found Chuck's reply eventually: 'Three months later

I happened to check the email and I saw he had responded back to me and I said, "Holy shit! Chuck D sent me an email!" I was freaking out like, "Oh my god, this has been in my inbox for three months, what the hell."'

In his reply, Chuck agreed that Ruffhouse wouldn't be a bad home for PE and he had been considering it himself. From that point on, C-Doc began to get more involved. 'A lot of people will say I was the first person to post on the enemy-board,' he says. 'I don't know if that's true or not, I can't remember, to tell you the God's honest. But there are many people who will swear up and down that I was the first one.'

Doc, who had been making music with his homies for around four or five years by that point, got hold of an a cappella of 'No', and he also had the twelve-inch of 'Give It Up'. Using his four track he remixed both. Soon after that, Chuck was the keynote speaker at a hip-hop conference in Cleveland, Ohio, only about a three-hour drive from C-Doc, who scooped up his boys and went down.

'After his keynote address I heard him saying, "I'll be hanging around out back if anybody wants to come by and say "Wassup".' They did just that. 'I was like, "Chuck, Chuck, it's C-Doc," and he said, "Hey C-Doc, whadup man?" Like I'm a long-lost friend . . . so me and the couple friends I was with headed out and chilled with Chuck and shit. We ended up building in the parking lot for four hours with Chuck and he was very, very accommodating.' That same night in the parking lot of Cleveland State University Chuck also met Marcus J from C-Doc's crew, the Impossebulls.

During that long chat Chuck mentioned SLAMjamz and how he was considering how to set it up again and the possibility of an internet label. Encouraged by this, Doc took the two remixes he'd done and posted them on the enemyboard. The feedback he received made him realise 'that there was this whole community of PE fans'.

Some of these people hollered back. One of them, a guy from the UK named Del, told Doc he had some beats. 'I said,

"Send me the beat on an MP3 and I'll record a verse to it, put that on an MP3 and send it back to you and you can mix the song together."' Once the tune was done, he sent it to Chuck and said, '"This is a little collaboration we did over the internet," and he played it on his internet radio show, the *Bring the Noise* internet radio show, and I just started sending him music and I said, you know, this "opens up a lot of possibilities".'

30

DJ Lord on the Ones and Twos

A year after *He Got Game*, *There's a Poison Goin' On* became the first full-length album by a major artist to be made available on the internet before it reached stores. After a period of contemplation Public Enemy signed with the web savvy Atomic Pop and linked up with Koch for the physical release. Atomic Pop was owned by Al Teller, the same person who had hooked up the SOUL deal back in the day. He was also the same person that Harry Allen was talking about in his interactive super highway phone call.

Unlike most in the industry Teller had the foresight to realise how central the internet was going to be to the music industry in the new millenium. The massive 'Do You Wanna Go Our Way???' was the big hit from this album, even if it wasn't really indicative of *Poison*'s overall sound. Unlike *He Got Game*, which featured a lot of big-sounding tracks like 'What You Need Is Jesus' and 'House of the Rising Son', *Poison* is a very sparse and stripped-down album.

To a degree, songs like 'Here I Go', 'Crayola' and 'Swindler's Lust' represent back-to-basics hip-hop. The beats are simple but very effective. Received similarly to *He Got Game*, *Poison* was cited by many as PE's best album since *Apocalypse '91*.

Lyrically, Chuck spent much of the album celebrating the freedom he'd wanted since *Yo! Bum Rush the Show* while simultaneously blasting the music industry and the direction that much major-label hip-hop was taking in the late nineties. 'Here I Go' found him complaining of how 'rap got pussy whipped' and how he was 'the opposite of jiggy'.

But it was 'Swindler's Lust', the album's closing track, that featured the most vitriolic and far reaching rhymes. In this tune, Chuck looks back at the history of music as a whole, complaining about how the mainstream music industry 'Stole rock'n'roll and ain't gave it back'. The song's chorus states, 'If you don't own the master/ The master own you'. Chuck ends the song by giving shouts to rock'n'roll pioneers like Little Richard.

Poison also marked the first time PE recorded using (then brand new) MP3 technology. 'Put it this way,' says Flav. 'Chuck was somewhere and I was on the other end. Chuck would do some shit, and send it. I would listen to what Chuck did, take whatever parts that I wanted, put my parts on it, then send it back. The chemistry of that album was slightly different. Chuck gave me a little bit of freedom.'

Was this freedom ultimately responsible for the brilliance of '41:19', which tackled the tragic situation when immigrant Amadou Diallo was murdered by the police, who mistook his wallet for a gun? It certainly wasn't usual for Flavor to be this overtly political. But since Flav has lived uptown for much of his life – Diallo was murdered in The Bronx – this tragedy was very close to home.

Flav collected some tracks, linked up with Gary G-Wiz, and knocked it out. 'That was the first record about forty-one shots,' he says proudly. 'I had the first forty-one shots record out. It was real fucked up the way that Amadou Diallo died. I had to write about that man, fo' real. The police shot at him forty-one times, but they only hit him with nineteen. Nineteen shots out of forty-one hit that kid, I had to write about that.'

Reminiscing about the track prompts him to ask DJ Lord if the beat is still in the machine. It turns out that it is. That night in Cambridge, in late October 2006, Flav performs '41:19' for the first time in a long while. It's quite apt that Flav should ask Lord about a track on *Poison*. The tour for *There's a Poison Goin' On* was the first time the new spinner in PE's life joined them on the road, on his way to becoming a permanent member of the crew.

Hailing from Savannah, Georgia, Lord Aswod had moved

to Atlanta and was making mixtapes, DJing at a few local clubs (like The Zoo and Mom's Lounge), and holding down a nine to five at Champs Sports shoe store ('It's hip-hop, you gotta have fresh sneakers,' he says, not unreasonably) when his roommate – who knew Professor Griff – came and told him PE needed someone to replace Terminator X.

He used to DJ under his government name, but 'people would always screw it up, they'd go Lord Aswad, Asswad'. So, after a while, his moniker shortened. The roommate who told him about Griff had been working on some production with the Professor, but he couldn't convince Lord that he was telling the truth about the opportunity that awaited. 'I was just a freshman in Atlanta,' he recalls, 'I was doing the job thing. I just didn't believe it. I was like, "Man, stop bugging, I'm trying to go to work."' When he came home one evening and Griff was chilling in his living room he suddenly took it more seriously. Griff confirmed they were looking for a new DJ, just as he had been hearing from his homie. And that was pretty much it. Lord couldn't believe his luck.

'It happened so fast. One week I'm at the crib, then I met Chuck, and got my passport in order.' After being given the right equipment to learn instant replay he was off on tour and was thrown in at the deep end. 'I had to go to Belgium with no rehearsal, it was crazy out there,' he says with a laugh. As at PE's very first show supporting The Beasties, things didn't go so well initially.

'It was a frickin' nightmare at first, I went onstage with no rehearsals, or show list, and all kinds of outside pressure 'cos Terminator's shoes are some big shoes to fill, man. It was crazy, I was missing cues, I was getting star-struck looking at the crowd, getting that rush from looking at the crowd, I was seeing people singing the songs word for word but they don't know English and that's bugged-out. I'm looking at all this energy and now I'm part of a group I idolised. I grew up listening to Public Enemy.'

Being a long-term fan – when Lord went to watch PE as a youth in Savannah he was very impressed with Terminator's blue flight cases – is what helped him the most on those first few intimidating dates. 'The good thing was I knew Terminator's scratches like the back of my hand so I did it just like it is on the record, but as I went on I started adding myself to it and do like different signature scratches that he does on record but freak 'em my way.'

Anyone who has seen Lord perform over the last few years has seen him do that with perhaps Terminator X's most famous scratch, the 'rock'n'roll' scratch from 'Rebel Without a Pause'. It didn't take long for Lord to find his feet. By his fifth or sixth show as a PE member he had it down and was freaking Terminator's scratches in all kinds of weird and wonderful ways.

Flavor, once again, inimitably compares the extensive qualities both DJs possess. 'When Terminator X left the group I felt like there was a tooth missing out of my mouth, and the tooth is still missing. But I grew an extra one in the back, my man DJ Lord. But Terminator? I mean, you know, nothing can ever fill that spot, nothing can ever take the place of Terminator X. There's only one Terminator X. Terminator X is the one that started making all that transforming shit famous. Can't nothing replace that. Terminator X had a certain look onstage that a lot of DJs then started having, can't nothing replace that. He had certain scratching styles that a lot of people won their championships with. But I know one thing. Can't nothing fuck with the DJ that I got today. Terminator, that's my man and everything, he got irreplacable shit. But Lord got shit you can't fuck with either. Lord is the up-to-date Terminator X.'

That said, in many ways 1999 was always going to be a tricky time to release a PE album. The hedonism of many of the *nouveau riche* clans, posses, camps and cliques left little space for music with real substance. Strangely though, the jiggy era still found a way to pay homage to the crew who put Strong Island on the map. P Diddy decided to recruit Flav for a remake of 'Public Enemy Number One' that he re-christened 'PE 2000'. It was the first single off his sophomore album *Forever*. This was not too outlandish, it being the height of Puff's jackin' for beats era. In the beginning of the video Flav rides with Diddy in his Lamborghini. When he notices helicopters following them he remarks to Puff how he's turning into a Public Enemy. Hurricane G, Redman's sister, then re-creates Flavor's famous 'the brother don't swear he's nice, he knows he's nice' routine.

The Poison tour was documented in the *Public Enemy – Live from House of Blues* DVD. The most interesting part of the DVD is the 'Architects of Rap' section where Chuck visits a number of important PE hotspots around Long Island. On a very snowy day, he drives by the Roosevelt youth centre where Spectrum first cut their chops, then goes to Hempstead, to 510 South Franklin Ave. If a person didn't know better they might think it was number 51, the '0' seems to have long since fallen off. Dr Gant's sign is still there. Chuck then drives to the Adelphi University campus, formerly home of the Thursday Night Throwdown and WBAU. The radio station disappeared in the early nineties. This clearly signalled that times were changing, that PE were moving into a new, radically different era.

Poison was also the very last PE album available to buy on cassette. MP3s and downloads would render CDs obsolete in a few years. The digital age had arrived.

31

The baNNed

In typical Public Enemy fashion they followed their most stripped-down album with a foray into noisy live music. The liner notes of *He Got Game* state, in bold capital letters, that even though their music has never been pretty, 'Public Enemy ... guarantee to always push the envelope in hip-hop.' In the new millennium PE continued to do just that by gradually incorporating live music into their sphere in a more meaningful and permanent way. True, live instruments had been a part of PE's wall of sound since Flav, Keith Shocklee and Bill Stephney did their thing on *Yo! Bum Rush the Show*, and many times throughout their career PE have demonstrated that they were always comfortable reaching beyond turntables and samplers, such as with the remake of 'Bring the Noise' and songs like 'Sophisticated Bitch'.

But employing full-time live musical accompaniment was a statement of intent. The leader of the live musicians, the baNNed, as they subsequently became known, is Brian Hardgroove. He's worked with Supertramp and David Byrne of Talking Heads fame. He played on Slash's first record. 'I did a number of things,' he understates. But he's most proud of working with Calvin Bell, a guitarist proficient in jazz, rock and funk fusion. Bell led a group called Calvinator, who were very popular in and out of the Black Rock Coalition, an organisation of like-minded artists who network, perform together and generally look after black rock musicians. Someone's got to. This association led to many recordings and a couple of European tours. 'He was well known among players in New York,' says Brian. 'He's an incredible player.'

It was a member of Calvinator who introduced Brian to the group he would join many years later. '[Calvin Bell's] bass player at the time was a friend of mine, Yossi Firen, he's from Tel Aviv. He actually played me the first Public Enemy record I ever heard, and that was *Nation of Millions*.' It was Yossi Firen who facilitated Brian's entry into Calvinator. When Yossi left he suggested that PE's future band leader be his replacement. 'That was a big honour 'cos Yossi Firen is an incredible bass player,' says a still-grateful Brian. The bass is actually his second instrument. Hardgroove is a drummer first. He has learned from some pretty heavyweight friends including Eddie Kramer who recorded and produced all of Jimi Hendrix's music as well as engineering some of Led Zeppelin's output. He was also Kiss's producer for live albums like the *Alive* series. Brian counted Jack Douglas, who produced John Lennon and Yoko Ono's *Double Fantasy* (he was also the engineer for *Imagine*) as well as many Aerosmith records including *Toys in the Attic*, as a friend.

While the aforementioned greats taught him about all things rock, Hardgroove learned about hip-hop through Kenny Lee, who has been one of Russell Simmons' right hand men for years. Lee hooked Hardgroove up with 'all of these groups that Russell had been trying to break'. This meant he ended up doing a lot of hip-hop production, something unusual for a man who admits he doesn't like much hip-hop. 'Personally, I was never a big fan of the genre until I heard Public Enemy. I liked LL Cool J, because he was a real talent, but the genre was a little too self-centred and that was just not me. When I heard Public Enemy they tapped into more of what's me: that's politics and social issues and their music was in-your-face and it was different.'

Even though he doesn't like a lot of hip-hop, he comes from a place steeped in hip-hop history. He hails from 100th Avenue and 196th Street in Hollis, Queens. Those familiar with the area will know that he was therefore very close to Jamaica Park. Even the members of PE who did not join until the new millennium were getting down to Run DMC in their formative years. 'I liked Run DMC cos I was exposed to them,' he says of his other favourite local group. 'I literally heard their parties in the park.'

Brian, like most kids at the time, wondered why on earth he was hearing Aerosmith's 'Walk This Way' again and again. Who the hell was playing this tune over and over? It's a good job it was one of his favourite songs. 'They'd start it, stop it, start it, stop it. I now know that was them rocking "Walk This Way" before they recorded it. Before they got big. When they blew up I checked up on them and one of my contemporaries Eddie Martinez played on one of their records.'

Many years later Kyle Jason spotted Hardgroove playing in New York and recognised that he would be perfect for his upcoming support slot for Frankie Beverley. Jason used the Black Rock Coalition to contact Hardgroove and they enjoyed a short working relationship. 'That's how I got to meet Chuck and, at some point down the line, he asked me to join a group that Chuck and Griff were putting together called Confrontation Camp.' Hardgroove became Confrontation Camp's bass player and they signed with Danny Goldberg's Artemis Records. 'We recorded the album and that's the first time I worked with Chuck.'

Confrontation Camp did a few shows here and there, most notably the Democratic National Convention in 2000 – and its Republican counterpart – but as Brian himself says, 'It was a short-lived project. There was a lot going on that kept us from doing much more. But Chuck had had the chance to see me work. He saw my work ethic, my [sense of] responsibility.'

These qualities prompted Chuck to call him up during the 2002/3 Revolverlution tour and ask him if he could do for PE what he did very well for Confrontation Camp. It certainly helped that Brian is around the same age as most of the PE crew and therefore grew up in the era before programmed music. 'I told Chuck this: I said, "Chuck, I'm the best guy you could get to do this, for this position, 'cos I don't approach it like a bass player, I approach it like a producer." I had to get Khari and Mike,' he says of Khari Wynn and Mike Faulkner, the baNNed's guitarist and drummer, 'to do this music the way I had to do it, I tried to keep them from viewing it as a drummer or as a guitar player, view it as a producer. Some things are out of tune. Some things are slightly out of time. I respect the music. I don't want him to be disappointed he ever asked me to do this.'

There doesn't seem to be much chance of that. 'Hardgroove bought an understanding of the nature and the sensibility of the Public Enemy cuts,' Chuck says. Before Hardgroove came along the live musicians would just play whatever they felt. 'Brian understood the nuances of the songs, the styles and the changes. There's an understanding of music theory and also the Public Enemy DJ/musician mess.'

Hardgroove was astute enough to know this was not simply a musical undertaking. Other skills would be required. 'When Chuck asked me to do it, I determined what the job description was simply because of what a band leader normally is. But that's not the role. What you're dealing with is various relationships that don't allow for being a proper band leader. What I found is being a politician is probably the best thing. Understand the relationships and negotiate those. Then I can do my job.'

When he's not messing with all things PE, Brian's other job, like Chuck and Kyle, is in radio. In Santa Fe, Hardgroove is known for holding it down on Indie 1015, a station in direct competition with industry behemoth Clear Channel. He seems to be drawn to people who fight the power. When the husband and wife team who had owned the station for years decided they wanted to sell it, they vowed that they were not going to sell it to Clear Channel. Fortunately, some former Clear Channel employees got together, got some investors and bought the station. Their slogan is 'the clear alternative'.

'It's a free-form station. It's not a college radio station, it's not public radio, it's a commercial radio station, so they have to make money, so it's very exciting. When they took me on they said, "anything you want to play". And so Brian plays what he likes. 'One of the station's slogans is "from The Clash to Johnny Cash" so you know they play a wide range of stuff. You can get the show online at indie1015.com.'

Gifted guitarist Khari Wynn met Professor Griff in Atlanta through a drummer who happened to be Wynn's former teacher. At the time, Griff was trying to put a band together, so he had put the word out. The band he subsequently formed would be called the 7th Octave. But Griff isn't possessive: 'When Public Enemy was putting their band together Griff was like, "Use my guitar player from 7th Octave,"' Khari recalls. 'The first gig I did with them was in 2001, for the "Gotta Give the Peeps What They Need" video in Boston actually. Long time ago. The first tour was 2002, the Revolverlution tour.'

Like DJ Lord, Khari met Griff in Atlanta though it isn't his home. His guitar playing is steeped in the city of Memphis, Tennessee. 'Memphis has a real rich musical history, with Stax and stuff like that,' says the youngest member of the baNNed. 'Kids nowadays come up rapping, but there's still that musical legacy, the musicians are still up there just 'cos of Stax being there. All the studios are still there and all the hits are coming out . . . it was definitely good to come up in Memphis 'cos I would say the level of musicianship is equal to any other major area. It definitely helped me as a musician.'

Mike Faulkner, aka 'New York City Mike', was the last member of the baNNed to join the fold. Mike and Brian hooked up through mutual friends in 2003 when PE's former drummer T Bone left the camp. Numbers were swapped and Mike and Brian hooked up.

'Brian asked me if I could play to a drum machine,' Mike recalls. 'I told him, "Yeah, that's no problem, I've done that previously."' Much like Brian, Mike has played with some real heavyweights. 'I played with Loose Ends when they toured years ago. I played with Steven Dante, he had "The Real Thing" on Chrysalis Records. I've been playing professionally since I was thirteen years old,' he says laughing. 'It's been a long time.'

Of course, playing PE songs (that were so revolutionary in terms of how they used electrical equipment) with instruments presents a musician with innumerable challenges. It also presents a whole new set of possibilities for Chuck, Griff and Flav. As Brian rightly says, 'to have a really tight band behind them gives them options they didn't have before. They take advantage of that.'

'It was different, man, 'cos I had to get used to, first of all, playing to pre-recorded tracks, and second, I had to get used to the way Public Enemy put their music together, which is really different,' Khari says. 'They have a lot of beautiful sections, especially the guitar parts and stuff buried underneath all this thick layer of noise. It's hard to reproduce the noise through instruments 'cos that stuff was done with samplers and stuff. So you have to find out where the real instruments are. Once you find that out you gotta find out what key it's in. It's totally different.'

All three players agree that 'Black Steel in the Hour of Chaos' is the easiest PE song to recreate. 'The piano parts are clear,' says Brian. 'You can hear the samples and you can hear what the bass does.' Songs like 'Fight the Power', or 'Rebel Without a Pause' which contain elements that are not so easy to identify are more of a struggle. 'I would definitely say "Rebel Without a Pause" is one of the most challenging ones,' Khari says of PE's breakthrough hit. 'There's the high-pitch thing and if you really listen close to the song there are guitar parts within the record. That one song is a challenge.'

Furthermore, there are the external factors and considerations that any group who plays in different venues across the world has to account for. It's not unusual for the baNNed to change the parts to certain tunes every day. Things can sound one way in one environment, then different in another auditorium. In venues where other frequencies are more prominent than usual, a keen ear will often detect something else that wasn't there before.

'That's one of the interesting things about some of these

Public Enemy records,' Brian says, 'there's a lot of things in there that you don't hear unless you listen to the record ten, twenty, thirty times. You realise, "Oh, that's what was going on."' The baNNed do their thing away from the stage as well. As Fine Arts Militia, Brian and Chuck have released one album based on one of Chuck's lectures. But as Koch only pressed up limited numbers, you'll have to look hard for it. The forthcoming second Fine Arts Militia record is going to include the one and only Bootsy Collins as part of the crew. Brian, Khari, Mike, DJ Lord and Johnny Juice released *BaNNed for Life*, the official debut album from the baNNed, in summer 2007. As may be expected, the subject matter is very much in line with PE's output. Standout songs include the televangelist baiting 'The Passion of the Heist'.

The debut 7th Octave record dropped in 2004. Khari has another side project called Solstice, which he describes as 'like a jazz rock thing which kinda mixes elements of jazz and kinda like what Miles Davis did'. Overall, the PE live show, always one of their greatest assets, has changed for the better. 'It's better probably for those reasons,' Brian says. 'There's more to work with [in the sense of] how it comes across to the audience, how it used to come across and how it comes across now. That's all individual opinions.'

'It definitely adds a thickness to the sound,' Khari says. 'It adds an organic element and creates more movement onstage.' The live drum-and-bass sound is also important: 'I think people kinda always have more response to that organic element. If they have live drums, the way a live kick sounds, it's just different. Even the lowest, lowest bass from a machine is different from the organic sound of a kick drum, so having the organic sound gives it a whole 'nother thickness that just hits people a certain way.'

While the trio of players are clearly enlightened individuals, rolling around the world with a crew like PE, who are one of the few hip-hop acts who think and tour outside of the box, cannot fail to broaden your horizons. While touring parts of Eastern Europe – in particular the former Yugoslavia – New York City Mike was shocked at the poverty and general despair he encountered. 'Usually when you're talking about some ghettoes it's some black people but it's not always just black people. With the travelling we've done, you can see the things that have happened in Bosnia and Serbia. They may not have our history of being oppressed but they're still living in dire circumstances day-to-day. We're not the only ones living hard, there's a lot of folks living worse than us.' Seeing such things for themselves, rather than watching it on the news or reading it in the paper, opened their eyes to the war that had occurred. 'When you see bombed-out buildings and people tell you that's because of America, you get a whole different light. Coming from America you don't really get to see first-hand what our government does that affects other countries.'

On a broad level they put Chuck in a space where touring was fun again. But despite this new lease of life – which he describes as a mixture between Run DMC, The Roots and Rage Against the Machine – he acknowledges the critics: 'Somebody might come along and say, "The classic things are this," meaning they don't wanna hear the live music. But it created a whole thing in itself.'

32

Jam Master Jay RIP

Despite changes in Public Enemy's personnel, some things remained exactly the same. The *MKLVFKWR* DVD features Flavor Flav once again proving that he's always got jokes. One of the backstage snippets shows him leaning over to James Bomb, and with a massive grin on his face, he asks the cameraman if he's ever filmed a human Rottweiler before.

Revolverlution, PE's ninth album, was released in 2002. A play on The Beatles' classic *Revolver*, Chuck first used the word 'revolverlution' on 'Crash' from *There's a Poison Goin' On*. The album demonstrated how PE were becoming one of the few hip-hop acts capable of the longevity that had previously been the province of rock groups like their friends U2 and Aerosmith. Like these groups, PE are able to release albums when they feel like it, and tour the world on the back of it. Their following is strong enough that a certain degree of success is guaranteed.

But once again, the album was different to what went before. Similarly to *Greatest Misses*, *Revolverlution* includes some remixes of some classic PE joints, including 'Miuzi Weighs a Ton' and 'By the Time I Get to Arizona'. But this time around the remixes were a result of a worldwide web competition where contestants sent in their reinterpretations – over 11,000 entries were received – and PE picked the best of the bunch. There are also some live performances and a few bits and pieces, like the phone conversation where Flav recorded his intro to 'Burn Hollywood Burn'.

Some loved the freedom of expression and the willingness to experiment. But, again as with *Greatest Misses*, others just wanted a new PE album and only paid attention to the new cuts, which were unfront-on-able. Chuck is unmoved. 'We

228 I Russell Myrie

wanted to make it historical. Everything we do is either totally historical or different.' Even those who criticised the record couldn't dispute this.

The opening track 'Gotta Give the Peeps What They Need' is just too wicked for words. Johnny Juice was now back in the fold as a producer and he proved he still had the skills with a truly amazing beat. 'Everybody has their different little thing,' Chuck remarks. 'Juice deals with areas of percussion and congas, dealing with herky-jerky motions. It kinda stops and goes.' Chuck is one of a very small number of rappers who would call for the release of political prisoners like Mumia Abu-Jamal and H. Rap Brown. Mumia, a former Black Panther and author of *Live from Death Row*, was convicted of murdering police officer Daniel Faulkner in 1981. He has always protested his innocence and the whole situation is obviously politically motivated. The case against him was riddled with inconsistencies and he continues to fight for his freedom. H Rap Brown, also known as Jamil Al-Amin, is a veteran of the civil rights movement. He, too, was convicted for the murder of a police officer, Ricky Kinchen. While his case is not so obvious a miscarriage of justice like Mumia's, there are still questions to be asked. The police believed the man who shot and killed Kinchen was injured in the battle. H Rap Brown had no injuries at the time of his arrest. Another man, Otis Jackson, has confessed to the shooting, but later recanted. Brown's supporters argue he is the real shooter.

'Gotta Give the Peeps What They Need' was banned from MTV for the lines 'Free Mumia/ And H Rap Brown'. MTV did not want the channel to be associated with the police killings in which they were implicated. MTV's Tom Calderone first demanded that PE remove the references to Mumia and H Rap Brown, and then the images of them projected in the background of the video. Chuck refused.

The guest verse from Bay Area rapper Paris on the remix was equally fiery and paved the way for the *Rebirth of a Nation* experiment.

The particularly scathing and self-explanatory 'Son of a Bush' – one of Professor Griff's best productions – showed PE had not mellowed with age. The song not only verbally lampoons both Bush presidencies, but Prescott Bush, Dubya's grandfather, gets it in the neck once or twice as well. But George W comes off worst. One of the song's most famous and provocative couplets is, 'I ain't callin' for no assassination/ I'm just sayin', who voted for this asshole of the nation.'

Another pertinent lyric is Chuck's assertion that as governor of Texas, Bush 'killed 135 at the last count'. He then criticises further by appropriating a Texas flow, saying 'Texas, Bounce, Texas, Bounce'. (For the record, Chuck was never going to get involved with all things crunk. During 'Put It Up' he notes that he's 'too old for 22s'.) No live performance of 'Son of a Bush' is complete without the chant that goes a little something like this: 'Fuck George Bush, fuck George Bush, muthafuck George Bush.'

The song also shows how the musicians who would form the baNNed were slowly but surely becoming an integral part of PE. 'That's actually me playing on "Son of a Bush"', Khari reveals. The version of the track that made it to the *Revolverlution* album was actually one of the fruits from the first session he ever did with Griff. The two were chilling in the studio listening to the drum track and a riff that had originally been sampled by Griff. Griff got rid of the sampled riff, Khari replayed it, and the rest is history. 'Son of a Bush' was meant to be for 7th Octave, but Chuck heard it, liked it and earmarked it for PE.

Flavor Flav represented on *Revolverlution* with 'Can a Woman Make a Man Lose His Mind?', another song documenting his unsettled private life. Nothing like 'A Letter to the New York Post', this time Flav's less controversial complaint was that he gets nagged when he wants to hang out with his boys.

However, even though *Revolverlution* was another album chock-full of quality material, not all of PE's members could enjoy the warm reception their first album of the new millennium received from their diehard fans across the globe. Things were not going well for Flavor. A gig on New York radio station Power 105.1 didn't work out – despite the fact that he was working with his old school homies Dre and Ed Lover: 'I started doing the traffic reports,' he recalls. 'It was called the geographic traffic, traffic that's geographic, the whole nine. I was working up there with them, then I started to feel negative vibes coming through the spot. I'm like, "Whaat". Put it this way, they kinda fired me.'

But there was some good news. When he was asked to appear on Wu-Tang's 'Soul Power (Black Jungle)' from their album *Iron Flag*, it wasn't just because the killer bees thought he was a dope emcee and recognised he was a hip-hop icon. It was because Flav found out he was a cousin to the late great ODB and therefore *his* cousin and Wu-Tang brethren RZA too. Flavor Flav's other cousin Timbo King Keys put him up on game.

'God bless him, I found out that me and ODB were related. His family and my family are the Cuffeys. I found that RZA is also my cousin, that's my family. When I found that out, about like RZA? I was like, "Wooooww". Word? Hey man, that's some mad cool shit. My cousin Timbo used to come and visit me in jail. He took me over to RZA and them. I got on the track, "2002, you know how we do, it's Wu". Papa Wu is married to my cousin from South Carolina.'

One of hip-hop's darkest days occurred in October 2002, when the hip-hop nation, and, more crucially, the Mizell family, lost Jam Master Jay, aka Jason Mizell. The hip-hop legend, an integral part of pioneers Run DMC, was brutally and tragically gunned down in a Queens studio. At the time Flav was in C-76 on Rikers Island, and this is one reason (apart from their extensive shared history) why he took it so badly.

'I went crazy that night. I went craaazzy,' he says, his mood changing noticeably. 'I had put the word out in jail that whoever did it, if they woulda came to the Island they wasn't gonna leave. They wouldn't have left. A lot of the correctional officers was waiting for that to come through there. Word up, serious, man, that really broke my heart. We was on our way to bed that night. They was like, "Yo Flav, your man Jay got shot." Whaat? I dropped the phone. I went crazy, man. They all had to hold me down.'

Flav found it hard to sleep. 'That next morning I went on the radio around four-thirty, five o'clock in the morning from jail. And the phones don't get cut on till eight in the morning. I had special privileges up in jail. I called Chuck too. I was in jail and was able to reach Chuck. I told him, "Man, that took a big piece out of me." I don't know who should have been holding him down but I know Jay shouldn't be dead.'

It was around this time that Flavor was battling various demons and something just had to give. An accumulation of small offences kept landing him in jail. About a year or so later, when Flavor was just about to get out of prison once again, Chuck ran into Prinses Hemphill while at a speaking engagement in Chicago. He appealed to her to try and speak to Flavor in the hope that he might leave New York and all his troubles.

'He told me that Flavor was about to get out of jail, Rikers Island, and he asked me if I would please convince Flavor, 'cos I have pretty good influence with Flav, to leave New York and come to Los Angeles. Every second Flav would always be in trouble 'cos he would never have a driving licence, he had a little drug problem, he had some issues going on. He just needed a chance to do something different, otherwise he was just going to end up in jail again.'

At the same time the combined force of Chuck and Hank were appealing to their old friend in the hope that he might swap the East Coast for the West Coast. 'My partners Chuck and Hank wanted me to go out, they gave me the idea to go out there to see what I could do out there 'cos my life was kinda stressful around that time,' Flavor reminisces. 'I wasn't doing too good out in New York, it wasn't happening for Flav.'

True to her word, Prinses linked up with Flav, convinced him to go out to LA and gave him keys to her apartment and access to her car. 'I took them up on their advice,' Flav continues with the satisfaction of someone who knows he made the right decision. 'I went out to California. That was the end of 2003, going into 2004.' Thus began one of the strangest and most interesting chapters in PE's history.

33

The Enemy and Reality TV

Fortunately for Flav and his ambitious nature, Prinses was, and still is, someone who has got the hook-up. As the national event co-ordinator of her own company (check out celebrityevents4u.com) Prinses knew exactly how to put Flavor on the right track. He didn't fall into TV by accident, it was his plan before he even left New York. And he knew he had to be seen around town. Soon after he arrived, Prinses and Flavor went to all the restaurants where the great and the good chill out on Sunset Boulevard's Sunset Plaza. As they were sitting outside on the patio they were easily noticeable.

'Once we sat down he's unmistakeable,' Prinses laughs. 'How many guys on the planet are walking around wearing a clock? People were just like, "Flav, wassup." At that point Flav didn't remember. I had to convince him again that he's a hip-hop icon, he's a legend. Once you've had some knocks, you're not believing that the people are feeling you. That was the hardest part. To get him to understand that people still have love for him.'

Flav's first step on the celebrity ladder was to attend Bernie Mac's Super Bowl party in early 2004. But old habits die hard. While Flavor hit it off with Bernie when he eventually arrived, leading to his first TV appearance on Bernie Mac's self-titled and extremely popular sitcom, he certainly made Prinses sweat beforehand. 'I must have called him about nine times, like, "Are you coming, when are you coming, what's taking you so long?" His mind still wasn't there.' Flavor did show up, but only just in time to catch Janet Jackson's infamous wardrobe malfunction during the half-time show. 'Most people show up at a Super Bowl party at the beginning,' Prinses observes.

The next big hook-up came courtesy of Will Smith and his wife Jada. Towards the end of February, Prinses found herself on a set near where the Smiths were filming their sitcom *All of Us*. Actress LisaRaye McCoy, a friend of Prinses' who played Neesee James, was the crucial link. She could help them gain entry, and, as Prinses well knew, Flav had been wanting to run into Will for a long time. They had already known each other for years, ever since DJ Jazzy Jeff and The Fresh Prince joined Public Enemy on one of the Def Jam tours of the late eighties. Once on the set, Prinses called Flav and told him that if he wanted to meet Will he'd better get over to the *All of Us* set in a hurry. Will just happened to be directing that particular episode.

'Flav is like, "Yeah G, that's my boy, that's my boy, aaaah," so I go up there and I ask Jada out of respect. I told her who I was, told her Flav was in town and that he wanted to meet Will, and you can imagine on this set, there's like maybe 125 people all moving around.' The large number of people on set didn't matter. Jada proved once and for all that Redman's line 'keep my family tight like Will Smith and Jada' (from 'Da Countdown (Saga Continues)') was not just empty rhetoric. Jada made a sound that was a little like a birdsong, or maybe a little like how U-God shouts 'Zoooooo' at the end of his verse on Wu-Tang's 'Protect Ya Neck'. Prinses was certainly impressed.

'All of a sudden Will just turned around and started moving in her direction. I was like, "Wow, what kind of call is that?"' As soon as Will knew what was up he arranged for some passes to get Flav in there. When Flavor arrived he received that rarest of things in Hollywood: a genuinely warm welcome. The studio audience started clapping at Will and Flav's camaraderie. Prinses was happy and could see light at the end of the tunnel. 'It was a very cool moment for Flav because Will greeted him really well and it was nice for him to see it all going down and be immediately embraced. I wish I'd had a camera!'

After *The Bernie Mac Show*, Damon Wayans's *My Wife and Kids* was the next sitcom that invited Flav to play himself. In that particular episode, Damon's son wants to be a rapper and so a couple of old-school rappers like MC Lyte and Flav were up in the mix. 'It was kinda cool,' says Prinses, 'and that time

I took my camera.' But, as is the way of these things, it wasn't all straightforward.

An appearance on Aries Spears' *Mad TV* show, though successful, didn't entirely go according to plan. Flavor was there to tell jokes, but the writers had scripted a disparaging joke about Michael Jackson. Flavor took issue with this, he didn't want to diss Michael, and it turned into a stand-off. The biggest problem was that the stand-off occurred as the live audience was entering the studio. Flav had finished rehearsing, he'd come through wardrobe and everything was ready to roll. But he didn't want to say this one joke. And that was not all.

It was *Mad TV*'s style to do one scripted take and one improvised take. Only thing was, they didn't tell Flav about the improvisational side of things. During the improvised take, Aries tried to be funny with Flav. He should have known who he was dealing with. Aries cracked on Flavor in the second take and Flav came back on Aries automatically. 'It was funny and everything but Flav didn't appreciate it,' says Prinses.

Before long, the chance to appear on the show that would change everything for Flav, and to some extent PE, arrived. One day a representative from *The Surreal Life* approached Flavor's manager and asked him if his client would like to appear in the reality show. Flav had a difficult decision to make because most people who appear on *The Surreal Life* (and most reality shows for that matter) are considered has-beens. But by now Flav wasn't really too worried about any potential haters.

'He had built up his confidence,' says Prinses, 'and he realised people fucked with him and were showing him love. He opted to just go for it and have fun doing it and that's how it happened.' So, once the formalities were sorted out, Flav headed out for filming, which only took two weeks. In the third season of *The Surreal Life*, which observes a bunch of once-famous celebrities in a Hollywood mansion, he was joined by Jordan Knight, formerly of boy band New Kids on the Block and former *American Idol* contestant Ryan Starr. Prinses wasn't around when the infamous Brigitte Nielsen episodes were broadcast where they got it together. But she caught wind of what was going down. There was no getting away from it. Tall, blonde and almost Aryan, Brigitte towered above the shorter, very dark-skinned Flav. More importantly, their characters didn't seem compatible. When she returned to LA, Flav picked Prinses up from the airport. While he was anxious to play her some of his new music – he had been working at DeVante Swing's studio – he also had to endure a grilling from her.

'I had been hearing about Brigitte and Flav and I didn't know what to think.' Unbeknown to Prinses, she was about to get a surprise of her own. 'We're riding in the car and the phone rings and it's Brigitte. Flavor is notorious for putting other people on the phone.' He didn't let the fact that Brigitte was calling from Europe deter him. 'He puts me on the phone and he wants her to say hello to me, so she's like, "Hi Prinses, how are you? Take care of my foo-foo."' Prinses hadn't seen an episode so she hadn't heard the hilarious nickname. 'But she's sounding like she's totally in love, she's telling me she loves him. "I love him, Prinses, take care of him," and I'm like, "Okay, nice to talk to you," so I give Flav back the phone and that was the first time I really realised, through his smile and the way he was acting . . . Flav really likes this chick!' There are some who will insist that the whole thing was a publicity stunt. But once she was back at her apartment, Prinses, at least, became convinced it was for real. 'I'm seeing that her and him are talking a lot on the phone and he really likes this chick. He really, really did.' Flavor's forays into reality TV prompted a whole heap of criticism for him as an individual and PE by extension. His response to this is as concise as ever. 'All the people that didn't like it? I didn't give a fuck. To all the people who did like it? I gave a fuck. The ones that didn't like it was not gonna stop me making my paper, wasn't gonna stop me from being successful. And a lot of people that didn't like it probably are the ones that wish that they were me.'

34

Is She Really Going Out with Him?

In 2005 Flav continued to roll with Brigitte in a new reality show, the aptly titled *Strange Love*. It created some problems. Even in the new millennium, a major part of the hype was the fact that Flavor and Brigitte were in an inter-racial relationship. But even worse than this was an episode entitled 'The Family That Flav's Together, Stays Together', which aired in late March. During the episode, Flav was shown arguing with some of his children and their mother about the lack of child support he was paying.

This episode in particular left Public Enemy vulnerable to accusations that while they talked the talk, not all members were walking the walk when it came to social responsibility. Chuck weighed into the debate that followed with a post on the PE website. He began by acknowledging that Flav has 'always been the same crazy cat from day one'. Nevertheless, he opined, 'the reality [of] dragging of his personal life excesses and children is uncalled for', and it 'doesn't bode well with what the group stands for with its fam. and followers . . . It doesn't bode well if Flav is yelling at his kids and his ex.'

The following extract from Chuck is particularly telling. 'In my prior conversation with Flav, he's still enamored with platinum sales and packed stadiums, and thinks that his TV profile will "bring Public Enemy back" to that material status. I remind him that travelling to fifty-three countries whenever he wants to play music and being "free" to make and produce recordings that are heard with respect across the world transcend that simple commercial status.' A few months later, Flav appeared alongside Keith Harris, Ron Jeremy and Lionel Blair in the UK reality show *The Farm*.

Despite these very real misgivings Chuck was still happy

that Flav was no longer doing the things that had caused him trouble before he left New York. 'Flavor comes from the black community where drugs are rampant and addiction is never beaten,' he told me in an interview for *New Whirl Odor* in November 2005. 'So it's very important to have someone at their happiest, and if fame makes Flavor happy, then hey, go for it, man. 'Cos there's no harm being done there, as opposed to something much worse that he could be doing. I think that's real.'

Towards the end of that year PE dropped *New Whirl Odor*, their first studio album in three years. By now, they were a full multimedia operation. Each release was accompanied by a DVD. In this case there was a selection of videos, a brief history of SLAMjamz and an introduction to the producers behind the beats, where you could listen to them recount how the album was put together – in the liner notes Chuck compared *New Whirl Odor*'s recording process to a 'Motown-ish assembly effort'.

In those same liner notes Chuck also deplored how, similarly to what occurred with the mid nineties incarnation of SLAMjamz, the trilogy of releases planned when *Revolverlution* dropped were thrown off track by the music industry. Distribution issues meant that *Revolverlution*, PE's fifteenth anniversary album, couldn't be closely followed by *New Whirl Odor* and *How You Sell Soul to a Soulless People Who Sold Their Soul*? There was nothing that could be done about the fact that, as Chuck puts it, 'Retail/distribution has a different idea of releasing records as opposed to our creative jones.'

Despite this setback, PE had a whole lot of output in the pipeline. There was the *It Takes a Nation: The First London Invasion Tour 1987* DVD, which features the Hammersmith Odeon concert from that year which PE sampled extensively for *It Takes a Nation of Millions to Hold Us Back*. It's a real trip to hear not only the famous intro to the album but also the intros to tunes like 'Terminator X to the Edge of Panic' and 'Black Steel in the Hour of Chaos'. That DVD also marks one of the few times you will hear Terminator X speak with his voice and not his hands.

Interestingly, the section where Flavor asks about being allowed to perform his dance illustrates the differences that have always existed between him and his lifelong close compadres. Chuck spits a very firm 'no' and Griff doesn't seem too keen either. Eventually they indulge him, as was obvious they would all along. His less serious personality was always the reason he was brought into PE and, also remember, one of the reasons why the group worked so well for so many years. All those who criticised his reality TV shows would do well to balance this fact with the more concerning aspects of the 'flavploitation'.

Also in the works was the *Rebirth of a Nation* collaboration project that would see Oakland rapper Paris writing Chuck's lyrics. SLAMjamz projects like Kyle Jason's excellent *Revolution of the Cool* CD/DVD and the Impossebulls' *Slave Education* were already making noise.

Chuck was enjoying this freedom. He'd been waiting years to build his empire like this. 'I realised, "Well, I wanna go through a creative period of just releasing a lot of Public Enemy content," because I realised things were shifting to the web and the internet and I wanted to ingrain myself into sometimes two albums a year, sometimes three, and then after the 2008 period I wanna go in a different direction.'

In the same way that the end of the millennium was perhaps not a good time for any conscious rappers, 2005 saw the tide begin to turn in favour of groups like PE and a release like *New Whirl Odor*. The anti-Iraq song 'MKLVFKWR (Make Love Fuck War)', recorded with dance music master Moby, showed exactly why PE were more necessary than ever.

Lyrics like 'Power to the people not the president/ Capitalists, communists, terrorists/ Swear to God I can't tell the difference/ Makin' new slaves outta immigrants' refer to how there isn't really much discernible difference between those who may appear to represent vastly different political doctrines.

Power is the main goal for all. The title track also offered much-needed perspective on the changing nature of prejudice. During the first verse of the Johnny Juice-produced track, Chuck complains about 'liberal friends who try to act like everything has changed, when nothing much has changed'.

Professor Griff spits on 'Revolution' but production-wise he probably made his presence felt most effectively with 'What a Fool Believes'. A brilliant tune where Chuck's unorthodox flow during the verses and the heavy guitars makes for something quite different to 'Sophisticated Bitch', 'She Watch Channel Zero?!' or 'Brothers Gonna Work It Out'. Producer Abnormal continued to represent for PE with hot bangers like 'Makes You Blind' and the wicked 'Bring That Beat Back'. 'Check What You're Listening To' is PE's dedication to Jam Master Jay.

The eleven-minute masterpiece 'Superman's Black in the Building' was another song that proved PE were still capable of making music that matched the quality of their classic earlier output. The song's genesis came about when Chuck sent C-Doc an email one night telling him there was going to be a new album. Doc remembered how recently on the enemy-board the peeps had let it be known they wanted some big drums and loud-sounding beats *à la* the album version of 'Shut 'Em Down'.

With this in mind, Doc created the first tentative basic backing track and sent it to Chuck. Twenty minutes later, 'Chuck was like, "This is serious, I'm writing to it already."' Originally, the lyrics that appear on 'Makes You Blind' were put on the rough beat. 'But then he changes his mind and said it's gonna be something like "Superman's Black" or something like that.'

Not too long after, Chuck had to do a lecture in Cleveland, Ohio. He and C-Doc found a studio and laid down the first part of the track, enlisting Bone Thugs-n-Harmony engineer and producer Mauly T, with a reference from long-standing friend and hip-hop writer Val-1. Originally, 'Superman's Black in the Building' was meant to be the first single from *How*

You Sell Soul to a Soulless People Who Sold Their Soul? But it then transpired that G-Wiz was going to do that record and C-Doc, Juice and Abnormal were going to put together *New Whirl Odor* and *Beats and Places*. Nevertheless, at the time C-Doc was listening to a lot of fifties rock'n'roll and Chuck had remarked on how he wanted to do something with some live jazz in the not-too-distant future. *How You Sell Soul* was originally going to be a little more souled-out than it turned out to be, a little more Stax-influenced.

All of these factors contributed to the second part of 'Superman's Black' which changes things up after the customary three minutes. As is nicely depicted during the *New Whirl Odor* DVD, this section of the song was a real labour of love for C-Doc.

'I went back and started messing about with the beat and stuff and when I came up with the second part I called Chuck and said, "I've got an idea."' Once Chuck heard the rough draft he was, as ever, down to try something new.

They got in the right musicians to execute this part of the track, but there was more. 'Chuck called me from Chicago like, "I got Gene Barge from Chess Records." I was like, "Holy shit, wow, okay."' Chuck had been taking part in a documentary called *Godfathers and Sons*, one of the documentaries in the Martin Scorsese-produced series *The Blues*. Alongside Marshall Chess, Johnny Juice and Kyle Jason he travels to Chicago to explore the past and present of everything to do with the music that birthed rock'n'roll, soul and, therefore, everything else.

Gene Barge's saxophone solo was duly incorporated into the whole. The way the song breaks down towards the end is audacious and intoxicating. Chuck switches from rapping to something approaching preaching. This part of the song – which changes the whole track from a regularly dope jam and takes it into new territory – was written by James Bomb. 'Superman's Black' was then earmarked to be *New Whirl Odor*'s first single, but Chuck was particularly taken with 'Bring That Beat Back' and he changed his mind.

That brilliant track wasn't C-Doc's main contribution. Chuck had told Doc that one of his main roles in The Bomb Squad was as an arranger. Chuck thought about albums like *Fear of a Black Planet* in seconds, rather than in terms of records or songs. 'He said this was so taxing and it was such an immense record that he kind of burned himself out on it and he kinda stepped back from doing it.'

Doc mentioned how it would be nice to get back to doing those kinds of dense arrangements with all the snippets of samples and so on. 'He said, "Well if you're interested, why don't you do it?" and I said, "Okay."' This is how C-Doc ended up sequencing the album. Chuck's only stipulations were that the first track had to be the title track, the second track had to be 'Bring That Beat Back' and the last one had to be 'Superman's Black in the Building'. Doc added the two snippets '66.6 Strikes Again' and 'Either You Get It By Now or You Don't' which recalled classic snippets interludes like *Fear of a Black Planet's* 'Incident at 66.6 FM'. These interludes consist of snatched and scratched-in soundbites and opinions often concerning the things various people love and hate about PE. A few weeks after the album dropped, Chuck D collected a lifetime achievement award at the 2005 MOBO Awards. In the immediate years that followed, PE would accept a whole host of awards that accepted them as legends, even as they continued to produce new work.

35

Rebirth of a Nation

Less than six months after *New Whirl Odor* hit stores, Public Enemy released *Rebirth of a Nation* on Paris's Guerilla Funk Recordings. As Chuck told me during an interview that appeared in the *Voice* in early 2006, the legend from the Bay Area 'is the only cat that I know who could actually write a Public Enemy record'. He's not wrong. When Paris released his debut album, 1990's *The Devil Made Me Do It*, he managed to seem super-militant in a hip-hop world where pro-black social commentary from groups like Brand Nubian and X-Clan was par for the course. But that was tame compared to 'Bush Killa', the B-side to the far mellower 'The Days of Old', the first single from his second album *Sleeping with the Enemy*. The song, a fantasy about the murder of the then President George H. W. Bush, was so controversial Tommy Boy Records dropped him.

The first seeds of *Rebirth of a Nation* were sown when Paris appeared on the remix to 'Gotta Give the Peeps What They Need' and PE returned the favour by guesting on his album, *Sonic Jihad*. Paris wanted to do a record with PE but Chuck was just too busy to handle it. 'I said, "Let me try one project where one guy does the music and the lyrics and he meticulously sticks it together."' In the liner notes Chuck mentions how Marshall Chess once put together an album for Muddy Waters, who more or less invented Chicago electric blues. He wanted to try something similar. So Paris began writing for him.

While *Rebirth of a Nation* contains songs like 'Can't Hold Us Back', 'Hard Rhymin'' and 'Rise' – joints that could sit alongside all the other classic PE songs – it also contains songs like the opener 'Raw Shit'. For the first time Chuck is heard rhyming to some West Coast funk. The collaborative nature of the record was extended to include appearances by like-minded artists. Dead Prez, Kam, The Conscious Daughters, Immortal Technique, NWA's MC Ren, and Paris himself all added their voices to proceedings. Chuck did contribute lyrically to *Rebirth*. That album was the first to feature a version of 'Hell No, We Ain't Alright', his response to the Hurricane Katrina debacle.

2006 was also the year that Flavor Flav's eponymous debut album finally dropped after years and years of waiting. 'It's a real crazy answer, it took that long because that's how long it took ha-ha-ha.' While the album surfaced a few years after he moved to LA and cleaned up his act, the part played by industry rule number 4080 shouldn't be ignored either.

The delays with his album have a lot to do with him being signed to Def Jam as a solo artist. At the time it must have made sense. PE were signed to the house Rick and Russell built and relations were reasonably good, if not great. Not only had things turned considerably sour towards the end of the nineties, which Flav blames on Def Jam's new direction and their refusal to entertain any ideas about the internet, but it has been widely reported how he had two completed albums rejected by the company, who were now more interested in promoting thug records.

It's one of the few subjects that visibly pisses Flav off. 'Being that they wanted extra projects out of Public Enemy they refused to put out my project until they got what they wanted. When they didn't get what they wanted the first time they were still supposed to put my album out, but they still held my fingers back and made me say, "Yeah, course I'll do another project," so that way I could put my album out. But after that they still never put my album out. Russell Simmons, Lyor Cohen, my partner Chuck D and Hank Shocklee weren't the best of friends around that time. So Flavor Flav was guilty by association.'

Hot joints on the album – where Flav either produced or co-produced every track – include 'Unga Bunga Bunga', 'I

Ain't Scared' and 'The Jooks'. There was also the Flav funk of 'Col-leepin', a remake and play on 'Cold Lampin''. On joints like 'Let it Show' and 'Two Wrongs' Flavor tried his hand at singing. While he has more heart, soul and passion than skill, he never tries to hit any unnecessarily high notes. Smooth B of hip-hop heroes Nice & Smooth guests on 'Baby, Baby, Baby'. 'Guess Whooz Bak' saw your boy relive the night Jam Master Jay was murdered.

Other projects in '06 included the 'Bring That Beat Back' remix project which C-Doc handled. He was also heavily involved in *Beats and Places*, another record which resulted from the 'jazzist approach taken to hip-hop' that Chuck mentioned in the liner notes. His concise and pointed reflections were as much a feature of the post-2000 albums as any of the other added extras. Mind you, the shout-outs on PE's albums had always been especially extensive. The shout-outs on Biggie's classic *Ready to Die* are probably the only thank yous that are as long as those on *Fear of a Black Planet*.

'Who's Your Hero?' is probably one of C-Doc's best tracks on *Beats and Places*. Chuck needed a theme song for the PE comic book that first made an appearance towards the end of 2006, and C-Doc was on hand. Chuck had been trying his hand at comics for years. In fact, it was through comic books that he originally met Harry Allen when they were both students at Adelphi University. Harry describes Chuck's comic book series *Tales of the Skind* as a 'serial drama, a story of the Spectrum mobile DJ crew who were battling the forces of evil trying to save the world. It was the funkiest thing in my week at Adelphi and I used to get the paper and just fiend for the next episode.'

One day in animation class he noticed someone drawing something remarkably similar to his favourite comic. 'I asked him, "Are you the person that does *Tales of the Skind*?"' The student confirmed he was. 'I said something that I still say to this day whenever I see Chuck: "I'm a big fan of your work." His response was, "Wow. I didn't even realise anyone was reading it." I guess that was the beginning of a quarter-century relationship?'

But there's a lot more to be found on *Beats and Places*. Johnny Juice in particular shines with joints like the raw 'Air Conditioning' and its remix. He made his scratching rhyme for a couple of verses on 'Grand Theft Oil'. He also produced the two spoken-word songs. Chuck does the preacher man thing on 'Like It Is'. 'Shit', also written by James Bomb, features a delivery that more closely resembles rapping. Every few bars, Flav pops up to remind us, 'The shit keeps on coming.' Perhaps best of all is 'If I Gave You Soul'. This was another joint originally earmarked for the original version of *How You Sell Soul*. Kyle Jason and Chuck's call and response chorus is probably the best aspect of a brilliant song.

2006 was also the year when *Flavor of Love* appeared on screens for the first time. In the show Flav spent the series coping with the 'challenge' of picking one of twenty women to be his girl. *Flavor of Love* became so popular that the second-season finale that appeared in October 2006 attracted 7.5 million viewers, the most in VH1's history. One out of every three African-Americans watching TV that night was tuned into Flav.

36

Twenty Years and Counting

In 2007 Public Enemy completed twenty years in the music business with *How You Sell Soul to a Soulless People Who Sold Their Soul?* It's a question many modern hip-hop groups who . veer from the commercial path might ask themselves regularly. The first single, 'Harder Than You Think', one of the last songs recorded for the album, featured Flavor marking this 'publicversary' by recreating the intros and ad libs from 'Public Enemy Number One'.

For PE, 'Harder Than You Think' was one of those beautiful records that just came together with a minimum of fuss. 'It happened with divine intervention,' Chuck says. 'G-Wiz had this track and I had this song and it was like "boom boom boom" and it was one of those rare times when two takes was all it took.'

G-Wiz recalls Chuck doing it in only one take. He made the trumpet-heavy track late one night and thought, '"Damn, Flavor would sound good on this shit." So we did some things with Flavor and I sent it off to Chuck and Chuck just knocked the shit out immediately.' Gary received written lyrics back in forty-five minutes. 'From there he did the cut in one take which is crazy.'

This is all the more crazy because when Gary says, 'Chuck is a hundred-take guy,' he literally means one more than ninety-nine. 'I remember when I first started recording Chuck and Keith would be in the studio, Keith would never pay attention to his first sixty takes. I'd be like, "Man, there's good shit in here," and he's like, "Nah man, we gotta let him just keep rhyming." So for Chuck to do a one-taker was a big deal.' Originally, 'Black Is Back', a tribute to Run DMC's early eighties shouting style, was going to be the first single. But as the lawyers had put a stop to PE reworking AC/DC's 'Back In Black', they chose 'Harder' instead.

The video, yet another PE visual directed by C-Doc, also celebrated the twenty years PE had spent in the game by showing Chuck and Flav travelling in a U-Haul truck, PE personnel like Eric Sadler and, best of all, 510 South Franklin Ave. In an age when even MTV doesn't play many music videos any more C-Doc is adept at understanding how to make a video for the small screen.

It also featured the brilliant show PE played at the Garorock Festival. Back home in the USA they were one of the main attractions at the Rock the Bells Festival. As a matter of fact, they shot the 'Harder Than You Think' video prior to playing at Rock the Bells with Rage Against the Machine, Wu-Tang Clan, Nas and others.

In a surprising but very welcome move Redman produced the funky 'Can You Hear Me Now'. Gary and his production partner Amani Smith had been doing the score for the short-lived sitcom *Method and Red* helmed by Redman and his fellow 'sky-highatrist' Method Man. The Funk Doctor Spock was going to the studio and hanging in the sessions and wanted to make something happen with Chuck. That's how 'Can You Hear Me Now' happened. Chuck remembers seeing a worse-for-wear Redman at Rock the Bells.

'He came onstage during Wu's set and Red was like,' he shuts his eyes till the pupils are barely visible. 'He had no clue. I was like, "What the fuck?" He's totally like, "Uncle Chuck, wassup."' Chuck thanked him for the hot track, but it didn't seem to register. 'He's like, "Huh what?"'

On 'Sex, Drugs and Violence' KRS-One collaborated with PE for the second time. When Gary G-Wiz – who, remember, has produced both of the PE joints that Kris has rhymed on – hit him up for 'Sex, Drugs and Violence' he was actually on the West Coast where Gary is based. Chuck was already at Gary's home studio, Kris came through, loved the concept and wrote his verse. It's particulaly great how, midway through

Kris's verse, the famous piano sample from his classic song 'The Bridge Is Over' suddenly appears.

Some songs from *How You Sell Soul*, like 'Escapism', were made a few years earlier when the trio of releases was originally planned. Chuck recorded the Gene Barge solo that appears in 'Escapism' on the same day that he recorded the parts for 'Superman's Black in the Building'. But joints like 'See Something, Say Something', a commentary on the whole 'stop snitching' fever, were bang up-to-date. Chuck rightly placed the term 'snitch' in its proper context by commenting on how black revolutionaries were the first to use the term for people who sold them out to the government. The album was sequenced and arranged by C-Doc and the outro, another spoken-word poem from James Bomb, ended things on the proper thoughtful note.

Harry Allen's exhibition was the perfect accompaniment to the twentieth anniversary. The fact that it was held at Eyejammie, the gallery founded and owned by Bill Adler, makes it all the more fitting. The exhibition came into being when *Wax Poetics* magazine did a famous piece on The Bomb Squad and were seeking pictures from the early eighties. After a while, they were pointed in Harry's direction. Back in the early days before he became a writer, Harry was documenting his local history with his camera. But when the writing took off, and in a way that he could financially support himself, he left photography behind. *Wax Poetics* ran through his collection and picked what they needed.

When Bill saw the issue and was really taken with what he saw, he reached out to Harry and asked if they could put on a show together. Harry agreed it was a good idea and the rest is history. The images are priceless. Without even really knowing it, Harry had documented PE's formative years and captured their last years of being music fans. Chuck is shown chilling with Kid Creole from The Furious Five, Keith was snapped putting the needle to the groove and there's a famous image of Hank looking up from the recording equipment he's surrounded by. Although there are pictures of hip-hop greats like Grandmaster Flash and T La Rock, these images are the best.

Dr Dre loves the image of him stood next to Jam Master Jay, DMC and Run. 'It was crazy to see a picture of Run DMC and myself from back then cos how would you ever know? It's like, "Wow."' Naturally, the images of Flavor are perhaps the most memorable. One features MC DJ Flavor performing to a nightclub full of people. Harry remembers taking it at the local roller rink.

'The roller rink was another Spectrum place,' he recalls. 'This was like a contest, a battle of the emcees that Flavor had entered. At that time, people didn't know what to make of him. Flavor had a lot of talent but it wasn't presented in the normal kind of package. But that night was just one of those nights where people were performing and being voted on. I think that's what was going on. And I just took some pictures and I was pretty thrilled, they came out pretty well. He was probably performing his record "Claustrophobia Attack".'

Even better, however, is the hilarious image where Flav is posing with a massive guitar around his waist. On that particular night Harry was up at the Adelphi University photo lab developing some photos. While he was there, a few people rolled through to get some pictures taken and to see how the lighting worked.

'Almost everybody in our local scene came up,' Harry says. 'Flavor, Shaheed, an Islamic rapper, The Classy Three Emcees, and Flavor came up and posed in his outfit with a guitar. He posed and I took pictures. I wish I'd taken a lot more pictures of Flavor. If I have any regrets from that time it's that I didn't take a lot more pictures of Flavor. Not only for the commercial value that they will have now, but also just because he was just something to look at.'

It was meant as a future publicity shot. 'Everybody kind of imagined they were gonna have a career or they wanted to be stars in a way and he wanted to be famous just like anybody else, and he had talent. It's a funny image now cos . . . it's just a funny image.' Harry even appears in the exhibition, standing to the right of Melle Mel with a big grin on his face. 'I'm very proud of that picture,' he says. 'I think that's the only picture I did not take. I think my brother took that picture. It's very gratifying to see these images, many of them have never been printed before at all, and so to see them hanging in a gallery and people seeing them and responding positively and buying them . . . it's just God-blessed, wonderful. You never know when something's gonna pay off.'

Bill Stephney attended the opening night and loved what he saw. 'Harry is a frustration to all of us 'cos he's such a brilliant artist and these brilliant photos were hidden for about twenty-five years! It's almost worthy of some level of execution,' he says with a laugh. 'I'm just wondering, how was I so much skinnier back then?' Of course, as a central figure, Bill pops up now and then. 'There's one shot that I'm in where we're in the front office of the radio station, it's me sitting next to Dr Dre and obviously Flavor's telling a joke. That photo really represents the amount of fun that we had and that Flavor was the laugh and riot that he continues to be.'

These days, Harry's main hustle is WBAI's *Nonfiction* show. If you find youself in either New York, Washington, Houston, Los Angeles or San Francisco between 2 and 3 p.m. Eastern Time, check it out.

Who else has brought the noise in the way Public Enemy always have? Perhaps Public Enemy's main achievement was causing hip-hop to grow up and develop a social conscience. At one time or another many successful groups have claimed to be 'the most dangerous band in the world'. Guns N' Roses and NWA are just two examples. But Public Enemy are one of the truly most dangerous groups of modern times. They are a group who have always spoken truth to power in a way that can't fail to concern the establishment. Their ethics have affected the way they have conducted themselves over the years. They are one of the few groups, of any genre, who never catered to the mainstream or the music industry, even when their message was no longer fashionable. They never sold out. They always pushed the envelope, and have remained one of the best live performers in the world. Best of all, the ride isn't over. They'll continue to do so for many years yet.

Chuck D's Selected Public Enemy Discography

Public Enemy was one of the very first rap groups to have a website. In 1998 the creation of www.publicenemy.com sparked what is now a decade-long run of CD, DVD and downloadable material. In 2000 www.rapstation.com was created and www.SLAMjamz.com served as a download home for PE instrumentals, remixes, sneak peeks and unreleased products.

BEYOND.FM is the official download store of SLAMjamz and Public Enemy.

The albums since 1999
1999 *There's a Poison Goin' On*
2002 *Revolverlution*
2003 *Public Enemy: The Millennium Edition*
2004 *Power to the People and the Beats*
2005 *New Whirl Odor*
2006 *Rebirth of a Nation*
2006 *Bring That Beat Back*
2006 *Beats and Places*
2006 *Fight the Power . . . Live!*
2007 *How You Sell Soul to a Soulless People Who Sold Their Soul?*: 'On our 20th year this record is an epic reach back into the ghosts and souls of PE past.'

The Def Jam years
1987 *Yo! Bum Rush the Show*
1988 *It Takes a Nation of Millions to Hold Us Back*
1990 *Fear of a Black Planet*
1991 *Apocalypse '91 . . . The Enemy Strikes Black*

1992 *Greatest Misses*
1994 *Muse Sick-n-Hour Mess Age*
1998 *He Got Game*

Chuck D solo material and related projects
1996 *Autobiography of Mistachuck*
2000 Confrontation Camp / *Objects in the Mirror Are Closer Than They Appear*
2002 Fine Arts Militia / *We Are Gathered Here*
2008 Chuck D, Kyle Jason and the Peeps of SOULfunk / *Tribb to JB*

Flavor Flav solo
2006 *Flavor Flav* (aka *Hollywood*)

Professor Griff solo material and related projects
1989 *Pawns in the Game*
1991 *Kao's II WizDome*
1998 *Blood of the Profit*
2000 *And the Word Became Flesh*
2006 *7th Octave* / *The Seventh Degree*

DVDs
2000 *Public Enemy Live at the House Of Blues*
2004 *London Invasion 1987*
2005 *MKLVFKWR: Live in Australia*
2006 *MKLVFKWR: Manchester UK*
2008 *Where There's Smoke . . .* The amazing World Tour Sessions of Public Enemy
2008 *What Side You On?*

The *New Whirl Odor, How You Sell Soul* albums and *Beats and Places* project were each accompanied by a DVD.

Look out for these upcoming releases:

DISCS

Bring the Noise 2000 Mastermix album in 1997 leaked over
an early website

Public Enemy Gold / 2-disc CD

Soul of a Nation / deluxe edition of *It Takes a Nation of Millions
to Hold Us Back.*

Afraid of the Dark / deluxe edition of *Fear of a Black Planet*

World Tour Sessions / compiled disc of the best PE live recordings

Louder Than a Bomb

The Complete Boxset of Public Enemy

DVDs

Power to the People and the Videos: Complete DVD and story
of PE

And the classic home videos to be re-released:

1989 *Fight the Power Live*

1990 *Tour of a Black Planet*

1993 *The Enemy Strikes Live*

Photography Credits and Permissions

Page 164: Anthrax and Public Enemy at the video shoot for *Bring The Noise* 15 June 1991 © Paul Nathan/WireImage/ Getty Images

Page 177: Cover of the *Juice* soundtrack

Page 196: Chuck onstage © Ian Dickson/Redferns

Page 215: DJ Lord performs with Public Enemy in Dublin, Ireland, 13 April 2003 © Getty Images

Page 252: Professor Griff, Chuck D, Flavor Flav and Public Enemy at the BET Awards, 26 June 2007 © Arnold Turner/ WireImage/Getty Images

Extract from *Howling at the Moon* by Walter Yetnikoff on p. 133 reproduced with kind permission of Little, Brown Group Ltd.

Acknowledgements

To my mum and family, thanks for everything. To the whole of the extended PE fam, thanks for taking the time out for my questions. Special shout out to Malik Farrakhan for being mad cool on Tour 55. Hope you enjoy the book.

Index